FROM THE STAGE
TO THE PRAYER MAT

FROM THE STAGE
TO THE PRAYER MAT

The Story of How a World-Famous Dancer
Fell in Love with the Divine

Rabia Christine Brodbeck

TUGHRA
BOOKS

New Jersey

Published by Tughra Books
335 Clifton Avenue
Clifton, New Jersey, 07011, USA

www.tughrabooks.com

Library of Congress Cataloging-in-Publication Data

Brodbeck, Rabia Christine.
 From the stage to the prayer mat : the story of how a world-famous dancer fell in love with the divine / Rabia Christine Brodbeck. -- 1st ed.
     p. cm.
 ISBN 978-1-59784-142-9 (pbk.)
 1. Brodbeck, Rabia Christine. 2. Muslim converts--Biography. 3. Islam--Appreciation. I. Title.
 BP170.5.B76 2008
 297.5'74092--dc22
 [B]

                                                          2008040828

ISBN: 978-1-59784-142-9

CONTENTS

DEDICATION

I wish to offer my sincere thanks to my friends who helped me wholeheartedly to realize this work. Living in Turkey, I wish to mention additionally all the people with the sweetness of their goodwill, with their general affection, with their encouraging inspirations, and with a heartfelt care, who made me feel that I am not alone!

I wish to dedicate this work to the beloved mother of all believers, Fatima az-Zahra, may God's abundant blessings be upon her, and to my beloved teacher, Safer Dal, may God bless his soul.

INTRODUCTION

Oh Lord, I wish to thank You with my incapacity to thank You.
Oh Lord, I ask forgiveness with my incapacity to ask forgiveness.

Abd al-Qadir al-Jilani

I am truly thankful of all the blessings of God Almighty as I was not seeking God when I was faced with His Reality, neither was it my intention to write a book when I first started to express some thoughts on paper. Through God's merciful guidance, this work of adoration grew into an unexpected size—and still today, inspiration flows constantly to my longing heart.

On the spiritual path, throughout my personal growth, I have felt a great need to communicate because I was brought face-to-face with God's perfection and beauty. I discovered inexhaustible treasures; I found pearls of wisdom and jewels of beings! I came across the most sublime saints in the universe, such as Abd al-Qadir al-Jilani, Ibn Arabi and Mevlana Jalal al-Din Rumi, may God's abundant blessing be on them. They inspired me endlessly to contemplate God's divine wisdom. It is through their divine guidance, supreme help and goodwill that the activity of writing grew in me.

Because I was confronted with so much beauty after almost two decades of being a traveler on the path, I began to feel spiritually highly inspired, so that I began to write down some impressions on paper. The more I advanced on the spiritual path, the more I felt the artist in me. It feels like intoxication with something "otherworldly," multiplying and growing constantly. Thus, I have come to the conclusion that the highest form an artist can aspire to is to become a believer, and the highest form of life is belief! This is why, at the present time, the artist in me is flowering delightfully.

Once one gets lost in the infinity of God Most High, there is no end to love; there is no end to divine grace; there is no end to aspiration; there is no end to divine knowledge; there is no end to beauty; there is no end to vision; and there is no end to faith.

I wish to share this great statement of a Sufi saint, ad-Darqawi:

> *A man who tries to find water*
> *By digging a little here and a little there*
> *Will die of thirst.*
> *Whereas a man who digs deep in one spot,*
> *Trusting in the Lord and relying on Him,*
> *Will find water;*
> *He will drink and give others to drink.*

I did not travel from the West to the East; rather, I came from my unawareness and encountered the reality of my own being. I did not change my belief; instead, I came from a misguided, meaningless life, to a life of eternal richness. This is why I feel this great need to shed light to the inexhaustible everlasting treasures within me. The mysticism of all religions speaks about the wisdom of the hereafter and the eternal values within human beings. There are inifinite possibilities. There is a source of eternal life. There is the treasury of divine beauty:

> I write because I was nourished so well,
> I write because I fell in love,
> I write because the source of existence is love,
> I write because I just followed my need,
> I write because using the pen does not mean writing for me,
> I write because I found saints who could express the inexpressible,
> I write because I found pearls of wisdom and jewels of beings,
> I write because our only salvation is selflessness,
> I write because I wish to remove misconceptions about religion,
> I write because our lives are verbally very poor,
> I write because I wish to reveal the wealth of inner dimensions,
> I write because Islam is the religion of adoration,
> I write because we are created for eternity,

I write because hunger is our food,
I write because we are part of the Breath of the Merciful,
I write because religion is pure joy,
I write because I wish to reveal the beauty in my life,
I write because I run from experience to experience,
I write because I was brought face-to-face with perfection and beauty,
I write because I feel there is no time to lose,
I write because mutual sharing of our spiritual lives is insufficient for different reasons,
I write because only a profound work can make a difference,
I write because writing discloses intimacy with the Only One,
I write because it was never more urgent to speak of the origin,
. . . And I write because I am honored to be a follower of the community of the Prophet Muhammad, peace and blessings upon him.

As a sincere believer wishes that his or her life becomes a prayer, I wish that this writing is felt like a prayer. As all life is divine, may these contemplations be a contribution to increase our sensitivities for the sacredness of all life.

My heart's truest wish is for intimacy with the One and Only, and intimacy with the highest priceless servant of God, the jewel of humanity, Muhammad Mustafa, peace and blessings be upon him.

PART ONE

Wonder and Admiration for
Prophet Muhammad ﷺ

The source of all existence is love,
Every movement in the universe is love,
The two most exalted lovers are God and Muhammad,
The two most exalted beloveds are God and Muhammad,
Never will cease their ever-blossoming friendship.

I wish to join all those who are longing for your beauty, O Muhammad, peace be upon you!

I marvel at you, O glory of the universe! Let us share the vision of your beautiful countenance! Let us quench our thirst in your truth! Let us drink from your infinite ocean of goodness and beauty! Let us breathe the beautiful scent of your most blessed presence! With this work of adoration, I am seeking to be near you, and I am seeking immersion in your gentle, kind and compassionate nature.

Our beloved Prophet wondered and gazed unceasingly at his Lord. He was the charmed admirer and the supreme adorer, embracing his Lord with marvelous deep affection. Nobody desired his Lord so endlessly and profoundly. However, he never asked anything for himself, never spoke a word about himself, never acted for himself, never prayed for himself, and never chose anything voluntarily. He was made to love and live by his Supreme Sultan.

He was the most blissful slave of all the creatures, offering his whole being infinitely in truest humility to his Lord. Never ceasing to prostrate himself, constantly seeking His nearness, he was in a state of perfect receptivity. He became the living truth of the grace of intimacy with his Lord. Only sincere slavehood allows true intimacy with its master.

Dressed in pure modesty, he was the center of all existing beauty, kindness, generosity and compassion, like pure water flowing from its origin. From his being, an inexhaustible divine, heavenly treasure reveals itself, limitless and unadulterated.

Nobody impressed himself so deeply on the whole of humanity. He is the key to divine knowledge, opening true seeing and hearing of the eye of the heart. He is the point where real human perfection starts, and he is the goal of all our possible accomplishments. With him we begin, and with him we end.

God hides Himself, hides His essence from His believers, but He lets us taste, know and find His reality through the beauty and goodness of Muhammad, peace and blessings be upon him. The key to God, the key to divine knowledge, is our beloved Prophet, peace and blessings be upon him.

There are 70,000 veils between the servant and his Lord. These veils are screens for the truth. In the words of Abd al-Qadir al-Jilani:

> *All created beings are a veil,*
> *With the exception of the Messenger, peace and blessings be upon him.*
> *For he is the doorway and the means by which the goal is reached.*

Ibn Arabi said:

> *All created beings have a shadow*
> *With the exception of our Messenger, peace and blessings be upon him,*
> *For he is the first light, the source of light.*
> *The source of existence has no shadow.*
> *With this light, we can see and understand God's truth.*

Our blessed master is the giver of all that is given, and he is the recipient of all that is received. He is the knower of all that is understood, he is the teacher of all that is transmitted, and he is the light of all that is enlightened. In true humility, he says:

My figure amongst the noble Prophets is this: A man builds a wall; he has finished it, except it needs one more brick; I am this brick. After me, there will be no more Messengers or Prophets.

Say of me: "The Servant of God and His Messenger," so that you do not fall into exaggeration that the people manifest with regard to my brother Jesus.

For the perfect lover of the real, he represents the satisfier of all our needs. To marvel at him represents an ascension for our souls. To hear of him makes easy what is difficult, because divine grace is radiating on whomever is contemplating him. Sending him salutations and blessings brings an immediate expansion of love in our hearts. Contemplating him brings the greatest joy and illuminates the face of our soul. Wishing peace for his soul means true salvation, touching the deepest interior of our hearts.

In the name, Muhammad, lives the wealth of all human goodness.
The name, Muhammad, is the key to inner purity.
The name, Muhammad, means real homecoming for the believer, our true origin.
The name, Muhammad, transforms and winds our nature.
The name, Muhammad, is the true remedy for our hearts.

"None of you is a true believer unless I am dearer to him than his father and his children, and all humankind," says the Prophet. God Most High says in the holy Qur'an:

The Prophet has a higher claim on the believers than they have on their own selves. (33:6)

There has come to you a Messenger from among yourselves; extremely grievous to him is your suffering, full of concern for you is he, and for the believers full of pity and compassion. (9:128)

[He was instructed to] lower your wings (of compassion and protection) for the believers. (15:88)

The Prophet's greatness does not lie in his superiority with regards to knowledge, wisdom, intellect and insight in every field, over every single man, but in his poverty, nothingness, humility, slavehood and modesty. He was the supreme authority on all levels, but in reality, he was the jewel of servants.

The greatness of his heart demonstrates that poverty is our greatest wealth. The more God blessed and favored our beloved Prophet, the more he became humble and submissive.

Every day, he asked for forgiveness a hundred times and prayed repeatedly to his beloved Lord:

> *Glory be to You! We have not been able to know You as Your knowledge requires, O Known One! Glory be to You! We have not been able to worship You as Your worship requires, O Worshipped One!*

All things begin with him, and all things are sealed with him. He is the most dignified of men. He is the pride of humanity, the honor of the universe, and the most beloved and the most desired Prophet of God Most High. But our most beloved of hearts acted like a man in a row—and this is the sublime secret of his being, the treasury of pure modesty.

In his tender heart, God's eternal beauty is reflected in the fullest splendor. Is there a greater beauty shining from a man's heart?

He never sought anything from his beloved Lord. During the heavenly ascension, God wished to give him all the riches of paradise in order to please him, but he answered with only one simple request: *"My community, my community."*

In essence, as soon as he was born, he prostrated himself and said: *"My community, my community."* Is there a greater beauty shining from a man's heart?

Once Jalal al-Din Rumi encountered Shamsaddin Tabrizi and asked him:

> *Who is greater?*
> *The Prophet Muhammad who says,*
> *"Glory be to You!*
> *We have not been able to know You*
> *As Your knowledge requires, O Known one!"*

Or the great saint, Abu Yazid Bistami,
Who says, in an instance of entranced ecstasy,
"Glory be to me! How exalted I am!"

Shamsaddin Tabrizi replied:

Both of these utterances show to what extent our Prophet is greater
than Abu Yazid Bistami. For the heart or soul of our Prophet was
like an ocean so deep and vast that it was impossible to satisfy. But
the soul of Abu Yazid Bistami was, in comparison with the
Prophet's, like a pitcher—easy to fill and quick to overflow.

The light of Muhammad is the essence of all creation. There
is nothing closer to God's Light than the reality of Muhammad,
peace and blessings be upon him. Both illuminated and illuminat-
ing he cried out: *"Oh Lord, show us things as they are!"*

The Prophet, peace and blessings be upon him, was designed
with such perfection that when he received the first revelation, he
found them in his heart. The beloved Prophet is the living Qur'an.
He gives meaning to all existence. He answers all questions. He is
the key to the secret between man and God Most High. All knowledge, light and perfection of all the Prophets are only reflections
from the noblest Messenger. But he prayed in utter humility:

Oh Lord, let me live as the poor, let me die as the poor, and resur-
rect me among the poor.

A wise man once said:

He is the sun of virtues.
Others in comparison to him
Are but stars that diffuse light
For people at night.

One of the greatest saints, Imam Ghazzali, said:

I stretched my intellect to such an extent that it almost broke apart.
I came to realize that it is limited. I experienced a kind of insanity
and I almost lost my mind. Eventually, I sought refuge in the spiri-

tual blessings of the Messenger of God, peace and blessings be unto him. Everything became clear. I discovered the secret and was saved.

At the point of the departure from this world to his beloved Lord, our blessed master uttered the following supplication:

God, God, God!
In your dutiful performance of the ritual prayer,
And in your treatment of what your right hand possesses.

In other words, our master wished us to pay great attention to "salat," the ritual prayer, and to fear God on account of all those entrusted in our care.

THE SOURCE OF LIGHT

God's first created act from His own Essence was the light of Muhammad Mustafa, peace and blessings be upon him. The very first divine creation represents the reality, the truth of Muhammad which originates from God's divine Light. Because the act of creation is symbolized by blowing, we can specify that God drew the reality of Muhammad out of the "Breath of the Merciful," *nafas al-Rahman*; therefore, the truth of Muhammad proceeds from the divine name *"al-Rahman,"* the All-Merciful.

The noble light of Muhammad, peace and blessings be upon him, contains God's Truth. The Prophet is the father of all creatures, even though his physical nature appeared afterwards. There is nothing closer to God's Light than the reality of Muhammad.

The Qur'an says of him:

You are surely of a sublime character. (68:4)

God the Almighty created the noble light of Muhammad from His Essence. It is God's first created act from the beauty of His Light. Prophet Muhammad displayed the source of light with a divine wonder. Thus, the source of divine love from Muhammad towards the Divine Essence, as well as from the Divine Essence towards Muhammad, was born. If God did not create Muhammad's light, the divine bountifulness would not be displayed on earth. So it is through this awe and wonderment towards the source of light that we can see the manifestations of God's Beautiful Names and Attributes.

Nothing can compare with the beauty of Muhammad's light, because there is nothing closer to the Almighty than the truth of Muhammad. This noble light, the limitless purity of Muhammad's luminous reality, reflects the beauty and glory of God Himself. It is Light upon light. Therefore, the source of light, the essence of the universe, represents the center of all existing beauty.

Bezm-i Alem Sultan said:

> *Muhammad originated from love.*
> *What would emerge from love without Muhammad?*

We have to understand that from the very beginning of creation, there is an eternal dialogue between God and Muhammad, because the world is born out of God's love and desire for our Blessed Glory of the Universe. That is why God created him in the most beautiful and perfect manner. This intimate dialogue of purest love, from pre-existence until all eternity, is the foundation of the universe. This richness of true adoration and wonderment is the inner wealth of the religion. For this reason, the writing starts with "the source of all existence is love." In other words, as our great saint Jalal al-Din Rumi, comments:

> *All things participate in God's Love, the motivating force of creation, so all things are lovers. In other words, each being is infused with need and desire for other beings and constantly striving to gain union with them. These individual loves are the immediate source of all movement and activity.*

Like no other religion, Islam is the religion of adoration. Our pride of humanity was the admirer par excellence, because the feeling of wonderment and awe is born through nearness to God Most High and certainly, our blessed master was the closest to his Lord, the Lord of the worlds. As it says in chapter *ar-Rahman*:

> *And the herbs and the trees both alike bow in adoration. (55:6)*
> *All those who are in heaven and on earth ask of Him. (55:29)*
> *Every day in (new) splendor does He (shine). (55:29)*
> *The whole world glorifies His praises. (55:29)*

The chapter talks about God's grace and favors given to humanity. The verses are revealing of the infinite wonders and treasures bestowed on God's creation. All existence shows heightened beauty of the All-Merciful, because everything is created in unity and grace.

The verses are of such artistic beauty that this passage is sometimes called the "Bride of the Qur'an," as the following words are uttered there 31 times from verse 10 to 77:

Then which of the favors of your Lord will you deny?

Thus, God reminds us to acknowledge His uncountable bounties and gifts. His workings and affairs are ongoing and show new splendor every moment. God has created the universe out of, and as the manifestation of, the mercy embodied by His Name the All-Merciful, and the whole of creation is immersed in the continuous worship of its Lord. Both earth and man are entrusted with the knowledge of God. The whole universe receives God's Glory! All things are one with Him, and all things are in harmony with Him. That is to say, all existence shows evidence of God Most High. Therefore, all life reveals His infinite beauty.

It is precisely a necessity of a believer to admire, to be astonished, and to be in awe of His endless favors given to humanity. To be blind to the wonders of His creation is equal to being ignorant and ungrateful. If the herbs and trees bow in adoration, should not human beings—endowed with intelligent speech, the capacity for understanding, and faculties of seeing, hearing, and taste—be utterly appreciative of His endless gifts?

Out of this source of light from God's Essence, everything else was created—the cosmos, the world, and all of humanity. In other words, God drew the entire universe out of the reality of Muhammad. Therefore, the noble Prophet, peace and blessings be upon him, said: *"I am from God, and the believers are from me."*

Thus, we are the fruit of God's tender care, and of His all-embracing love for the jewel of servants, Muhammad Mustafa, peace and blessings be unto him. In another tradition, the Prophet, peace and blessings be upon him, said:

> *Even though I am a son of Adam in form,*
> *In him I have an essence of my own*
> *Which testifies that I am his father.*

After God's first creation, our Prophet's light, the preceding creations evolving from this source of light are linked to his. Sheikh Muzaffer Ozak Al-Jerrahi describes in unfolding marvelous stages, God's creations from the Prophet's light, such as:

> *On his forehead, all the destinies are written; his generosity is in his palms; his forbearance is in his chest; his eyes show his conscience…*

> *When the Lord made Himself manifest to His blessed creature of light, a sense of shame produced drops of sweat from every part of his sacred body. These drops became the embryos from which all creatures were brought into being. The angels were created from the sweat of his head, the Throne and the Seat, Tablet and Pen, the sun, the moon and stars from the sweat of his face, the Prophets and Messengers, martyrs, champions, saints and righteous men from the sweat of his breast…*

Our blessed master owns the most supreme station because he is the source of light. He was the first to be mentioned, and he was the first to be desired by God Most High. He represents the highest, most excellent rank—the nearest to God of humankind. He is the most dignified, the most complete being of the human race. For this reason, all things begin with him, and are sealed with him.

Thus, of the one hundred and twenty four thousand Prophets, our blessed master is the forefather and the final seal. In the Prophet Muhammad's own words:

> *I am the first to have been created and the last to have been sent.*

The essential reality of our Messenger is unique, incomparable because his essence coincides with God's Essence. He was the most evident symbol of his Lord. Therefore, the Prophet represents the doorway, the means, and the goal.

Muhammad, peace and blessings be upon him, is not only the wine of God's wisdom that he gives us to drink; he is also the cup in which the drink is offered.

Muhammad, peace and blessings be upon him, is not just the possessor of the jewels of divine wisdom; he is also the setting of the ring in which the diamonds are held. Muhammad, peace and blessings be upon him, is not only the recipient of the revelations of the holy book, the Qur'an; he is living the entire truth of its messages.

In the book of *al-Tawasin*, referring to the "Verse of Light" (verse 24:35 of the Qur'an), it says:

> *All knowledge is but a drop of his knowledge, all maxims are a mouthful of his river, all epochs an hour of his time...He is the first to have been included in the divine presence, and he is the last to have been sent as a Prophet!*

Only Muhammad Mustafa, peace and blessings be upon him, could convert his ego into that of a true Muslim. His whole inner nature submitted towards God, and was in service to Him. He transformed his inner faculties into believers.

Thus, for the true believer, the noble character of Prophet Muhammad, peace and blessings be upon him, is the greatest miracle that exists.

MY BELOVED

God the Merciful calls our blessed master, "My beloved." He created all and everything for love of him. Without him, nothing would have ever existed. He is the reason for the entire creation, the whole universe and all humankind.

God says:

I created all and everything for you; I created you for Myself.

God placed the Prophet's noble name beside His own Name. In every part of paradise, from the beginning of creation, it was written: *"La ilaha illallah, Muhammadur rasul-Allah* – "There is no god but God; Muhammad is the Messenger of God."

Because the two names are linked together forever, our blessed master is raised to the rank of praiseworthiness! God Himself, His own divine Essence and His angels praise and bless His beloved and He commands all saints, all righteous servants and all believers to wish peace and convey blessings on him as well. We can never praise our blessed master as he deserves, because his greatness has no end!

He was dearer to God than all the other Prophets, for his noble character, his utmost proper behavior, and his modesty. Our blessed master always experienced deep concern and sadness about unbelievers, never asking his Lord to lift the cruelties done to him. In deepest thankfulness, he never wished anything from his Lord. For this reason, throughout his whole prophethood, God comforted His beloved without him asking; nourished His beloved without him pleading; granted His beloved without him worrying; and enriched His beloved without him wishing.

As God Most High exalted His remembrance
And made his Prophethood the most excellent,
He sent His dearest beloved as a favor to all believers,
He sent him as the seal of all the Prophets,
He sent him as a mercy to the entire world,
He made his community the best of all communities,
He sent him to perfect good behavior,
He made him chief of the Prophets,
He sent him as a light of guidance,
He gave him the most excellent of all the heavenly scriptures,
the Qur'an,
He gave him the station of the intercessor on the Day of Judgment,
He made his religion prevail over all religions,
He is dispensing His unconditional mercy through His beloved
Prophet to all the believers.

God Most High did not give all of these particular favors to the previous Messengers. It is of the highest value, and an unimaginable privilege, to walk in the footsteps of the Prophet Muhammad, peace and blessings be upon him. The previous prophets who came before our blessed master were all eager to be part of his community, too. No other community was honored with such infinite richness and with such divine favors.

According to a tradition, at the time when God most High created the Archangel Gabriel in the most beautiful manner, a conversation took place between them. Archangel Gabriel performed two cycles of prayers, each cycle taking 1000 years, in gratitude towards his Lord who created him in such beauty:

> The Almighty said: "No one has worshipped Me like you, but at the end of time, a noble Prophet of Mine, My dearly beloved, will come. Although his community will be feeble, sinful and not very devout, two cycles of prayer performed by them for all their absentmindedness, mistakes and forgetfulness, will be dearer to Me than this prayer you have performed for the sake of My Honor and Majesty. Their pre-eminence is due to their being the community of My beloved."
>
> Angel Gabriel asked again: "O my Lord, what favor will you grant for the prayer they perform?"

And the Exalted One replied: "I shall give My Paradise."

Gabriel then replied: "O Lord, would You give me permission to look around this resort of Paradise You are going to give the community of Muhammad?"

After Gabriel had flown around for three thousand years and again for thirty thousand years, he grew weary and alighted in the shade of one of the trees of Paradise. Prostrating himself to God, he begged to know what distance he had covered: "O my Lord, my strength deserted me. Tell me, how much of this Paradise, which You will the community of Muhammad, have I traversed? Is it half, a third, a quarter?"

The Almighty told him in reply : "Even if you flew on for another thirty thousand years, at ten times this speed, you would not cover one tenth of the bounty I have conferred upon the community of Muhammad. Such, O Gabriel, is the bounty I reward a prayer of two cycles."

For the believers who follow truly our blessed master, the following statement becomes valid: he is for everything, and everything is for him! Thus, let us share our gratitude in our actions as devoted servants. May we become worthy to be members of his blessed community!

THE NIGHT OF THE ASCENSION

In one of the most difficult phases of our blessed master's life, when he was most threatened by his enemies, God bestowed on His most beloved Prophet Muhammad, peace and blessings be upon him, the greatest of all gifts: He took him to Himself in order to show His abundant love and affection and to profoundly please him. This was the night of the heavenly ascension. Our noble Prophet was lying in his bed, feeling distressed and sad about the hostilities of the unbelievers. Knowing too well the condition of his purest heart, God conferred the greatest favor on His beloved, pleasing him with union that night, although not the slightest complaint about the cruelties done to him came from his lips.

Our Prophet Muhammad, peace and blessings be upon him, was transported by the heavenly stead, Buraq, to his dearest Lord. On his travels, he was allowed to see all the levels of hell and heaven, and all the holy treasures and hidden mysteries of paradise were revealed to him. The major Prophets came before him, and all the angels ever created were in service to him. They greeted him with the greatest honor, being in awe of his beauty.

After traveling through the whole of God's kingdom, the Prophet arrived at a place where there is no time and space. This stage marks an essential point called "The Lote-tree of the Boundary" (verse 53:14 in the Qur'an), *Sidrat al-Muntaha*—an unsurpassable limit, with the exception of our Prophet, for any created being. Not even the Archangel Gabriel could transgress this barrier. This is the realm of God's Essence, of His unsupportable Presence to any creature.

For this reason, our Prophet Muhammad, peace and blessings be upon him, continued his ascent alone and entered into the divine Presence. Lover and Beloved were united. In this moment,

the unity of divine Essence was shown to Him. In deepest intimacy, without any veils, they conversed about all the secrets of divine
Knowledge.

This highest privilege to look at the Eternal Face, to converse
with God Himself, was never given to any other creature. Only our
Prophet could endure the Sight and the Might of God Himself,
while still living in this world. This dwelling place is called the "indescribable nearer," evoked in the *Surah* of the Star (Chapter 86 of the
Qur'an).

God wished to give His most beloved all of Paradise and the
treasures of heaven; the Pen, the Guarded Tablet, and the Throne,
but Muhammad, peace and blessings be upon him, wished only for
his community. His only concern was the salvation of all human
beings. Our blessed master's tender-hearted truest wish was simply,
"Oh Lord, what I ask of you, is nearness to my community!"

The Prophet was blind to the wonders of heaven. When his
profoundest wish, the salvation for his community, the intercession on the day of Resurrection was granted, he prostrated himself
in deepest thankfulness and pleaded to his Supreme Sultan once
more: *"Oh my Lord, let my Fatima, my Hassan, my Hussein and the
people of my household intercede for my community as well."*

The Prophet's family lived in total union with each other. We
may say that the Prophet Muhammad was part of them, and they
were part of him. They participated with all their hearts in the
Prophet's deepest concerns, which is the salvation of humanity:

> On that night, God said: "He is Mine, and I am His."

The intercession was granted to everyone in his community and
not only to some chosen people. This promise from God Most High
was made way before the creation of the world, where He said:

> My Mercy encompasses by far My Wrath. I will give you before you
> ask. I will forgive you before you ask forgiveness.

In a holy tradition, it is also reported that:

On the day of Resurrection, all people are in distress about their state asking all the Prophets to intercede for them. From Adam, upon him be peace and blessings, up to Jesus upon him be peace and blessings, they answered: "I myself, I myself, have to fear God's Judgment."

Only to our Prophet Muhammad, peace and blessings be upon him, the intercession for his community was granted. How could God refuse His desired and His most beloved's profoundest wish, which dominated his whole being, as he pleaded endlessly for the salvation of his community?

On that blessed night, God had the following conversation with His beloved. God asks His Prophet: *"My beloved, what did you bring from amongst your community?"*

Our blessed master replied: *"O my Lord, I brought something that You do not have."*

God said: *"O my beloved, what do I not have?"*

Our blessed master replied: *"O my Lord, the only thing that You do not have, is poverty. This is what I have brought to You."*

This state of poverty is what God most desires from humankind, as our blessed master said: *"My poverty is my pride."* When a believer is completely naked, and not a single particle of the world or himself remains, God will rush towards him and close him with the robe of true servanthhood. This is what God is most pleased with.

Thus, only through the state of poverty may we reach nearness to our beloved Lord. We will be able to live in His eternal Richness. Therefore, our biggest gift we may give to our Lord is "giftlessness"!

In Muzaffer Ozak's book, *The Irshad*, another significant conversation is reported to have taken place on this night:

The exalted Lord said to our master: "O Ahmad, to be aware of doubt is the beginning and end of religion. Worship has ten parts: eating lawful food accounts for nine of those parts, and silence is the other. I develop the hearts of those who observe silence, while I wreck the hearts of those who talk too much. Do you know the reward due to a servant of Mine is if he fasts and keeps silent to please Me?"

> *Our master said: "My Lord, I do not know."*
>
> *So the Exalted One explained: "The reward for fasting, keeping silence, and not talking too much is wisdom. The legacy of wisdom is esoteric knowledge. The end of esoteric knowledge is closeness to Me. I have three rewards for anyone who conducts himself to please Me and earn My divine approval: I shall teach him such knowledge that no ignorance will remain in him. I shall give him such intelligence that no forgetfulness will remain in him. I shall give him such affection that he will love nothing other than Me. That servant of Mine will have his heart so full of My love that there will be no space in it for any other. I love those who love Me. I also cause them to love My servants. I make them kings of the heart."*

And according to Imam Ali, may God be pleased with him, the blessed Messenger said:

> *On the Night of my ascension, I asked God: "What action is dearest to You?"*
>
> *The Lord of Majesty replied: "O Ahmad, the most meritorious of all actions, and the one dearest in my sight, is that of entrusting everything to me. O Ahmad, no action is higher than being content with what I have given. I love those who are content with Me, I love those who love one another for My sake, and I love those who bring people to Me."*

The event of the heavenly ascension, our Prophet's arrival in the divine Presence, confirms a fruitful dialogue between the Creator and the created. The intimate conversations prove a most creative relationship of "God to man," and "man to God." There is a secret connection between the Lord and His servant. Thus, a sincere believer can rise to the level of real friendship and intimacy with his Lord.

God gives us the possibility to transcend the duality, to make a divine synthesis of the Creator and the created, Lord and slave, Sustainer and sustained, the invoker and the Invoked. Those with wisdom call this highest station, "the kingdom of singularity."

When a true believer's soul on an inward journey arrives in the divine Presence, his purified soul will meet the divine Light. In other words, his soul travels through inner spiritual states and gradually arrives. There, he is alone in the contemplation of unity. They also call this station, "the paradise of intimacy." It is where the truth of Muhammad, upon him be peace and blessings, is gathered. This is where God wants man to be, this is the end of the believer's ascension.

The paradise of intimacy is the true believer's total bliss. God's veils are lifted and endless gifts and grace pour over him. There are no paradises with rivers of milk and honey and jeweled palaces. It is only Him. Ibn Arabi says about the highest level of the ascent:

> At the end of this miraj, the ascension, man is reduced to the inde-structible divine secret which was lodged in him at the beginning of time by the breath of the Spirit breathed into Adam's clay...Then the even and odd come together, He is, and you are not... And He sees Himself through Himself.

God Most High says:

> My servant, if you wish to enter the sanctuary of My intimacy, do not pay attention either to this world or to the higher world of the angels— not even the higher world where you receive My divine attributes.

A true believer has to offer all of what he is, and the offer must be sincere. As Abd al-Qadir al-Jilani comments:

> The true believer belongs entirely to God the Almighty. Not a single atom of his being belongs to creatures. God is in charge of both his outer and his inner dimension. He makes no movement except because of Him, and he does not come to rest except because of Him—for he has his being entirely because of Him, from Him and in Him.

As we see, each believer's soul is given the experience of the ascension inwardly. But our beloved Prophet Muhammad, peace and blessings be upon him, is the only human being receiving the honor of actually being transported by his Lord to his Lord physically—that is to say, with his earthly body. As mentioned before, no other creature could endure God's divine Presence while living in this world. Further, the event of the heavenly ascension is said to have taken place in one single instant. When he returned to his bed, it was still warm. Our great saint Jalal al-Din Rumi comments:

> *On the Night of the Ascension, the Prophet in his selflessness traveled a 100,000 years journey.*

The actual ascension, being lifted up from the earthly plane into the Divine Presence, symbolizes our Prophet's absolute purity. Before the ascension, God had already re-absorbed the divine treasures in his blessed breast, washed them clean with the waters of paradise, and put endless love and mercy in him. The chest is the seat of secrets, according to the saying of the Prophet:

> *Abu Bakr, may God be pleased with him, does not outdo you with fasting or with prayer, but with something deposited in his chest.*

In the Surah *al-Inshirah*, which translates as "The Expansion," Yusuf Ali gives a marvelous description in his commentaries, which reveal the significance of the human breast. In the first *ayat* (verse) it says:

> *Have We not expanded your breast? (94:1)*

In addition, Yusuf Ali comments:

> *The breast is symbolically the seat of knowledge and the highest feelings of love and affection, the treasure-house in which are stored the jewels of that quality of human character which approaches nearest to the Divine. The holy Prophet's human nature had been purified, expanded and elevated, so that he became a mercy to all creation.*

We can never imagine this highest bliss which the prince of the universe experienced that night! No other human being would have wanted to leave the highest paradise—the paradise of God's Essence—and return to the world. When the Prophet arrived back at his household, there was not even a mark appearing on him.

Our Prophet returned as a humble slave to us poor sinners, giving his life to his community. His return to the world gone astray represents true and abundant servanthood, the greatest act of love.

The highest form of obedience, the most pleasing action to our Lord, is returning to the world of duties and responsibility after having attained unity with Him. Wearing the crown of illumination, being absorbed in Him, and then descending to creation, the world of multiplicity, in order to serve, teach and guide, is a higher level than staying in unity with Him. It is an act of true generosity and compassion towards all existence, which is the essential reality of our blessed master, *"ubudiyya,"* absolute servitude.

There is nothing more valuable than serving humankind in God's sight! The end of our search for God is not arriving in God. Rather, it is accomplishing nearness to God with other human beings. A saint is not a saint unless he is close to human beings.

The great saint, Abu Yazid Bistami, may God be pleased with him, dwelling in unity with the Only One, took a step back towards creation and fainted. He could not bear the separation. In reality, the highest ascension a believer is able to experience is the descent, because he is honored to be God's agent, representing his beloved Lord on earth.

This is especially true of the first human being created, the first Prophet Adam, upon him be peace and blessings. He had a lapse, was expelled from paradise and had to descend to creation. If he had not lapsed, he would not have been honored to be the vicegerent of God.

There is a divine policy: the more a sincere believer separates externally from his Lord, the more he is with Him. In his exile, he will radiate God's divine attributes through his noble character, because his heart will be full of love for the Almighty and his beloved Prophet, peace and blessings upon him. We can say that all external separation of a believer from his Lord represents a form of retreat, then, and the most effective retreat is done among crowds, because we please our Creator most by being useful to His creation.

Therefore, the aim of an obedient servant is to become a true representative on earth. Those who return are the most perfect!

There is a significant statement made by Sheikh Abu Madyan, may God be pleased with him:

> *To flee from created being is one of the signs of a novice's sincerity. To reach God is a sign of the sincerity of his flight from created being. To return to created being is a sign of the sincerity of his having reached God.*

The Lord of Majesty says to one of His beloved servants, who asked Him:

> *Oh my Lord, why do you not speak to me, as you spoke to Moses, upon him be peace and blessings?*
>
>   *God replied: "Is it not enough that he who loves you, loves Me, and that he who sees you, sees Me?"*

There are further significant essential realities of the descent to mention, which demonstrate again that the ultimate spiritual level a sincere believer can reach culminates in a "downward" movement. One is the prostration in the ritual prayer. This act expresses the profoundest humility, symbolizing the total deliverance of a believer into God, the union with Him. It is the culmination of the exalted experience of a believer, because in this ritual position, he is nearest to God. He puts his head on the lowest level, descending from a standing position, lowering his whole body to the earth itself. What beautiful wisdom arises within this greatest act of worship of a believer. As we mentioned previously, the Prophet, peace and blessings be upon him, never ceased to prostrate himself, as he represents the perfection of humility and gratitude!

Another downward movement happened in the Night of Destiny or Power, "*laylat al-qadr*," during which the Holy Book, the Holy Qur'an, first descended. The Muslim community celebrates this night as one of the most important nights of the Islamic year, representing the absolute fulfillment of all divine Revelations ever given from God the Almighty to humankind, because all previous prophetic messages are contained in it.

It is as Ibn Arabi says about the Night of Power:

> *It is nothing other than the Prophet Muhammad, peace and blessings be upon him, himself, who descends.*

The believer is able to experience something like a second birth, through which he becomes that which he was from all eternity, because he can receive from God's Wisdom. Everything is given to the Prophet's community, all the methods and all the graces to enable us to become perfect human beings. Consequently, with the beginning of the Prophet's community, the true followers are able to reach the ultimate level of spiritual evolution.

To comfort His beloved on the night of the Ascension, the Almighty gave a great gift to our noble master, the ritual prayer, "*as-salat,*" the gift of continuous intimacy with Him. Because our Prophet had to separate himself from the paradise of the highest bliss of union with his Lord and descend to the world, whenever performing the ritual prayer, he could re-experience the nearness to his Lord as in the night of the ascension. In this way, his tender heart would find the light of his eyes.

This great heavenly gift which God offered to His Prophet represents, therefore, the symbol for the heavenly ascension itself. For this reason, the ritual prayer signifies the ascension of the believer and the highest form of divine remembrance.

As our beloved master, on the Night of the Ascension, exclusively wished for the salvation of his community, he immediately pleaded to his Lord to give all sincere believers the exalted experience of the ascension as well. Thus, God granted His most beloved's wish:

> *God said: "In that case, they shall perform the ritual prayer."*

The Prophet is a perfect model for all and everything in our earthly existence. He is the spiritual master par excellence, representing the ultimate perfection of the human being. The believer is able to imitate him in all the finest, microscopic details of his life and is, therefore, given the possibility to reach enlightened sainthood.

The followers of the community of the Prophet Muhammad, peace and blessings be upon him, inherit with the ritual prayer, consequently, the greatest privilege, because the ascension of the believer symbolizes the stages of the spiritual journey of the human soul that leads to human perfection.

SERVANTHOOD

The world is born of love for perfection. The world is born of love to be known.

The most honorable creation in the entire universe is the human being, because he is created in the concept of the Perfect Man! God breathed into man His Spirit, which means he is of divine origin. He becomes a manifestation of God's activity. The perfect man is the purpose of creation!

Because of his perfect nature, he is also called *Khalifah,* the deputy, the representative of God on this earth. Through him, God preserves His creation. Man is chosen to guard God's kingdom. He is entrusted with His knowledge. The world will be preserved as long as the perfect man subsists therein. The world subsists in virtue of his existence. The end of sainthood is nothing other than the end of the world!

However, the ultimate fulfillment of spiritual life is only reached by serving humankind. That is to say, the perfection of a human being culminates in servanthood. God's purpose of creation is the perfect man as a servant. God announced Muhammad as a Prophet as well as a servant to our world, peace be upon him.

In the testimony of faith, all believers say:

Ashhadu an la ilaha illallah, wa-ashhadu anna Muhammadun 'Abduhu wa Rasuluh

"I testify there is no god but God, and I testify that Muhammad is His servant and His Messenger."

This title and function was never given to any of the previous Prophets. With the coming of our blessed master Muhammad, peace and blessings be upon him, the world was endowed with the source of light! Truest humility, profoundest love, infinite mercy, abundant grace, and supreme adoration poured unceasingly towards all human beings. These compassionate qualities are the essence of servanthood.

In other words, his essential mission consisted not only of transmitting God's revelation to humankind, but most of all, demonstrating true slavehood to his Lord and abundant service to his community. Displaying a great authority in preaching, proclaiming or declaring became secondary.

With our blessed master, human perfection begins and human perfection ends. He is the wealth of human goodness. He demonstrates like no other being that through the perfection of servanthood can we reach God Most High the best. Consequently, for the true believers, the way to God means the way of sacrifice.

If we put the value of the Prophet's servitude on one scale and all the worship ever performed by all the angels, Prophets and believers on the other scale, our Prophet's servanthood would outweigh these by far!

For this reason, our beloved Messenger became the master of all people, because the master of the people is their servant. What a sublime function his Prophet-hood fulfilled—a slave leading humanity! No other Prophet showed such infinite concern for his own community, as well as abundant compassion and love towards all existence. He was sent as a mercy to all the worlds. He was sent to perfect good character. From whatever way we contemplate his life, the Prophet Muhammad, peace and blessings be upon him, represents the jewel of servants. This is the message to humanity from our Lord of all the worlds!

For a sincere believer, servanthood is the condition of man and it is the meaning of being human—our whole existence is based on it. Servanthood means to do everything for God's sake, thus to please God with all our actions and our behavior. A man without a trace of servanthood is lacking humanity. The true servant earns God. If he sincerely serves and submits, he will win

God's pleasure; he will win everything spiritually and materially; and he will win humankind and the entire universe.

There are three stages of surrendering your life to God. The first stage is surrendering your possessions, your property and your money. The second stage is surrendering your family, your friends and your children. The third is surrendering yourself, meaning body, health, mind, status, affection, heart and soul—which is expressed through servanthood as *"ubudiyya."* Consequently, the very art of life is giving oneself totally!

THE UNLETTERED PROPHET

The Qur'an talks about Prophet Muhammad in the following way:

> [He is] the unlettered Prophet (7:157, 7:158, 62:2).

Under the unfavorable conditions of his time, the Prophet did not attend any school and was not formally educated; consequently, he could not read or write. But God endowed him with the whole of His eternal Wisdom, because our blessed master is the source of light, which God drew directly from His own Essence.

Although in his earthly life, he was not versed in human learning, our blessed master put the wisdom of the learned to shame, because his knowledge was inborn, meaning his knowledge was not acquired. For this reason, he represented a great example for natural scientists, medical researchers, historians, astronomers, and so on.

When people asked our beloved master, "Where did you learn all this?" he replied:

> Since I had no one and I was an orphan, that Someone of nobodies became my tutor and taught me, for the all-Merciful taught the Qur'an.

Jalal al-Din Rumi says about God's eternal Wisdom:

> If a person wanted to learn this knowledge from the creatures, he would not be able to acquire it in hundreds of thousands of year. But if he did learn it, his knowledge would then be acquired and imitative. He would not possess its keys. It would be the outward picture of knowledge, not the reality and spirit of knowledge. Anyone can paint a picture of man on a wall. It has a head, but no intellect; an eye but no sight; a hand but no generosity; a breast but no illuminated heart.

Having no formation from any school, nor from his parents, and growing up as an orphan, our dear Prophet's heart was totally empty, clean and of spotless purity. No other authority than God became his Teacher. His brilliant inward capacity to receive divine Revelations was incomparable. Just as Mary, the mother of Prophet Jesus, upon them both be peace, had to be a virgin, untouched and pure, the Prophet had to be unlettered, like a blank clean page. They were pure receptacles for God's manifestations in them.

Additionally, God enriched His beloved Prophet with His eternal Wisdom and His divine Knowledge on the Night of the Ascension, as well.

Sheikh Muzaffer Ozak describes beautifully the passage of the Prophet's father passing away, while our blessed master was still in his mother's womb:

> *All the angels in tears begged God to explain, and He comforted them as follows: "My angels, a father's function and duty is to bring up, train and protect his sons, but My beloved needs no one but Me to bring him up, train him and take care of him. While other children call "daddy" when they need help and support, My beloved Muhammad will call for Me, saying: "O Lord!" I have left him fatherless so that he will not turn for help and assistance to anyone but Me.*

Our blessed master said in a holy tradition:

> *My Lord trained me, and He trained me well.*

POVERTY

The Qur'an talks about the extreme gentle nature of the Prophet, because he embodied the mercy and compassion of God Most High. Throughout his life, he was extremely anxious for the believers. The Prophet felt deep sorrow for the ones going astray, but patiently watched over them; and when anyone returned showing faith, he welcomed them with kindness and mercy.

He took special care of all those in utter need—the poor, the sick, the oppressed, the neglected, the slaves and the orphans. He shared their sorrows and their sufferings:

God most High says: *"I am with those whose hearts are broken on my account."*

The Prophet was the glory of the universe. His majesty and compelling power, and his supreme greatness is infinite, but he spent his entire life at the side of the poor and needy. For this reason, if we show love for the sick, the politically tortured, the needy and the poor, it is a sign of love for our blessed master.

The Prophet Muhammad, peace and blessings be unto him, lived in extreme poverty, as did his family and closest companions. Through his example, God showed us that poverty is our greatest wealth. He was poor in this world, so his poverty could rest in God's eternal Richness. Slavehood and poverty are one. Loving to be the poorest slave before the Infinite Greatness and Glory of God was his inspiration.

Here are some examples from our blessed master's simple life:

He always slept on the floor on a straw mat.
Whatever was given to him as a gift from wealthy people did not stay for more than one moment in his hands. He immediately gave everything away to the ones in need.

One day his most beloved daughter, Fatima, came to her father with a necklace, and he said to her: "Do you want people, the inhabitants of the earth and the inhabitants of heaven, to say that the daughter of the Prophet is wearing a chain from Hell?" Our Prophet wished to prepare his daughter to be the mother of all believers, meaning the mother of the whole chain of the highest grades of saints ever to come and to guide us in this world. The wearing of jewelry is not unlawful, but she had to represent a life of simplicity and purity for the coming generations.

Abu Hurayra once saw our blessed master performing his prayers in a sitting position and asked him whether he was ill. The reply was of the kind that made Abu Hurayra weep: "I am hungry, O Abu Hurayra. Hunger has left me no strength to stand up for prayer." Hunger was common to his household and his companions. One night, Abu Bakr and Umar, blessings be unto them, met with the beloved Prophet unexpectedly outside their homes. "What brought you to come out at this time of night?" They asked one another and replied: "Hunger!"

Each major Prophet represents a basic quality. Abd al-Qadir al-Jilani mentions eight of them:

– Generosity	Prophet Abraham (on him be peace)
– Cheerful resignation	Prophet Isaac (on him be peace)
– Patience	Prophet Job (on him be peace)
– Symbolic expression	Prophet Zachariah (on him be peace)
– Exile	Prophet John (on him be peace)
– Wandering	Prophet Jesus (on him be peace)
– Poverty	Prophet Muhammad (on him be peace)

Our Prophet's needs for this world ceased completely, so his inner state of poverty allowed him to dwell in intimacy with his Lord. God offered him all the riches of this world, but he preferred to be nourished by His Nearness. Whatever God gave or took from our blessed master, he accepted everything with gratitude, and treated every situation in the way most pleasing to God. In his noble behavior, he showed true humility and submission. His will was completely tuned in with the Supreme Will.

In God's eyes, the highest quality a human being can reach is poverty because it means self-sacrifice, the extinction of one's being unto God. In the state of poverty, meaning selflessness, one becomes automatically an admiring slave of the One and Only. Is not our beloved master the most honorable creation in the whole universe, and the most beloved of God Himself? The reason for his exalted station is exactly his pure selflessness, meaning the highest stage of annihilation. Through his sublime state of humility and slavehood, our beloved of hearts became the wealthiest of all men in the universe. This is the significance of his saying:

> *My poverty is my pride.*

As the Prophet wished for nothing but his dearest Lord, a sincere believer can clean the dirt of this world from his heart and empty it of all creation, so there will be room for the Only One. In a true slave's heart, God can become the most honored guest. Recognizing our nothingness and God's Greatness and overwhelming Power is the secret of reunion between the Lord and His servant. Two beautiful teachings about the essence of poverty are given by our supreme saint Abd al-Qadir al-Jilani:

> *The real meaning of poverty is not depending for your needs on other people, while the real meaning of riches is being able to do without other people.*
>
> *Spiritual culture,* tasawwuf, *is not acquired through long palaver, but through going hungry and giving up things that are familiar and pleasant.*

To reach the station of poverty, the Prophet gives us the following advice:

> *Die before you die.*

It is the prescription for sainthood. Saint Junayd al-Baghdadi says:

> *Sufism is that God should make you die away from yourself and live in Him.*

When a true believer reaches this state through the secret prescription, his self-will ceases to exist and he will act in the way God orders us to act. In one of the most famous holy traditions, God the Almighty says:

> *My servant comes close to Me with the worship of good works until I love him; and when I love him, I become the hearing in his ears; I become the sight in his eyes; I become the words on his tongue; I become the hand with which he holds; I become the strength of every part of his being.*

We find true life when we surrender our lives. In the spiritual realm, there is no death without resurrection. There is no negation without affirmation. There is no god but God, and all things perish except His Face. After extinction and annihilation, we remain in subsistence, eternity. To "die before dying" is far sweeter than anything we have ever tasted, because we find awareness of Him. The state of poverty delivers us from the suffering of existence. When we leave the cage of this existence, we will find eternal bliss and happiness. Then we can truly experience His never ending generosity.

The great saint Jalal al-Din Rumi writes in his exquisite poetry:

> *For these martyrs have no patience without death; they are in love with their own annihilation.*
>
> *Of all the different kinds of knowledge, on the day of death, only the science of poverty will supply portions for the way.*
>
> *Poverty is not for the sake of hardship. No, it is there because nothing exists but God.*
>
> *All the hearts of God's lovers have formed a circle around poverty: poverty is the sheikh of sheikhs, and all hearts are its disciples.*
>
> *When annihilation adorns a man because of his poverty, he becomes shadowless, like Muhammad.*
>
> *The dead man has been annihilated in one respect through loss of life, but the Sufis have been annihilated in a hundred respects.*
>
> *Fear is not even a hair before love. In the religion of love, all things are sacrificed.*

Only selflessness can illuminate the universe!

PERFECTION ON THE EARTHLY PLANE

The religion of Islam is simple and practical. For every believer, all questions are answered, from the simple social order to profound spiritual truths. Our Prophet declares the One and Universal God, guiding man in what is right and forbidding what is wrong.

The Prophet Muhammad, peace and blessings be upon him, demonstrated by his way of life the deepest penetration into all earthly matters, like no other messenger. In the same way that the whole Qur'an embraces every aspect of human life, the Prophet showed in all his actions the most appropriate, perfect behavior.

Our noble Master's mission was forever linked with eternity. This extreme sensitivity to the hereafter was combined with the fullest earthly plenitude. He gave advice on how to guide our private and public lives, from the ordinary man to the highest saint. He joined the busy life of the city, worked hard, and lived an exemplary family life. There was no need for any magic, miracles, supernatural powers, or fortune-telling. Through his noble character and his beautiful conduct, all measures, directives, discrimination, sense of proportion and values were shown. His patience, gentleness, and trustworthiness, as well as his truthfulness, were extraordinary examples.

Our Prophet proves that he is not only the perfect man on the mystical plane; he is, most of all, the perfect man on the earthly plane! The Prophet does not teach us to get lost in the ocean of God's love, but recommends the believer to strengthen his personality—to strengthen it with love, worship and service.

To perfect our behavior within our daily lives, *Hadrat* 'Ali, may God be pleased with him, gives us splendid educational advice:

May God shower His Beneficence upon the one who knows his worth, who knows to stay within his bounds, who watches his tongue, and who does not spend his life in idleness.

Your words depend upon you until you utter them; but once you have uttered them, you will depend upon them.

Man's salvation depends upon the use of his tongue! Our words can destroy a person's morale, or they can bring the greatest happiness to another's heart. Therefore, the Prophet warns us that the tongue can be more harmful than our hands. He also lets us know that if we hurt our fellow beings or break their hearts, it is as if we destroy the House of God, the Ka'ba. The Prophet Muhammad, peace and blessings be upon him, is reported as having said:

Offending the believer is fifteen times more serious in God's Sight than violating the Ka'ba, the Ka'ba.

The importance of rightly guided conduct is immense, because what we plant in this world, we will harvest in the hereafter. The only opportunity to prove our goodness and win God's pleasure is given to us within our earthly lives. Only the human being is endowed with a will of his own. He is, therefore, charged to carry the responsibility over his own words, behavior, and actions.

As Ibn Arabi says:

The human being's subtle nature is resurrected in the form of knowledge; the bodies are resurrected in the form of their works.

On the Day of Resurrection men will see God according to the degree of knowledge they had about Him below.

MEDINA AL-MUNAWWARA
THE CITY, THE ILLUMINATED

Our blessed master's whole mission was guiding humanity to perfection. As human perfection culminates in servanthood, he gave the greatest importance to the refinement within the earthly plane. Not satisfied only with providing the best education for our human characters, our beloved of God founded a perfectly functioning social system for his newly initiated followers. At all levels of life, he introduced practical social rules of behavior. In other words, he founded a model of society, a social organism, which grew into a city and a state. This model included advice on all social levels, covering environment, health, education, justice, administration, trade, religion, and so on. At the same time, the social order was very solid and compact and very practical and simple. Consequently, our blessed Prophet represented an excellent example as a doctor, teacher, craftsman, judge, father, salesman, husband, scientist, warrior, and so on. No previous Prophet was able to create such a healthy functioning civilization.

Our Prophet Muhammad, peace and blessings be upon him, was sent during one of the darkest ages of Arabian society. At that time, men were allowed to have as many as forty wives, female babies were buried alive, and slavery was common among all rich families. Human rights were completely violated. However, our blessed master turned these vulgar people into a universal loving community of sincere believers. These supreme achievements can be considered as one of the greatest miracles, to make the impossible possible, to penetrate within the deepest regions of people's hearts in such a miraculous manner. This exquisite capacity of transformation is only given to our most noble of men. He not only changed the "arrogant" into the "humble" within one moment, but through his supreme eternal wisdom, his majesty of being, he made equality between the highest ministers and the poorest beggars. His universal community became an organism of living, flourishing unity.

The revolutionary change of character, making primitive people into the highest grades of saints, is certainly our Prophet Muhammad's most outstanding miracle.

How could such transformation of hearts be achieved? His teachings were not about words! His tenderness, his mercy and compassion, his sweet and kind behavior—nothing other than pure love instantly created a complete change in the depths of people's hearts. It was his noble character, the true miracle of his being, which transformed people into truthful believers.

It is no one other than God Most High, with His eternal grace and His limitless divine favors, who made such a perfect functioning society achievable. Our prince of the universe was God's beloved. With our blessed Prophet, God completed His divine favors onto humanity, perfected His religion, and united all the hearts of His universal community. The most magnificent civilization in human history was achieved!

The realization of this miraculous community took place in the city of Medina al-Munawwara. Medina translates as "the city," and *Munawwara* as "the Illuminated."

As the Qur'an says, addressing the Prophet Muhammad, peace and blessings upon him, and his companions:

> *You are the best people that have been brought forth (as a pattern) for mankind. (3:110)*

> *Today I have perfected your religion for you and completed My favor upon you, and I have been pleased with Islam for you as a religion. (5:3)*

Our blessed master said concerning the illuminated city of Medina:

> *Medina is the dome of Islam, the seat of faith, the land of emigration, and the place of the distinction between the lawful and unlawful.*
>
> *Faith recoils into Medina as a snake recoils into its hole.*
>
> *The last city of cities of Islam to be mined is Medina.*
>
> *I was commanded to go to a city that swallows the cities. They say that Yathrib, which is Medina, expels people just as the furnace expels impurities from iron.*
>
> *None shall plot evil against the people of Medina but he shall be dissolved as salt is dissolved in water.*

ALL LIFE IS DIVINE

Our enlightened master demonstrated so beautifully that all life is divine. As the Holy Qur'an often stresses, there is no separation between the sacred and the profane, between the worldly life and the hereafter, between the material and the spiritual. Once we can cast away the shadows of our unconsciousness, our way of life will become the way of life of the hereafter! Contemplating the hereafter will open up the understanding of the earthly life, and vice versa. The human being can realize eternity through his limited existence. When we perceive His infinite Greatness and Perfection and our limits and nothingness, we can reach the truth. We will be able to experience the divine Reality in this world and behold the beauty of paradise in this earthly life. When human perfection in this world is reached, eternity exists here and now. The sweet taste of heaven is given to those sincere believers who obey and love their Lord!

For the lover of the Real, the material and the spiritual become inseparable. They are in such deep slavery with their Lord that they cannot separate the world from God any more. Therefore, their way of life becomes the way of life of the hereafter. Their struggle to find Him, and their eager desire for Him, brings them the taste of pure heaven, because on their way, they gradually find themselves in greater nearness to their Lord. We can say that they surpass creation, because their selves cease to exist. Their bodies become a holy channel, subtle matter and purified. They have died before death, so as the holy tradition reports:

God becomes the eye with which they see, the ears with which they hear, the tongue with which they speak, and the feet with which they walk.

For the ones who have found God in this life, the world becomes perfect and beautiful, and they fall in love with all of existence. Wherever they look, they see the manifestations of God's Beautiful Names, because they see with the eye of their hearts. For the knower of God, the world becomes a divine mirror. Whenever the true lover looks at creation, he contemplates his Well Beloved. Living in this world, they find a secret taste, a hidden satisfaction. As Ibn Arabi says:

The whole universe is from Him, in Him, with Him, through Him. The world becomes a means to dive into the infinite ocean of Oneness.

As a result, the perfect lover of the Real shows the greatest respect, the utmost care, for all things that surround him. All seemingly lifeless matter becomes meaningful—like clothing, furniture, houses, and so on. He is compassionate with vegetation and animals. He is in admiration for the earth, water, minerals and the whole cosmos, stars, planets, sun and moon.

What a heightened level of sensitivity man can reach is truefully expressed by a companion of the Prophet, may God be pleased with him, who exclaimed:

> Each leaf that falls in autumn gives me as much pain as my arm being amputated.

However most of all, the lover shows the profoundest respect for his fellow beings, because they are God's most honored and valuable creation within the universe. His overwhelming love for the Prophet Muhammad, peace and blessings be upon him, and his family, makes him imitate their praiseworthy, loyal character. Holding life sacred implies the best of character traits:

- Treating every situation with the greatest care and respect
- Showing humbleness in all our actions
- Being moderate in all things
- Showing care and love for others
- Thinking well of everybody and everything

- Giving to the ones in need below our material level, being concerned to serve them
- Receiving from the ones in unity above our spiritual level and being concerned, to learn from them
- Spending our sustenance, materially and spiritually, in God's cause

The most noble of men, our Prophet Muhammad, peace and blessings be upon him, with his purest tender heart, was able to see, experience and act the unity of being like no one else. The following tradition of our blessed master allows us to see most clearly his highly increased sensitivity to the hereafter, combined with his deep penetration into earthly life:

When rain started to fall, he exposed his head to it and said that it came fresh from his Lord.

The water drops come from the realm of God's cleanliness, sinlessness, and purity. The rain felt like a divine inspiration, receiving a great divine benefit. As mentioned in the Qur'an, water is the essence of all material life, and from water, God made every living thing (21:30, 24:45).

Furthermore, does not the statement of Aisha, blessings be upon her, our blessed master's wife, give proof to the believers of the sacredness of all life? When she was asked about how the Prophet was as a person, she reported:

He is the living Qur'an.

Ibn Arabi describes the two divine Mercies: the unconditional Mercy, *"ar-Rahman,"* which refers to God's Words:

My Mercy embraces all things. (7:156)

In the conditional Mercy, *"ar-Rahim,"* God prescribed Mercy to Himself and He made it a law to be merciful towards His purified servants, who deserve His divine favors. In other words, through their acts of good works, they are guaranteed God's divine Mercy.

The works done for God's sake are precisely called "works of adoration." Furthermore, speaking about love, a noble saying is reported from our blessed master, which highlights his utmost divine awareness:

> *I was made to love three things from your world: women, perfume, and the freshness of my eyes is in prayer.*

With this beautiful utterance, our blessed master showed us the significance of the highest form of divine love; that is to say, he showed us the reality of his love. On the external level, the three things the messenger mentioned are part of the world, but in meaning, they belong to God's divine realms of eternity. They radiate the sweet scent of the hereafter, they represent infinite nourishment for the soul, and they bring the good news of eternal life—women as divine beings, perfume as divine scent, and prayer as divine communion.

So all things of this world represent a source of contemplation for him; that is to say, with these three most precious things, our noble master could admire, desire and reach his Lord best and enjoy nearness to Him.

The beloved of God, our Prophet Muhammad, peace and blessings upon him, never claimed superiority. He acted as a humble servant, in utmost humility, always in a state of perfect receptivity! This was his nature, the treasury of pure modesty. Therefore, our Prophet Muhammad, peace and blessings upon him, was drawn towards divine love and divine beauty. His essential reality was such that he was given the inspiration to love. He was made to love things of this world by Divine love. They gave him the vision of divine beauty. They brought him close to witness the eternal Beauty of his Lord. That is to say, things were rendered to him worthy of love by God. This means that in all things, the object of his desire was exclusively God the Almighty. Therefore, throughout his entire life, he never chose something voluntarily. He was made to live and love by his Lord of Majesty and Bounty.

So the love the Prophet Muhammad, peace and blessings upon him, felt for things in this world was part of his divine love for God.

In the same way as God loves His creatures, he loved women. He was made to love women as the whole loves its part. They were a source of inspiration of divine beauty for him. He could exercise perfect contemplation of God through them. Goodness and beauty are feminine attributes. God created women in utmost beauty and endowed them with His most essential attributes of mercy and compassion due to their station of motherhood. God's mercy encompasses all things. God fashioned human beings with His two Hands, and this divine touch endowed them with a generous and kind nature. He called the human being *"bashar,"* which refers to tenderness. The Prophet was drawn to women because they radiate God's attributes of mercy, love, beauty, tenderness, compassion.

The Prophet, to whose speech the whole world was enslaved, used to say to his wife:

> *Speak to me, O Aishah!*

And our saint, Jalal al-Din Rumi, comments about man and woman:

> *If, like water, you outwardly dominate over woman, inwardly you are dominated by her and seek her.*
>
> *But ignorant men dominate woman, for they are shackled by the ferocity of animals.*
>
> *The Prophet, peace and blessings be upon him, said that, women totally dominate men of intellect and possessors of hearts.*
>
> *She whose beautiful face makes man her slave – how will it be, indeed how, when she begins acting like his slave!*

God's act of creation is by blowing the divine breath of mercy. The world is a manifestation of His divine breath of mercy. All of existence is contained in the divine Breath. Because of the light of the breath of mercy, beauty is in every breath. The divine breath of mercy emanates from the source. At the source purity reveals a sweet fragrance; it is the perfume of divine existence.

God's love and desire for the Prophet Muhammad, peace and blessings be upon him, is beyond our imagination!

He named him, "My beloved." The divine favors of the All-Merciful on His most desired Prophet were without measure. As a sign of His love, the Almighty bestowed the secret of the perfume of existence unto him, which is the "divine breath of Mercy."

So the Prophet was made to love perfume after women. The divine scent has a secret presence. It manifests itself due to the purity of divine love and divine friendship. The sweet scent of divine friendship emanated between the Prophet Muhammad, upon him be peace, and his best friend from Yemen, Uways al-Qarani. It was also between the Prophet Jacob and his son, Prophet Joseph, upon them be peace and blessings, before they re-united after many years. The perfume of divine realities was brought to the Prophets as good news of their most beloved Lord. In the *Mathnawi* of Jalal al-Din Rumi, we can read an excellent description about the secret presence of the divine scent:

> *Did you ever smell the scent of a rose where no rose was? Did you ever see the foaming of wine where no wine was? The scent is your guide and conducts you on the way; it will bring you to the garden of Eden and Kawthar. The scent is a remedy for the sightless eye; it is light-making; the eye of Jacob, upon him be peace and blessings, was opened by a scent. The foul scent darkens the eye, and the scent of Joseph, upon him be peace and blessings, succors the eye. You who are not Joseph, be a Jacob; be familiar, like him, with weeping and sore distress. Hear to this counsel from the Sage of Ghazna (Sana), that you may feel freshness in your old body.*

God the most Gracious holds His servants who love each other for His sake in the highest esteem. He bestows on them the gift of divine fragrance. The sweet taste of heaven is given to those sincere believers who love each other for His sake. As the truthful believer becomes the mirror of the truthful believer, the sweet scent of divine friendship will spread from lover to lover. When lovers inhale and exhale, they are living the perfume of remembrance. Such lovers are the perfume of this world. For this reason, the same miraculous sweet scent can hit us sitting in the presence of holy men and, especially, in visiting their sacred graves.

The ritual prayer is the pillar of the religion. It is the basis of faith. Concerning the ritual prayer, our blessed master says:

Everything has a symbol. And the symbol of faith is the ritual prayer. The ritual prayer is the light of my eyes.

My heart ardently desires these forms of worship. On account of this longing of mine, my Lord gathered together the various acts of worship performed by the inhabitants of the seven heavens to form the prayer, which He made a religious obligation for my community in honor of me. Any member of my community, who properly performs these five set of prayers will accomplish the worship of all inhabitants of heavens.

Salat, prayer, has a double meaning: to pray and to bless. While we pray, God reveals Himself and dispenses His Mercy towards us. In other words, God blesses the worshipper with His Presence. According to a tradition, God says:

I witness the invocation of he who invokes Me.

The ritual prayer is designed in such perfection that the invoker will accomplish immediately a deep communion with God most High. It is the highest form of remembrance, designed to penetrate through earthly limitations and arrive in God's divine realms of infinity, where time and space get suspended. Having transcended earthly conditions, the believer will get a taste of the divine scent of the hereafter, the everlasting values.

Therefore, the ritual prayer is the one where the extinction of the worshipper into the Worshipped is reached, transcending the duality of the Creator and the created. Only God is left praising Himself in the heart of the worshipper. In this greatest of all prayers, the worshiper will be totally overwhelmed by his Beloved up to his own annihilation in Him.

Therefore, the ritual prayer represents the biggest favor to all the believers. It represents the most exclusive, most unifying, most elevated, most mysterious, most unique, and special of all prayer rites due to the worshiper's ascension.

The prostration is highly significant for the self-annihilation of the worshipper into the Worshipped, and his complete deliverance unto Him. This ritual posture carries the quality of complete submission and intimacy of a slave with its owner. Prostration is the symbol of loving union of the servant with its Lord. This is precisely the nature of the Prophet Muhammad, upon him be peace and blessings, himself! Therefore, our blessed Prophet was made to love prayer after perfume.

As we see, the prayer symbolizes the contemplation of the adorer towards the Adored, the praiser towards the Praised. The perfect prayer is accomplished when the adorer dissolves in the Well-Beloved. Our Prophet was consumed by the love he had for God. He was the adorer par excellence. Therefore, the Prophet said:

The freshness of my eyes is given to me in prayer.

With this tender, loving statement of adoration, our blessed master reveals to the followers of his community what beauty and great joy he found while praying. In Arabic, the expression, "the freshness," meaning "the coolness of my eyes," signifies intense pleasure.

As we see, throughout his whole life, our blessed master stayed perpetually in deepest communion with his Lord. His sacred body became the purest heavenly channel, possessing an extraordinary sanctifying magnetic presence. An ocean of light, grace, compassion and love poured out ceaselessly in great abundance.

How precious is our body! If we understand that our physical being is God's treasure house, that our body is a divine instrument, how careful we should be in its use! Our body, our senses, our organs, our mind, and the inner faculties have to be educated. This work will be the work of purification from matter towards light. We have to train our eyes, tongues, ears, hands, speech, stomach, sexual organs, mind, concentration, and willpower. Through the constant struggle with our lower nature, we will be able to gain control over our physical condition and reach the desired purity of body and soul, so God wills!

THE NOBLE CHARACTER OF THE PROPHET

The holy Qur'an does not give great importance to the miracles of the Prophet. Nevertheless, there are two remarkable wonders worth mentioning: one was the Night of the heavenly Ascension, where he was transported by God to God and brought before His eternal Presence; the other was splitting the moon in half. However, the Prophet only split the moon in two because of the weakness of the people's perception.

Throughout history, we can observe that most previous Prophets were possessors of certain miracles. In the Prophet Moses, on him be peace, miraculous powers were manifested, like his stick; and at the same time, he destroyed the magical tricks of the wizards. With the Prophet Jesus, on him be peace, healing powers were demonstrated and he revived the dead to life. The Prophet Joseph, on him be peace, was the master of the interpretation of dreams. The Prophet Solomon, on him be peace, was granted the direct power of command over the wind, animals, and the jinn.

But with the coming of the Prophet Muhammad, upon him be peace, the need for miracles to prove the truth of the Revelations ceased. It is precisely his noble character, his own personality, his heart, his mind, and the faculties of speech, hearing and seeing, which reveal the greatest of all wonders. That is to say, God's greatest miracle of creation is nothing other than the truth, the hidden reality of Muhammad, 'hakikat-ı Muhammedi,' and his noble character, 'ahlaki Muhammedi.' In other words, with our blessed master, God wished to shift the attention of all the believers from the outer spectacle to the inner reality within ourselves! It is important to see that God Most High holds our noble master beyond every kind of worldly authority and sovereignty.

Nevertheless, let's just mention a few of the visionary capacities our blessed master possessed:

- The art of perfect knowledge of all the sciences
- The art of highest eloquence, and penetrating speech
- The art of seeing all of the past and future events. (This knowledge is precisely written down on the 'Guarded Tablet,' 'Lawh-i mahfuz,' a synonym for the Universal Soul, on which God engraved all things happening in the past, the present and the future.)
- The incomparable capacity of his heart to receive divine Revelations, combined with the art of effective miraculous penetration into the hearts of his followers.

And here are some of his miraculous character features:

- The Prophet was illiterate, but he knew and understood all sciences, and all divine knowledge.
- He made his ego into a Muslim.
- Before the ascension, his breast was split open as an initiation ritual which purified all his inner organs.
- He was sent as a mercy to the entire world.
- He will be the intercessor for all humanity on the Day of Judgment.
- His modesty was the glory of the universe, and he was the most noble of men.
- He made dead matter and animals into talking creatures.
- He made stiff-necked arrogant, ill-mannered, uncivilized people bow their heads in submission and transformed them into the most praiseworthy guides of humanity.
- He made equality and brotherhood between kings and beggars, poor and rich, ministers and shoe-shiners, sultans and vagabonds.
- He built a universal community, a believing society of unbreakable unity, out of vagabonds and Bedouins.

- By the light of his wisdom, he made humanity into a living organism of flourishing unity, as every pilgrim in Mecca is given the privilege to experience. All believers breathe the same breath and have the same goal. A hundred thousand become one.
- Sent as a mercy to the whole of mankind, grace and blessings poured ceaselessly in abundance from our blessed master. Being the source of goodness, every moment of his earthly life, he nourished and illuminated all of existence, such as the mineral, vegetable, animal and the human beings. He symbolized the bounty of bountifulness:

One time, his beloved daughter, Fatima, may God be pleased with her, was extremely hungry; our master said prayers and put his hand on her chest. After his supplication, Fatima, may God be pleased with her, never felt hungry again.

Another time, when he dug a young date tree into the earth, its fruits immediately emerged from the small branches.

When the governor of Iran, Husrev Perviz, received a letter from the Prophet, he tore it furiously apart. Upon his tearing the letter, our blessed Prophet made a prediction concerning this incident that the governor's possessions and status were going to be destroyed as well, which happened years later.

We have to mention that within his daily contact, the Prophet ran away from extraordinary things, like special crafts, fortune telling, magic and miracles. He only wished to be a good example to everyone in all matters of life. He demonstrated with his behavior, that to be created as a human being is sufficient to make spiritual progress up to the level of pure illumination. In other words, the human being is created in the concept of the perfect man. He carries the seat of sainthood in himself.

God did not wish to impress large crowds with wonders or special effects, but to teach humanity through His beloved messenger about how perfection in man can be reached. All of the wonderful qualities our Prophet possessed are within us. We are created in "God's Image,"[1] so we are of divine origin and blessed with divine wisdom and secrets. Divine treasures are placed within us in abundance.

Through sincerely loving him, yearning for his beauty, we have the possibility to get closer to his supreme degree of existence. Our most sincere intention should be to imitate his noble character, and to adopt his fine qualities and his perfect behavior.

When we are able to reach some beauty of character, some light of wisdom, it will be like a spotless mirror in which the eternal light of God shines at us. We will be able to see God's Truth in the pure mirror of our hearts. We look at it with the light coming from it. The same is true on the material level, for we are able to see the world only by the reflection of the light coming from the sun.

---

[1] Bukhari, Isti'zan, 1; Muslim, Birr, 115, Muslim, Jannah, 28.
Important note: Image in this hadith stands for the manifestation of God's beautiful names as reflected in human creation, not in the sense of likeness of physical attributes. God's Essence and nature of existence is beyond our comprehension and outside our imagination.—Ed.

MODESTY

Nothing touches our hearts more profoundly than our blessed Prophet's exemplary humbleness! It is the inner treasury of pure modesty which makes all followers shedding tears of love, admiration, bewilderment.

God gave him all divine wisdom but very often, he simply prayed to his Lord:

God, give me more knowledge.

He was an unlettered Prophet, but all people learned from him. He slept on a mattress of straw, but he was the prince of the universe. He put himself in rows with ordinary people, but he carried all the wealth of his Lord in his breast. All creation praises him, but he called himself only God's servant. He reached the highest point of the ascent, the indescribable 'nearer,' the reunion with his Lord, and then descended to the lowest level of human evolution, to teach the perfection of Shariah, and he shared his life with the needy and poor. God wished to give him all of paradise, but he wished only for his community.

During the battle of Uhud, his companions requested the Prophet to invoke God's curse on the enemy. Although his face was bleeding, he prayed for forgiveness:

Oh God, forgive my people for they do not know.

He is the praiseworthy, but he prayed countless nights to his Lord until his feet were swollen. God created him in the greatest purity, but every day he recited one hundred *'Astaghfirullah,'* saying, 'I seek forgiveness from God.' In between every recitation, he contemplated his nothingness and his baseness. As the seal and the chief among other Prophets, he simply said:

I am just the last brick, which finishes the wall.

He leads humanity to God's Light, but cleaned up his neighbor's dirt in front of his own door. He is the chief of all the Prophets, but his humility is infinite.

God named him as His beloved, but he insisted on the company of the needy and the poor.

His slavehood was without measure, but God exalted his name beside His Own. He is the reason for creation, but attributed nothing to himself. He was the supreme head, the chief of the Imams, but he worked as an ordinary man.

How can our blessed Prophet not be the master in conquering all of our hearts? Our blessed master's home is in the heart of every truthful believer.

SECRECY

In the Qur'an, God the Almighty says:

Call Me in humility and in secret. (7:55)

Our Prophet Muhammad, peace and blessings be upon him, is the treasure-house of generosity. He is the river of truth. His greatness has no end, but he hides the divine treasures behind ordinary behavior. His devoted followers, who sincerely wish to become like him, hide behind simple and undistinguished appearances as well. They are champions of the truth, but they conceal who they are. Their self-sacrifice is of such perfection, that they have lost their own existence. They belong entirely to the Only One. Their state is that of an abundant slave obeying its owner. They are in a state of pure servanthood without free will. Such submitted slaves become unrecognizable. Their servitude reaches such perfection that one hardly notices them. Because they have reached the highest level of human perfection, their appearance blends in with everyone. Their servanthood is flowing so naturally that their offerings become one with their surroundings.

In Islam, secrecy is a principle. The intimates of God are the holders of divine wisdom. They keep God's treasures safe behind good locks, because what they carry within their breasts is highly precious. They never reveal divine knowledge without God's order. They preserve God's truth, so God preserves them. Their secret wealth is hidden through their state of poverty, their nothingness.

As our great saint Jalal al-din Rumi comments:

I have preferred Your Pleasure over my own; Your Secret is mine, so I keep it hidden.

The perfection of secrecy is, again, our beloved Prophet peace and blessings be upon him. He was the supreme master in all earthly and spiritual matters, but simple pure modesty reflected from his appearance. Within the religious obligations such as fasting, praying, the Prophet did not leave any trace of his behavior. It was very hard for his household and companions to see him fasting, or catch him breaking the fast, or to see him performing voluntary prayers during the night, or giving alms to the poor. He never made a demonstration of his supreme sainthood and his exquisite divine knowledge.

He always acted as a man in a row, blending in with everyone. He moved very naturally, and he was very human. He did not give the opportunity for people to say: "Look what a great thing he did!" However, to the seemingly unimportant matters of daily life, he gave us deep insight and inspiration of the beauty within them!

Our Prophet showed utmost care at every moment, in all of his behavior and actions. When he was talking, eating, working, going to war, being consulted, and in whatever he did, his goal was to please his Lord and to be an enlightened example of how to live a good and simple life. In other words, our blessed master showed us that giving high respect to every moment of our days and nights makes our lives into a prayer. As we see, we could not witness voluntary actions of the Prophet, nor did he manipulate the people to do so. However, the light of his generous devotions, done in secret, spread far and wide; and in this way, all living souls benefited. The Prophet Muhammad, peace and blessings be unto him, nourished all humanity with his eternal light of goodness!

The devotees, who perfectly resemble our blessed master in their modesty perfectly, become God's brides. He covers them with veils of His protectiveness. God carries such servants in the greatest esteem. He hides His most precious brides from creation. Their intimate love discourses are held in the highest privacy. They are for Him; He is for them. They know nothing but Him and whom He alone knows.

The ones who most resemble our beloved of God in his essential reality of servanthood, secrecy, humbleness, and humility are the *'malamiyya.'* They are called the "men of blame," because they take all blame on themselves while secretly keeping innocent. They fully satisfy all the conditions of pure servanthood to all humanity. Another description of the *malamiyya* is given as 'the children of the night,' whose sainthood is hidden from man's eyes, whereas among 'the children of the day,' their spiritual perfection is visible. Because they are the most hidden, they become the most pure.

Here are a few beautiful examples of such essence of saintly secrecy:

A hadith quoted by Abu Nu'aym:

> *The servants whom God loves best are the pious and the hidden. When they are away, no one misses them, and when they are present, they are ignored. They are the imams of good guidance and the torches of Knowledge.*

The saint, Abu Yazid al-Bistami says:

> *The saint of God has no feature by which he is distinguished, nor any name by which he can be named.*

In a holy tradition, God most High says:

> *The most enviable of My* awliya *close to Me is a believer whose possessions are few, whose joy is prayer, who accomplishes the service of his Lord to perfection, and obeys Him in secret. He is obscure among men and no one points at him. Know that God has servants who are neither prophets nor martyrs and who are envied by the prophets and martyrs for their positions and their nearness to God. On the Day of Resurrection, thrones of light will be placed at their disposal. Their faces will be of light—these are the* awliya *of God.*

A hadith quoted by Abu Hurayra:

> *I went in one day to the Prophet. He said to me: "In a moment, a man will come towards me through that door; he is one of the seven men by means of whom God protects the inhabitants of the earth." And behold, an Ethiopian* (habashi) *came through that door. He*

was bold and his nose had been cut off. On his head, he carried a pitcher of water. God's Messenger said, "This is he." Now this man, explains Abu Hurayra, was the servant of al-Mughira Ibn Shu'ba, and it was he who washed down and swept out the mosque.

Hasan, blessings be unto him, the grandson or our beloved master, used to go frequently out at night with his face covered, so that no one could recognize him, giving food to the poor, leaving it at their doors. Once he had passed away, from that day on, the poor people noticed that there was no food left at their doors any more. No one else than our beloved martyr could have been the mysterious donor. Our blessed grandson of the Prophet had to leave this earthly existence before they became aware of his charitable acts!

Sheikh Muhyiddin Ibn Arabi comments about the state of secrecy:

There is nothing higher in man than the mineral nature, for it is the nature of the stone, when left to itself to fall, and this is true of 'ubudiyya,' servanthood. True servants are the pebbles in the hand of God.

The earth carries the same nature of submission. It simply exists for humanity to inhabit, to build on, and to give birth to vegetation. Flowers reveal their sweet scent and color, as their harmonious beauty touches us unnoticeably. It is the essence of the flower which serves us by its existence.

All creation receives God's divine grace and mercy. All life is in harmony with Him. All existence turns by His Breath, glorifying, praising and celebrating the oneness of being. Thus, all things by their nature are living true servanthood.

The whole essence of being secret points to the fact that when one loves deeply, one becomes shameful and humble. When one is in union with one's Lord, one becomes private and secret—because what is most precious for oneself has to be carefully protected.

God Most High reveals Himself in the same manner. He makes Himself known from what He hides from us. Through

His concealment, He reveals His secrets. He is the Greatest and the Most Powerful, but He reveals Himself as the most Merciful and Compassionate. His Revelations contain immense and infinite knowledge, but the meaning remains hidden.

The Prophet's very being is the key to the secrets that is shared between God and man, and he is the living truth of secrecy. He is the highest authority on all levels, preserving and hiding God's divine treasures behind his modest appearance.

THE SACRED LAW

In the Qur'an God most High says; *I have not created the jinn and humankind but to (know and) worship Me (51:56).*

The Sharia symbolizes the highest ethics of the religion of Islam. It signifies the spiritual journey to the Ka'ba of the heart. It represents the greatest divine design ever given to humanity from God most High. The performance of the Sacred Law is equal as to mount on Buraq, the heavenly stead of love! And to fly with the wings of intelligence of Archangel Gabriel, peace be upon him.

The abandoning of the sacred obligations means to break away from the light of Muhammad! The abandoning of the religion, to deny the Existence of God means to deny the reality of mercy! If believers do not think and reason in the light of prophethood, in the light of the holy Qur'an, there will be disorder, chaos, confusion, disharmony, injustice, ignorance.

The worship activities of fasting, pilgrimage, charity, prayer is an exercise to strengthen the truth in ourselves! How can we ever be truthful in life and in worship if we do not find the secret essence buried within our hearts? Through the performance of the religious duties the falseness of the self will gradually be pealed off and the truth will start to appear. It is the light of our soul which will shine in full splendor.

The All Glorious One gave us a miraculous prescription to reach the ultimate goal, the perfection of the human being; it is the Sacred Law, the Sharia. The Sacred Law is the foundation of all the worship activities for God. Within it lies the inner wealth of the religion Islam. In order to establish harmony within ourselves, all human beings have to live in accordance with the divine order. The five pillars of the religion are the foundation to build up our spiritual life. Our lives will not become sacred if we do not submit to the Sacred Law. A believer's life without the five pillars of the religion is like a house without base, walls, windows, and roof. Without the source of strength of the religious obligations, a believer's life will become disordered and lose its spiritual value and meaning.

The law of the religion represents the way for human perfection. All doctrine and method are given to reach spiritual maturity provided that one includes the sayings from the prophet Muhammad, peace be upon him, and his way of life, conduct, and behavior. When our most noble of all men honored this world with his holy appearance, pure love descended and the world got enlightened. As the prophet of God said; *"I came to perfect good behavior."* He brought the law of religion, the Sharia, and completed it with the example of his life, namely the example of his noble character, his conduct his practices, his sayings. The religion of Islam is to the highest degree a flowing, uninterrupted, dynamic education, ever-present, because it is based on the practice of God's Messenger!

The teaching of the religion of Islam lies in the wisdom that the fruit of eternity and divine harmony are only earned through the struggle in daily life. This is why our Prophet became the Sultan of the Sharia, because he was sent to perfect good behavior. He was sent to teach nothing other than the sacredness of Sharia, because the way of human perfection ends in simple conformity with the Sacred Law given by God Most High. Through the Prophet's life we see that perfection of the law paired with the acquisition of a noble character will bring us to the highest station. Our blessed master represents therefore the illumination of our earthly existence. As Sheikh Muhyiddin Ibn Arabi says: *"Sainthood is earned through works of the Sacred Law, not those of thinking."*

More precisely, Islam demonstrates that the worth and honor of a human being does not lie in the perfection of knowledge, rather in the degree of love he shows to submit to God's commandments and the degree of his struggle to achieve the highest ethics of character trades. Praying to the Almighty has to be an expression of one's love, admiration and longing towards the Only One. The secret for successful worship lies therefore in the desire we have for Him, in the wish to become intimate with Him, in the degree of one's yearning to communicate with Him, in the profundity of one's longing to be raised to the level of friendship with Him. Worship subdues the ego, surpasses mundane passion. If our worship does not leave rational thinking, calculation, we cannot be intoxicated with something other-worldly, we cannot get a divine taste, we cannot penetrate into the realms of the unseen, we cannot perceive images of the eternal realms of beauty. If our worship does not leave the desire for position, possession, rank, status, family, children, friends, we cannot enter the ocean of God's mercy. We cannot look at the divine mirror of generosity. We cannot get lost in the infinite sea of God's oneness. We cannot see the beauty and perfection with the eyes of our hearts. If the worshipper is not in love and admiration with God's Beauty and Majesty, he cannot perform the true prayer!

Thus it is through the earthly perfection, living a life of joyful devotion for the Almighty Creator and servitude towards His creation, a believer can realize the highest levels of human spiritual evolution. If we perform the religious duties and the voluntary acts with love, religion becomes pure joy.

No one else than our blessed master, the Prophet Muhammad peace and blessings be upon him, expressed the love for the Sacred Law and the beauty of servanthood so perfectly. It is our glory of the universe who gave meanings to all existence and most of all, taught us the value of the law of the religion, like prayer, fasting, pilgrimage, and charity. Without his supreme example, his beautiful conduct, and his noble character, the law of the religion would just be a mechanical routine. He filled the divine duties with pure love for his beloved Lord and his infinitely desired community.

The sacred law is not separate from the one who brought the sacred law to humanity, the Prophet Muhammad, peace be upon him. God most High send him not only as a prophet, but as a servant and for the perfection of good character and as a mercy for all the worlds. This means, the treasury, the essence of the sacred law bears his noble character, his infinite mercy, his abundant servanthood. It is through the sacred pillars that the religion of Islam got perfected. It is through the sacred law that the religion of Islam differs from the previous religions. In other words, the sacred pillars of fasting, charity, pilgrimage, the ritual prayer, the testimony of faith, symbolize the noble character of the Prophet.

Our blessed master is the perfect mirror of God the Almighty. He is the living Qur'an. God hides Himself, His essence from His believers, but He lets us taste, know and find His reality through the beauty and goodness of Muhammad, peace be upon him. The key to the door that opens to finding God, the key to divine knowledge, is our beloved messenger. His whole life gives witness to the glorious unity of being, that is to say, the reality of Muhammad finds expression in the deepest regions of his earthly existence, which is servanthood. So the sacred pillars are a direct mirror to his servitude.

As our blessed master is sent by his Lord as a mercy for the whole world, so is the sacred law a manifestation of God's all-comprehensive mercy. As he was sent for the perfection of character, so is the sacred law a manifestation of his noble character. As he was sent as a servant, so is the sacred law a manifestation of servanthood. As he was sent to bring a universal message to humanity, so is the sacred law an expression of universal blessings, favors, bounties for all humanity.

The sacred law is the door to enter the King's palace, the palace of the glorious realms of the hereafter, the eternal realms of beauty. The lack of human eternal values, the lack of the connection with one's own roots, that is to say, the lack of religion can only be replaced by the foundation of the sacred law of the Almighty. In other words, a life devoid of the living grace of spirituality can only be replaced though the submission to His divine commands!

Does not the entry to the Palace of His Majesty necessitate a price to pay? The ticket for its audition is the performance of the sacred duties, the submission of our small will towards His great

Will. This is the price we should pay in order to get true spiritual success as believers, namely to gain His approval and contentment in executing our religious duties with the joy and love we feel to be His servants.

In order to reach the ultimate goal, we have to see the sacred law as a means to reach the awareness of fasting, reach the awareness of the pilgrimage and alms giving and the ritual prayer. The sacred law is nothing else than to exercise the sensitivity for the Divine Presence, that is to say, to gain divine awareness! The prayer rituals help to approach the indestructible divine secret, our soul, they help us to find and understand the rank of our soul. Divine awareness is the awareness of our inner nature, our divine origin, our roots, our soul.

We are created with the essence of fast, pilgrimage, alms, and prescribed daily prayers, they are the deep seated quality within us!! That is to say, praying, fasting, alms giving are part of human nature. These essential divine attributes are exactly the nourishments of the angels. The angels are the divine manifestation of devotional worship activities. As long as the believers act in accordance with the commandments of the Sharia, they will be part of a virtuous circle of the angels. Divine blessings, sacred powers, infinite grace will flow from the Almighty towards the hearts of His beloved creatures to the degree of their worship, their devotional activities. Neglecting the religious duties, means to be deprived of the light of God's wisdom. We can compare this uninterrupted flow of living spirituality with the divine flow of the heavenly bodies of the universe. Sun, moon, stars, galaxies are all conforming to the divine order of God's creation.

In the five pillars the light of God's wisdom is manifested. God most High created the human being with the need for His knowledge, the need for divine awareness, consciousness, with the need to see with the eyes of the heart, with the need of breathing the divine scent of the hereafter, with the need longing to hear the divine sound of "Am I not Your Lord?" "Yes indeed You are," with the need to return home to our divine origin. It is the greatest longing of the soul, a desire, a yearning, implanted in the deepest region of our beings at the time of creation of man. It is the essence of who we are because we are created in His Image.

Jalal al-Din Rumi states:

> *"The thirsty man laments: "Oh sweet water! "The water also laments: "Where is the drinker! This thirst in our souls is the attraction of the Water, we belong to It and It belongs to us."*

The nourishment for the divine thirst and need is given in total abundance within the Sharia. Our soul can find infinite satisfaction with the divine light of the Sacred Law. For these reasons, pilgrimage, alms, prayer, and fasting are exactly what man misses most, knowingly or unknowingly. Being deprived of its divine nourishment, man lives in his own tyranny, oppression and cruelty. Deprived of the sacred worship duties, his spiritual self will decay, degenerate. Thus the Sacred Law is a treasury of divine healing!

We need to conform ourselves to the divine order of the cosmos. All existence, the universe, our planet, our body is made out of the same substance matter, the four elements, earth, water, fire, air. They are all in constant movement making millions and millions of changes every moment. With the divine substance of the prayer rites, we oppose these heavy transactions and therefore cut off the material attachments to the material realms of the body, the world and the universe.

For this reason, the body is most involved in the worship rituals and the performance on the exact time is highly required. For example giving alms to the poor is an excellent method to cut off the attachments to personal possessions, status, fame and wealth. The fast of Ramadan is an exquisite training to reduce the activities like eating, drinking, as well as trying to fast with our senses like with our eyes, ears, tongues. The pilgrimage represents a most profound physical struggle, turning one's back to the world and becoming aware of the hereafter.

The human being is a highly sensitive creature, with a very delicate balance. He is a creature sliding between light and clay, between his physical and spiritual nature, his soul and his body. The inner balance is very difficult to establish. The regulations of the body's chemistry is of the highest complexity. Millions of changes happen every moment simultaneously. In one second there are 30,000 new cells created. It is for this reason that our Creator gave as miraculous prescription to attain control over the inner organs and senses, the sacred law. The prayer rituals are the medicine to regulate all bodily functions day and night, cleaning the senses and the inner organs, regulating all of the bodily functions, bringing tranquility and peace of our psyche, thoughts and mind, they bring divine satisfaction, spiritual joy to the heart and soul.

With the practice of the pillars we exercise the internalization of our human state, the transition from the outer physical transitory temporal realm to the inner spiritual eternal realm. It is the work of purification of matter towards light, of the heaviness towards lightness, of material towards spiritual, of the low towards elevation. Our body, our organs, the inner faculties get educated, transforming its chemistry, renewing the cells, changing the blood, changing the skin. The substance of the prayer rituals is like a divine infusion into the body. The blood circulation penetrates the human organs and they get washed clean. We train our eyes, tongues, ears, hands, speech, stomach, sex, mind, concentration, will power in avoiding wrong decisions, wrong actions. The ultimate goal of a believer is to become a holy channel, an instrument of His Will, a receptacle of divine grace, where God will become the eyes with which we see and the ears with which we hear.

We have to adopt the consciousness that we live in exile. Man on earth is the 'fallen man', he is separated from his original home, the realms of the souls. He lives a separated existence from his Creator. If he becomes aware of this separation and experiences its pain, he will be dominated by the wish to go home, he will wish to return to his origin, the state of innocence and purity.

The practices of the sacred law are given to rehearse the return to the One and Only, to re-emerge, re-center our original being. They offer believers the opportunity to remember their divine source. The religious practices signify the spiritual journey to the Kaʿba of the heart. In other words, whilst performing the sacred rituals, we rehearse that we come from God and that we will return to God.

The ritual prayer, fasting, charity, service to the needy, the pilgrimage, are all designed to exercise our sensitivity of the unseen worlds. Our modern societies lost the connection to the divine realms of the hereafter. Being busy with the world like superficial occupations, sensual pleasures, excessive sleep, bad habits, laziness and so on, keeps us away from sacred realms. We have to cut the attachments to the world like intense consumerism and idle occupations and reduce eating, sleeping, and talking. Islam gives perfect measures and guidance on how to deal within the daily 24-hour routine in all spiritual and material matters. It gives the spiritual training of fasting from the activities of the world and increases the activities of the hereafter. The increase of worship, remembrance, service towards one's Lord and the decrease of the satisfactions of the lower self will reveal qualities like patience, peace, contentment, tranquillity, endurance, silence of mind and heart.

A wise man said: *"True comfort is freedom from the desires of the lower self! Your prison is your own lower self. As soon as you escape from it, you will live in the comfort of eternity."* And our great saint Abd al-Qadir al-Jilani gives us the following advice; *"Spiritual culture, Sufism, is not acquired through long conversations, but through going hungry and giving up things that are familiar and pleasant."*

If we obey wholeheartedly with the submission of a loving slave, namely pure joy, we will surpass the stages of simply complying in obedience towards the Sacred Law, and we will reach the stages of the perfection of love! All works of believing servants lies in winning His approval, His contentment, His love. When we meet God's contentment, we will arrive at the door of His intimate conversations. And then so God wills, the believer will be given the chance to see and hear his beloved Lord whilst performing his religious duties. Such lovers are impatiently waiting after having performed one of the ritual prayers for the next one to come. This state of eagerly expecting the next "rendezvous" with the most Merciful is the greatest sign of love. Those sincere servants are waiting impatiently to be led into the divine Presence of their beloved Lord, because when they are praying they have reached the ultimate wisdom; they are able to stand in front of the light of God most High!

Is there any greater way to show our love towards our Supreme Creator than the performance of the Sacred Law with utmost joy of obedience and sincerity?

THE HOLY QUR'AN

As we see, the miracles of the Prophet are not given much value in the Holy Qur'an; on the contrary, the holy verses reveal the actual miracle of creation. They stress how and why God manifests His creation. Here we touch upon an essential reality of God's messages to humankind. When we contemplate the mysteries of creation itself, how God meant the universe to serve us, and how and how we are created in His Image, how we belong entirely to Him in order to serve Him, we will gain consciousness of Him. When we contemplate further the divine mysteries of man and the mysteries of earthly and cosmic nature, we discover a sea of knowledge which will open the eyes of our hearts and bring us to the true purpose of life.

To contemplate the miracle of creation is our essential duty. If we look at the marvelous wonders of God's manifestations, we cannot help to be in awe of their unfolding beauties. Is not the growing of an embryo from two drops of liquid into a whole human organism the greatest proof of the all-embracing Power of God as the Creator? Is not our beloved Prophet Muhammad, peace and blessings be upon him, proof of His never-ending love and compassion toward humankind?

The greatest source of meditation is the holy book, the Qur'an, as well as the life of the Prophet Muhammad, peace and blessings be upon him. The Prophet's nature represented the Qur'an and, therefore, the messages of the Qur'an were carried out through his actions. The meditation on the holy Qur'an and the life of the Prophet are as important as the blood in the veins of our body. Sheikh Muhyiddin Ibn Arabi comments:

> *He who – among the members of his community who did not live*
> *during his epoch – wishes to see Muhammad, let him look at the*
> *Qur'an. There is no difference between looking at it and looking at*
> *God's Messenger. It is as though the Qur'an had clothed itself in a*
> *form of flesh named Muhammad Ibn 'Abdallah Ibn abd al-Mut-*
> *talib. This identification of the Prophet with the divine Word itself*
> *is explained by the words of his wife, Aisha, may God be pleased with*
> *her, who, when questioned about the Prophet's nature, answered:*
> *"His nature was the Qur'an."*

The Qur'an was the last book to be sent. Our master was the last Prophet to be sent. Therefore, the message of the Qur'an represents the seal for the completion of scientific investigations of nature and its mysteries. The exemplary life of the Prophet represents the seal for the perfection of human nature. The Qur'an, as the last book to be sent, contains all the other prophetic books. The Prophet, as the last Prophet to be sent, brought the total of all prophetic revelations. If we drink from it, we are blessed from God's wisdom.

Further referring to the Qur'anic verse, *'Dhuha,'* Chapter 93, "The Morning Hours," an even greater promise from God is given to a sincere believer who recites and contemplates the revelations in the depths of his heart. He can increase his knowledge of his Lord at every moment:

> *And verily the hereafter will be better for you than the present. (93:4)*

In his commentary on this verse, Yusuf Ali says:

> *To the truly devoted man, each succeeding moment can be better*
> *than the one preceding it. In this sense, the hereafter refers not only*
> *to the future life after death, but also to the soul of goodness in*
> *things in this very life. His soul will be filled with more and more*
> *satisfaction as he goes on.*

A beautiful way to describe God's response to His sincere servant, who is trying to be present to his Creator, immersed in reciting and contemplating the Holy Qur'an, is given by Martin Lings:

In every flow there is the promise of an ebb, the grace of the Truth's irresistible power of attraction!

God's Revelations are flowing. The verses flow from God back to God, like waves of the ocean flow and ebb. The messages flow to the human soul, the purest drink it can taste, the ultimate fulfillment. In tasting the divine Words, the soul is drawn back towards God's divine Presence. The Almighty overwhelms us with the Truth of His Messages and carries us back to the eternal realms of His Nearness.

For a lover of the Truth it is a duty to see God by observing all of His creation. It says in the Qur'an :

> *Wherever you turn, there is the Face of God. Verily God is the Infinitely Vast, Infinitely Knowing. (2:115)*

Like never before, the mysteries of knowledge are being opened out to the greatest extent through the holy Qur'an and the personality of the Prophet. In effect, the Prophet brought the full sum of the words *(jawami al-kalim)*, and he spoke in all languages and on all levels. This means the revelations of the Qur'an descend directly into the hearts of the believers in the community of the Prophet Muhammad, whereas the signs given to the children of Israel were visible, they were manifested externally, as stated in the Qur'an:

> *We will cause them to see Our signs in the distance (macrocosm) and in themselves. (41:53)*

A perfect balance to reach spiritual maturity was only given to the followers of our blessed master's community. It is the model for the perfect man, *al-insan kamil*, which leads into the science of unity. So man has this special position in creation, which is referred to as a trust, *'amanat.'* God the Almighty is charging man with divine safe-keeping. Thus, man becomes the holder of divine wisdom. He preserves God's Truth. In the Holy Qur'an, it says:

We offered the Trust to the heavens and the earth and the moun-
tains, but they refused to carry it and were afraid of it; and man
carried it. (33:72)

We have honored the children of Adam. (17:70)

In other words, God honors man to be His vicegerent on earth.
What a supreme responsibility for the human being! His Trust is
our honor.

Therefore man can be described as the true manifestation of
God's activity; man is entrusted with God's safekeeping; man is the
mirror in which God's attributes are reflected; man is the pillar of
heaven, man is the brother of the Qur'an; and man brings together
the divine reality and the created realities.

Man thinks he has to reach nearness to his Creator. However,
He is Ever-Present—He is with you wherever you are. All truths are
present at all times and at all places for those who have eyes to see.
Search for yourself in everything, and search for everything in yourself. When we have knowledge of God, we perceive Him in all
things.

The wisdom of the Prophet and the wisdom of the holy
Qur'an are immeasurable. The Qur'an stresses the source of all creation. The revelations are a restoration, a revival of the very beginning of existence. As the holy Qur'an is the purest form and most
complete of all divine Revelations, the Prophet demonstrates the
purest form of all human beings, restoring the saint in man, and
reviving our divine origin!

God's Revelations are His Light generated from His Essence,
never static, never finished, never exhausted, but constantly unfolding, infinitely flowing as a never-ending divine manifestations towards
all eternity.

Once we arrive in true belief, all discussion will disappear, illusion will disappear, imagination will disappear, reasoning will disappear, and heaviness, worries, and concerns will disappear. The result
is peace of heart, and absolute certainty.

THE BIRTH OF THE PROPHET

Only selflessness can illuminate the universe!

The night of the Prophet's birth is valued very highly because our prince of the universe honored the world with his holy appearance.

The event of the birth of the most blessed creature of all times shook the entire universe. The world looked into an enlightened future. The whole world experienced a manifestation of divine beauty.

As it is narrated in the traditions, God most High says:

> Had I not created him, I would not have created universe. For him
> I created My all, for Myself I created him. He is Mine, I am his.

The world was faced with the source of light. Pure love descended. All existence experienced a spiritual earthquake at the time of his physical appearance. God's abundant mercy and compassion revealed itself to the entire universe. We can compare it to a second birth of the cosmos. The whole world was flooded with endless mercy.

Doctor Haluk Nurbaki so wonderfully describes it in his book about the holy birth of our beloved Prophet, of which he says of 'the holy moment':

> As if the heart of the sun would stop, because it had been burning just
> to serve our blessed Prophet. The sun was running only to reach this
> precious moment throughout billions of years. On that day, the sun
> radiated its rays from the deepest of its ember heart. Now it would
> reach the glory of the universe and would caress his face as if praying.
>
> And on that day, the earth was whirling in a trancelike state of
> ecstasy. The angels were showing exquisite enthusiasm for their
> prayers. The atmosphere reviewed its harmonious order once more to
> itself and gathered the most sensitive molecules around our beloved

*master. All existences in the universe were eagerly waiting with a
feeling of tenderness to see this holy moment.*

*Still the lovers return to the fourteen century in order to experi-
ence the magnificent joy of that moment, because this holy event
became everlasting in time. Thousands of beauties were displayed.
After the ecstatic experience of the souls in the realm; "Am I not
your Lord?" The whole universe experienced a second festival. And
at that moment, all rebellion and denial towards God diminished.
All ways of the universe were surrendered with another light. At
this most precious moment, all creatures emitted their pure supplications by playing most exquisite tunes...*

This night, very unusual things happened. For instance, all the
idols in the Ka'ba fell down on their faces and shattered; the fire of
the worshippers extinguished; the palace of Chosroes collapsed.

With the coming of Muhammad into this world, humankind
received infinite riches, the fullness of God's divine gifts, supreme
consciousness, infinite grace, the highest illumination, and the treasures of divine generosity. Human beings were faced with perfection in every field. Sainthood was restored in man, and our divine
origin was revived. Our blessed Prophet raised all minds and hearts
to the exalted places of God's Majesty and Beauty. All the pure
hearts of the lovers were overfilled with joy.

It is God's love towards His most beloved Prophet Muhammad,
peace and blessings be upon him, which gave birth to the cosmos
and all it contains. Our blessed master is the reason for the entire
creation. The love of God for His most honored Prophet made
Him say:

But for you, I would not have created the universe.

All creatures have been created for the love of him.

THE PROPHET'S FAMILY

I f we did not contemplate the life of the Prophet's family and his closest companions, we would exclude part of our beloved master's essential truth. This writing about the Prophet's personality would be insufficient, because his family and his companions embody his inner wealth and his secrets.

When the Prophet was asked who his family was, he called first Ali and Fatima, may God bless them both, to his right and left sides, and Hussein and Hasan, may God bless them both, below their mother and father. He took them close to his body, opened his cloak and closed it around his beloved ones. Externally they appeared as one body with him, which demonstrates that they are internally part of each other.

As we hear, our blessed master saying about his grandson, Hussein, may God be pleased with him:

I am part of Hussein, and Hussein is part of me.

Our blessed master had the greatest admiration and love for his two grandsons, Hussein and Hasan, may God be pleased with them both. He honored them to such a high degree that he carried them on his shoulders while praying:

> *One time his Caliph, Umar, may God be pleased with him, came into the Prophet's house and saw our beloved of God's grandsons on his back. Seeing this intimate family embrace, he said, "What a beautiful mount you have!"*
>
> *The Prophet immediately added, "What beautiful riders they are."*

His daughter, Fatima, may God be pleased with her, is called the mother of the believers because she is the first of the descendents and the first inheritor of the truth of the Prophet Muhammad, peace and blessings be upon him. Of all the members of his household and companions, she most resembled his noble character, his movements, his behavior, his way of talking, and his appearance. Once, our blessed master looked at her face and said:

Oh my daughter! When I look at you, I remember myself.

He loved her like no one in this world, and she loved him more than she loved her own self. She was only twenty-six years old when she passed into the realm of eternal beauty to join her beloved father:

Shortly before Prophet Muhammad left this world to unite with his most beloved Lord, he told his daughter about his passing away into her ear. At first, she got very sad, and then she smiled. That was because the first thing that he told her was about his leaving this life to join his Lord, and the second thing was that she would be the first to join him.

Ali, may God be pleased with him, the Prophet's son-in-law, his daughter's husband, is called the "king of saints," because he represents all the saints from the Prophet's descendents. Our noble master said to him:

Oh Ali! The offspring of every other Prophet came from himself; however mine will come from you.

There is a wonderful supplication of Ali, may God be pleased with him:

The one who seeks finds me, the one who finds knows me, the one who knows loves me. I love the one who loves me, I am the companion of my lover, the fault of my lover is mine, the caution (responsibility) of my lover is mine.

Anas bin Malik, who performed services for the Prophet for ten years said:

I have never seen a man who was more compassionate to his family members than Muhammad.

His own family shared his essential reality, which is *"ubudi-yya,"* servitude, in a heroic way. Such abundant sacrifice of body, mind, feeling, soul, properties, status and belongings is very particular to the religion of Islam. This highest degree of submission is born especially in our Prophet's universal religion, because our blessed master represents the pure servant among all human beings and the pure slave of his Lord.

Our Prophet's greatest concern was exclusively for his community. His family and his companions showed the same extraordinary service to humanity. We can say that they were an extension of his greatest need, the salvation of his community. They were the embodiment of his noble character and beautiful qualities, and of his compassion for humanity. God created them in such incomparable purity that their complete participation in the Prophet's own life enabled them to become perfected like him.

Receiving direct transmission of God's Revelations through our blessed master, and living constantly in his presence, his family and companions demonstrated how to practice God's newly revealed messages. They reflected our blessed master's supreme wisdom, and his excellent behavior in the smallest, finest details of their lives. The purity of their intention was of the Prophet's level of illumination.

Therefore, his family and closest companions are our first supreme teachers! Through their light of guidance, and their miraculous self-sacrifice, all believers in later times can learn how to live in a righteous and sincere way. In their heroic example, they showed us how to establish the Prophet's qualities of compassion, generosity and love in our lives. They were the first human beings to transmit the religion of Islam. They were the highest grade of saints, the purest of the pure!

A true lover of the Prophet becomes a lover of his family! We certainly owe them our deepest longings, as well as all of our love and goodwill, and our profoundest respect and admiration. In fact, we owe them our lives!

In religion, a believer who is ready to give up his life in God's cause on the battlefield is called a martyr. There are certain believers who reach such a level of purity and faith that they attribute nothing to themselves, not even their own goodness and their own faith. They live their lives entirely in God's cause, keeping nothing for themselves, sacrificing whatever they are and have. They never do anything for any reason, for ulterior motives, and expect neither results nor divine favors. They only wish to conform to the divine Will and to please their Lord. All rewards for their good actions, God distributes among their fellow beings. This is true humility, true generosity.

Sincere believers can be called martyrs, too, which means that they inherit the truth of Muhammad, peace and blessings be upon him. These are the greatest martyrs! Nothing touches us more than their supreme courage, their readiness to sacrifice all and everything in God's cause. Their generosity is of such infinite glory that it extends towards all existence, like God's Mercy and Compassion extends to the whole of the universe and what it contains. These devoted servants are living miracles, as we know our prince of the universe, the reason for creation, Muhammad Mustafa, peace and blessings be upon him, to be. Such supreme self-sacrifice is called heroic generosity, *'futuwwat.'*

For a believer who belongs to the community of the Prophet Muhammad, peace and blessings be upon him, the infinite heroic generosity for humanity of his closest ones is absolutely heartbreaking. As we mentioned, the noble character of his beloved family and closest companions is identical with our blessed master's supreme character traits. That is why, within their daily lives they wished to support, protect, help and serve their beloved Prophet, to carry out the messages revealed by God Most High.

Through their devoted servitude:

- They neither worried nor were afraid to get hurt, tortured, mistreated, sick or even killed
- They answered only with goodness to anyone who treated them badly
- They were content with misery and poverty
- They covered the faults of their fellow beings
- They never complained, even though they were tortured or in the greatest danger.
- They had nothing left to eat or wear, yet they still gave away their very last pieces
- They continued their worship like nothing happened, even when coping with the greatest troubles

In other words, they were immune to what happened to them, and insensitive to pain, because they were filled with the highest love for God and the Prophet Muhammad, peace and blessings be upon him. A certain righteous man would often say:

> *My God, other people may love You for Your gracious favor, but I love You for Your trials and tribulations.*

Another humble servant of God, if there came a day when no affliction befell him, used to say:

> *My God, what sin have I have committed today, that You should deprive me of my trials and tribulations?*

We can say that the more they suffer, the higher their love and affection for God and the Prophet grows, and the stronger their faith becomes! So if you put the faith of all believers on one scale, and you put the faith of the Caliph Abu Bakr, may God be pleased with him, on the other scale, his faith would weigh heavier!

The most touching example of heroic generosity is certainly the beloved grandson of the Prophet, Hussein, may God be pleased with him, who died as a martyr with all of his followers on the battlefield of Karbala, the most tragic event in Islamic history. They were left for many days without water. His followers and his children were dying of thirst as they waited to be admitted to the city with due respect. Yet he submitted to God's divine Will in order to demonstrate the enlightened behavior of a sincere believer. In consequence, Hussein and all of his followers were brutally killed.

His heroic example is held in by Muslims. It is believed that the Prophet, peace and blessings be upon him, himself will intercede for us poor sinners on the day of Judgment and his own family will contribute to our salvation as well.

Abu Bakr, may God be pleased with him, begged God to make his body big enough to cover all of hell, so no one would be able to enter.

One night, when enemies were trying to kill our beloved Prophet, peace and blessings be upon him, Ali, may God be pleased with him, was told by our master to sleep in his bed, so when the enemies came to murder our blessed Prophet, they would find Ali, may God be pleased with him, in his place. Therefore, Ali, may God be pleased with him, waited patiently in the Prophet's bed to be killed. When the enemies came, they found Ali there instead and let him live. As soon as they left, Ali, may God be pleased with him, was eager to rejoin his beloved master, who was on his way emigrating from Mecca to Medina with his Caliph Abu Bakr, may God be pleased with him, to avoid being killed by his enemies. Ali, may God be pleased with him, walked rapidly for many days and nights, without ceasing, through the desert, so that his burning heart could rejoice with his beloved master as soon as possible. When he finally arrived in Medina, he embraced his enlightened master, but his feet were covered in blood from the terrible burning desert.

In one of the holy wars, the Prophet, peace and blessings be upon him, himself got hurt:

> *A woman, Sumayra, although her two sons and her husband were killed as martyrs on the battlefield, was more concerned when she heard that our blessed master had been hurt, as she asked in the greatest distress: "Where is my beloved Prophet?"*

Running to look for him, she forgot her own family's losses! When she spotted him, enemies with spears encircled him. She courageously picked up a spear and fought her way through the hostile crowd to the Prophet. And even though she was wounded, she finally managed to get to her beloved master's side. Only by rejoicing with him could she comfort her distressed soul.

Prophet Joseph, upon him be peace and blessings, represents such a remarkable example to us believers that his whole life is described in a *Sura* (chapter) of the Qur'an, to teach us the heroic generosity of a sincere faithful believer. He was thrown into the depths of a well by his own brothers; he was sold as a slave; he was thrown into a prison; and he was separated from his most beloved father for 40 years—but he never said to God, although he was a Prophet: *'Save me from my distress, save me!'* However, he was finally reunited with his whole family after having experienced this greatest examination from God. Then he made the following supplication to his Creator:

Rafiq al-ala! – O supreme Companion!

After having reached true happiness, and being reunited with his family, and as the king of Egypt, having suffered for 40 years, he did not claim to enjoy his luck. He only wished to be a true servant.

Even though the Prophet Joseph was betrayed by his own brothers, he kept on praying to God for ten years, day and night, making the following supplication:

Oh God, if you forgive them, so be it. But if not, then I will fill the world with mourning. Punish them not, Oh Lord, for they are full of regret for the sins that suddenly overtook them!

Joseph's feet became blistered from his night vigils, his eyes full of pain from weeping and wailing. But his lamentations went to the highest heaven, and the Lord of all Worlds rewarded him with endless grace and mercy.

The Prophet Muhammad, peace and blessings be upon him, many times did not eat or even cook some water for two or three days; or, as Aisha, may God be pleased with her, reports:

> *One night at his bed, he found a date, picked it up and immediately ate it. How hungry he must have been! However, as he tried to sleep, after putting this date into his mouth without thinking, he could not sleep the whole night. He felt devastated, not knowing if the date was apportioned for charity or not.*

When the Prophet Abraham, peace and blessings be unto him, was to be thrown into the fire by his enemy, Nimrod, Archangel Gabriel asked him if he wished for something from God. He responded that he was not in need of anything from his Lord; it was enough that He knew his situation. A similar emotion is related in the following:

> *A man who had cancer of the skin and bones was lying in the hospital, and wiped from time-to-time the open sores on his face with cotton and said: "Look what a big present God gave to me!"*

There was a truthful follower of the Prophet peace and blessings be upon him, who was the owner of this supreme level of faith, because of his affection for our most noble of all men, and he said:

> *I have known nothing of worldly pleasures in my life of over eighty years. All my life has passed on battlefields and at various other places of suffering. There has been no torment, which I have not tasted and no oppression, which I have not suffered. I care for not for paradise, nor fear hell. If I witness that the faith of my nation— that is, all the Muslim people—has been secured, I will have no objection to being burnt in the flames of hell, for my heart will change into a rose garden while my body is being burnt.*

These highest grades of saints are the true founders of 'the school of love.' May God give us the honor to be one of their devoted followers! How blessed we are to be part of the Prophet Muhammad's community, peace and blessings be upon him, and have such exalted examples to learn from! Ali, may God be pleased with him, although he was the door of knowledge, shows us with his famous statement how exquisite the divine favors pouring on us are:

> *If you teach me one letter, I become your slave.*

Similarly:

> *When the Prophet, peace and blessings be upon him, was asked: "Who is your family?" He responded: "Every beautiful believer is part of my family."*
>
> *When the Prophet peace and blessings be upon him, was asked: "Who are your closest ones," he replied: "You are my dear friends, you share your lives with me; but all believers who will come in later times, who did not see me but believe in my religion and love me wholeheartedly, are closer to me than all of you who are able to be with me."*

For a true believer, to live the truth of Muhammad, peace and blessings be upon him, is pure necessity! It is like the heart to the body. The body is the religion of Islam, and the heart is the reality of Muhammad, peace and blessings be upon him, which feeds the arteries with life.

To live this highest level of truth, we must put God before paradise, the Sustainer before the sustenance, and the Creator before the creation. We must put the Prophet Muhammad, peace and blessings be upon him, before our own blood relationships. If we do not love our blessed master more than anything, or anyone, even ourselves, we do not reach the perfection of faith!

Our blessed master Muhammad, peace and blessings be upon him, is trembling for us! In all of our behavior, we should be worried not to hurt him; we should be ashamed not to love him with the profoundest of feelings; we should be ashamed of not contemplating him with a burning longing; and we should be enslaved by his exalted speeches.

We should be in pain of separation from Him. His inexhaustible beauty should bring us to the greatest admiration, bewilderment and helplessness. His supreme light of unity should wash away our impurities like a heavy storm. We should tremble to win his compassion and guidance, and wish fervently to be part of his intercession.

Our Prophet Muhammad is the pure source of the divine eternal truth. Especially in our present time, I believe we can comprehend the reality of Muhammad much more profoundly than in the past! We are able to perceive his supreme value and beauty more fully, because the world today is in greater need of him. And as the most enlightened man in the universe, he brought an enlightened and enlightening religion. The Prophet Muhammad's inner potential is incomprehensible for the human mind. We can only catch a glimpse of his greatness. But through trying to love him, we can get a taste of his beauty within ourselves. His home is in the pure hearts of his lovers.

UNTIL WE FIND HIM

Until we find the Prophet Muhammad, peace be upon him, we are blind. All suffering comes from not understanding and loving the Prophet Muhammad. If we love the Prophet more than anything else, our lives will change. For a true believer, the noble character of the Prophet Muhammad is the greatest miracle that exists.

In one sense, paradise is nothing other than clearly knowing, seeing and tasting the divine reality within ourselves. Moreover, for a true lover, paradise is to see and taste the beauty of the Prophet Muhammad, peace and blessing be unto him!

I wrote so many pages out love for him, out of longing for his beauty. But we need purity to reach him. Therefore, I am only an admirer from far away. We are living in the end of times. We are of the 'weak' ones. May God Most High judge us by our intentions!

PART TWO

The Dance of Life

LIFE STORY

I was nourished so well!

Before I was faced with the reality of God, I did not give any thought about religion. Is there a God? Is there none? Is there any necessity to join any group conducting religious activities, or to go to church? Is there any truth in the three main religions, Judaism, Christianity and Islam? What are the differences between them? Do souls and the hereafter exist? Is there any destiny, or is our life all free will? Such questions did not interest me.

The only time I touched on these religious matters in the environment in which I was living were during meditation circles, which were part of the Buddhist movement. This was the only activity that was common amongst my friends. Today I know why the western mind feels more familiar with Hinduism, Buddhism or Zen Buddhism. To explain the meaning of human life, they offer a logical, rational set of philosophies and the concept of reincarnation, whereas in all monotheistic religions, one has to believe in the unseen!

Why was I in such a seemingly state of 'disinterest'? I was very busy and very fulfilled! I was a modern dancer, a pure artist. In fact, I was not just a famous dancer, but within the dance world, I was something of a pioneer. In 1980s, I founded a new movement in Switzerland called 'Dance-Performance.' This movement was common in the beginning of the 20th century as freestyle dance or natural dance.

Having had a ballet and modern dance education, I felt that I could not join a company, although choreographers wished to employ me. Something in me said, "No!" This was the crucial point. I was extremely dissatisfied with the Ballet Academies as such, and the working conditions of the present Ballet companies. I strongly felt the 'narrowness' of this profession. I knew instinctively that there could be much more freedom of expression and richness within the movement vocabulary, and deeper levels of personal experience than I encountered at that time. Therefore, I went in search for some kind of 'opening,' a true way of expressing the needs and concerns of our human lives. All artistic renaissances throughout history manifest themselves in order to bring about a deeper method of communication. This specific conflict I encountered within myself is essential to explaining my whole life story.

After puberty, realizing things about one's own way of life, about one's environment, family, school, friends and so on, one either begins to question everything, or one continues to live in exactly the same way as everyone else, never trying to change anything. I belonged certainly to the first category of young people, because I was extremely unhappy within myself. Life seemed meaningless and empty. I even, now remember this feeling. How could this be? Switzerland is such a perfect country—economically, politically and socially. Again, this is the crucial point!

When I started to grow up, when my personality began to develop after puberty, after I had just finished my ballet education, I discovered amongst my friends and my family, in work places and hanging out in places like bars and restaurants, a great heaviness and narrowness. Life felt insufficient and very low. Today I know that it was love that was missing, it was respect that was missing, it was beauty that was missing.

Of course, there was no solution, no place to go, no one to consult. However, inside of me, there was this very powerful certainty, that life is not as it appears to be! I knew that there must be people who knew much more than I did, that there must be places where 'interesting' things were happening, and this feeling became the driving force for my ongoing search. Therefore, I went instinctively to big cities like London and Paris, because I thought that surely there must be people there from whom I could learn something 'new.'

At the age of nineteen, I went alone to London for one year. It was the first time that I had been separated from my parents and sisters. It turned out to be a little catastrophic, because of my extreme loneliness and the fact that I had no one to share my deepest concerns. Young people like me, who were very dissatisfied with their life situations, were mainly trying to resolve their problems with drugs and alcohol, and so on. Thanks be to God that I had a natural instinct that 'getting high' with narcotics and other things was not the solution!

This seemingly small but actually immense difference highlights the fact that I was drawn to seeking the truth, whereas many of the young people around me did not seem to be.

If certain things in one's life should be changed and one wishes to do something about it, it is absolutely necessary to become aware of one's insufficiencies and become dissatisfied with the situation one lives in. The wise men say the biggest problem is not the problem itself; it is not knowing where the problem comes from. In other words, to be a seeker means we have to develop the awareness of the situation we live in and take appropriate action according to what is required.

These were some of my thoughts at that time as a dance artist:

- It is necessary to struggle for what is missing in our lives.
- Where something is prevented, we must begin to work.
- We have to evaluate our own worth.
- We have to resist the emptiness with a creative substance and strive for knowledge and values, to improve the quality of our lives.

At the age of twenty, my dissatisfactions were great. I could not help questioning, searching and experimenting. I felt heaviness and emptiness, a kind of degeneration, because society was mainly oriented towards consumerism, the material side of life. In short, I was

bored and felt very lonely. When one is an 'outsider,' not being inte-
grated in any way into a social structure, either professionally or pri-
vately, one suffers great internal losses. The following years, I went
through many physical and psychological problems; for example, I
did not wish to eat and I walked around almost like a skeleton.
Even now, I still have to work out the last remains of bad habits
and unbalanced psychological states.

After many years of searching within the dance world and my
circle of friends, I wrote an article that was published in art maga-
zines with the title, *"We must take refuge into life!"* This was exactly
what I felt living in 'dry' Switzerland. I had formulated what was
wrong, in my opinion, with society—the way we treated our bodies, and the way culture and art were handled. After puberty, I just
felt that something was wrong; and at a later stage, I became aware
of 'what' was wrong.

During these years, I went alone into the studio, using it like
a laboratory. I instinctively looked for a new way of expression, a
new body language, and some form that could capture my deepest
concerns. With my friends, I did the same research. First of all, I
looked for substantial friends, some interesting people. But how
could I find them amongst those artist groups, which were not
able to find for themselves. Because we did not fulfill each other's
needs as friends, we became very busy constantly discussing art
events, politics, cultural movements, new movies, books, theatrical
performances, new philosophies and psychologies. We nourished
ourselves especially with the celebrities from the music scene, such
as the Beatles and the Rolling Stones. The entire music scene was
completely fulfilling! Although, on the surface, we were occupied
with an extreme 'busy-ness,' underneath, I was very hungry for
something 'new,' some unknown knowledge, to discover 'other
worldly' realities about our lives.

However, we never talked about religion, because it was not
of any interest amongst artist groups. I was very busy, my life was
very exciting, and I did not need any 'God.' These art events and

discussions amongst my friends occupied me externally; but sub-consciously, I was looking within human relationships and in the dance world for a new way of expression, for a deeper fulfillment, for mutual sharing. I only realized much later that I was looking for love, which means that I was looking for God! But in all these years of searching, I could not find any solution. There was no concrete result. In short, nothing changed except my way of per-ceiving.

Now I know that we will never find anything, even if we des-perately fight for it, because it is 'the water that looks for the thirsty,' meaning God looks into our heart, at the purity of our intentions, and when we are internally ready, He will reward us with His divine favors.

My search went on for a long time, for about ten years, until there was a kind of 'opening.' At that moment, a serendipitous situ-ation occurred which led into a new way of life! I was in the right place, at the right time, with the right people, doing the right thing! However, today I say, "God put me at the right time in the right place..."

After this period of rootless wandering with no certainty, con-viction, trust, peace, comfort, or solution, a man came into my life and found great value in the way that I worked. He was the director of the modern museum of my city, Basel, who used to go and look around in artist's studios, to discover new young talents to display at his museum. He saw some of my work, as I had some small dance pieces ready to present, and he immediately gave me an engagement in his exhibition hall. The place was completely filled with people; they had to sit on the floor, and many stood on ledges on the walls. I will never forget this wall of people staring at me! My dance per-formance was very successful because I did something very new. Usually, dance, theatre and opera were only displayed on official stage theatres. But I danced in an open room, with no curtains, no public stage, no lights, and no distance from the spectators—in short, no 'theatricality'—which meant that I simplified the dance into pure qualitative elements.

This was exactly what I wanted, to become intimate again with the audience—to talk to them at a natural distance, without make-up or costumes, just through movement, breathing, and human emotions vibrating from me to them! Without knowing it, I was not only searching for a new dance style, but at the same time, I was looking for a new form of representation and communication. In short, the method of presentation was more important than the dance itself. Again, I say that it was warmth, trust and closeness that I needed. Does not the artist with his work wish to embrace his audience or his reader?

I continued dancing for another six years, until I became a famous dancer in my own country, Europe and especially, New York. They say that New York is the Mecca of the dance world, and this is where I worked from the beginning of my career until the slowly-approaching end.

At this point, God made Himself known to me! He knew my innermost needs. Only He knows the right moment for His servant to be caught in His divine net. As I was reading in a book about Sufism from one of my most beloved authors, Martin Lings, who lives in England and converted to Islam:*"...and the fishes of the soul swim without distrust into the divine net." (Frithjof Schuon)*

This was my time to be chosen by the Only One, to wake up from the false perceptions and to encounter His divine Presence. However, I did not swim without distrust towards the realm of His Nearness, but the Almighty One took me like a mother cat with her kitten, carrying me by the nape of the neck. God pulled me out of my busy artist's life and put me right into the heart of divine celebrations, an act of His greatest generosity and compassion. He singled me out from millions of souls and put me on the straight path, the path of His eternal light and love.

And this is how it happened. While staying for another performance in New York, my two best friends, unemployed downtown movie actors, walked one day past a strange looking building. They were both born in New York and had walked along this street hundreds of times before, but on this day, they stopped in front of it, wondering about the color and unusual appearance of the building. They discovered that the door was open, although this building had no store. They entered, but could not understand how, in downtown New York, a building could be left unlocked. They saw many shoes on the floor and behind the stairs; there was a large room with oriental carpets and no furniture. Right away, some people came to greet them with a very loving welcome. They began to explain the meaning of this place. It was a mystical circle, practicing divine remembrance, spiritual conversation and prayer in downtown New York. After going there a few times, my two friends got a good taste of these spiritual gatherings and they started to like them very much.

That is when they began to tell me about it, making up a funny story as if it was from a movie, and they asked me if I wished to come, too. Of course I said, "Yes," because we always did most things together. One night, all three of us went together, but I do not remember how I reacted. However, I shall never forget the night I went again and experienced a remembrance ceremony. My face flushed bright and red from the excitement, and afterwards, sitting in a restaurant talking about it, I still had red cheeks for the entire evening.

Something very powerful had happened. I guess the fire of love had struck me.

From this moment on, the three of us went there whenever there was an open night. We loved it. We found what we had been looking for all of our lives. We found the truth! We were seekers, because subconsciously we felt the longing of our souls for our Lord. As I said, all need is need of God, but without realizing this fact, nothing can be done. Who else other than God can make you realize that all you need is Him! Jalal al-Din Rumi comments:

All the hopes, desires, loves and affection that people have for differ-
ent things - fathers, mothers, friends, heavens, the earth, gardens,
palaces, sciences, works, food, drink - the saint knows that these are
desires for God, and all those things are veils. When men leave this
world and see the King without these veils, then they will know that
all were veils and coverings, that the object of their desire was in
reality that One Thing. All their difficulties will be solved, and all
the questions and perplexities they had in their breasts will be
answered. They will see all things face-to-face.

All three of us were brought face-to-face with the truth about the most basic questions: What is a human being? What is the soul? What is religion? What is God? What is the hereafter? What is the real purpose of life on earth? What happens after death? And so on. For a person who does not find answers to these fundamental questions, there will never be any rest. That is why there is so much activity in the west, and there are so many 'workaholics,' because most people are driven by their egos instead of love. The selfish person will never satisfy his desires—he always wants more. The hunger for possessions, power, money, position and fame is insatiable.

Now our lives became enriched and meaningful! I realized that throughout my whole dance career, I had been looking for this certain content—I had been searching for this certain substance. Now I found these qualities in the teacher of this mystical Sufi centre. He was showing us how to live in the way of God. He did not need to demonstrate anything with his teachings; he lived the truth he was talking about. There was no difference between what he said and what he was! Especially, when he was reciting verses from the Holy Qur'an, the internal richness of the holy verses overwhelmed the souls of all the listeners. This marvelous fact is exactly what caught me in the 'divine net.' Here was a man whose talk and whose being were identical! Never in the art world or in my life had I experienced such beauty from a human being! In the west, we lack truthfulness and sincerity, but this man felt like pure love.

I learned that to grow towards spiritual maturity is a 'becoming.' In the west, to have knowledge of things generally means the end, because we think that all matters of life can be handled with the mind. But for the lovers of the path of the truth, the end means illumination and purity. This state requires the whole of man. Therefore, the way of personal growth is first an awakening, and then, a gradual becoming. The lover becomes a traveler on the long spiritual voyage to eternity.

Looking back, I realize how happy I am to have left the art world in exchange for the divine world. Art is praising the ego, the individuality. In the art field, one slips very easily into arrogance, self-praise and competition with others. Many artists become 'prima donnas' who are very difficult to work with. This is one of the reasons why I became a solo dancer.

However, this spiritual encounter in downtown New York was just a small introduction, like a glass of water taken from the infinite ocean of love.

After one or two years traveling between Switzerland, Europe and New York, I finally began to be very curious about the origins of these spiritual activities. New York was one of the branches of this mystical order, but the centre was located in Istanbul, Turkey. There I would meet the so-called 'Efendi,' the Sufi master, the head of this spiritual order, the man whom I would love more than anything or anyone in this world—the man who changed my life!

As always, I could not share with anyone the things that interested me deeply. Therefore, I went alone from Switzerland to Turkey, and for the first time in my life, I traveled eastwards instead of westwards. The hotel room in Istanbul was greasy and in a terrible tourist quarter, and the streets were very chaotic. If there had been a plane back to Switzerland that first night, I would have taken it.

Some days after, with great difficulty, I found the 'headquarters' of these Sufis. When I entered into the small building, there was a room full of people, and in the midst of them a tiny, simple, unnoticeable man. I then discovered that this was the spiritual master; he looked similar to his photograph, which I had seen in downtown New York. What a humble appearance for a man who was the spiritual master of a worldwide Sufi order! When I told him that I came alone from New York, he asked me often if I needed any help and if I was all right at the hotel. He obviously was very concerned about me, a woman alone in Istanbul.

From this moment until his passing away into the realm of God's eternal beauty, he showed continuously his deep respect for me, seeing my great longing to sit in his presence, whatever the cost. Visitors always came with their friends, with their families or in groups. My love for him was so great that I did not care about being alone, and I was blind to the inconveniences and dangers which a woman alone could encounter in a foreign place.

After this experience, I remember very well that I could not sleep the following nights; I was completely restless, wandering in the streets of Istanbul. At this point when I first encountered my beloved master, my life story continued only outwardly, but inwardly, my life story ended and my love story began:

When the 'truth of Muhammad' hit me,

When I paid allegiance to the lineage back to the Prophet Muhammad, peace and blessings be unto him, and to God Most High Himself,

When they took over my life,

When I found a love that I had never known before,

When I met the 'perfect man,'

When I experienced generosity and compassion from my most humble master,

When I met my true spiritual father, my true guide, my true friend,

When I was touched by the reality of all the Prophets and the purest of saints,

When I was smitten with God's generosity and endless bounties,

When I beheld the face of my master shining with the radiance of God,

When I inhaled the divine scent of the hereafter,

When I saw the king of hearts, the prince of the universe in my dreams,

When I met the gardener who gave me life and growth,

When I saw glimpses of the eternal light,

When I met the man who stole my heart,

When I tasted the secret mysteries of the unseen world,

When I encountered divine beauty and perfection in a human being,

When I felt everlasting greatness and my own nothingness,

When I met the agent of the compassion which embraces all things,

When I tasted true humility,

When I sat in his luminous presence,

When I became intoxicated with his impeccable manners,

Then the sun on my past life set, and the sun on my eternal life rose.

Writing these lines 15 years later, after my first encounter with the man I came to love more than anything else in this world, I am now able to make the following statement: know that the love for a spiritual teacher stretches to infinity, and each moment he becomes dearer to you.

The nature of this love is above the ordinary love for things and between human beings. Although one's master is a human being, one does not feel human love for him. What a mystery! The first seeds of this higher love began to grow for the teacher from downtown New York, because of his profound state of 'oneness.' Then when I met my true master in Istanbul and committed to him, I was smitten with intense multiplied light, beauty and power. This light and beauty is God's divine love—limitless, endless, and inexhaustible. When the purity of God's divine light appears to shine in the deepest regions of our being, the darkness of unconsciousness disappears, and the inner meanings of the truth will shine in luminous brightness.

This is exactly what happens to a person who becomes a sincere follower of his spiritual teacher. With true commitment, one gains access to the spiritual chain. This means attachment to the chain of transmission, starting with one's own master, connecting with his master, to the master of his master, and so forth, leading all the way to the Prophet Muhammad, our prince of the universe and then to God, Lord of all the Worlds, Himself. Through this chain, God's eternal Light flows directly from the enlightened soul of the master to the Eternal Presence. Wholehearted commitment enables the initiated to drink from God the Almighty's Divine Light, which is the source of all existence. What a great honor it is to have found a master who is submerged in the nature of the holy Prophet Muhammad, peace and blessings be unto him!

Our great saint, Abdul Qadir Jilani, describes in a commentary about the nature of 'divine light,' from the Qur'an's "Verse of Light" (24:35):

> *When the light from God, (Who) is the light of the heavens and the earth . . . begins to shine upon the regions of your heart, the lamp of the heart will be lit. The lamp of the heart is in a glass, the glass is as it were a brightly shining star . . . Then within that heart, the lightening-shaft of divine discoveries strikes. This lightening-shaft will emanate from the thunderclouds of meaning, neither of the East nor of the West, lit from a blessed olive tree . . . and throw light upon the tree of discovery, so pure, so transparent that it sheds light, though fire does not touch it. Then the lamp of wisdom is lit by itself. How can it remain unlit when the light of God's secrets shines over it?*

I visited my beloved master many times during the following four years in order to learn and make progress on the path. These years of extreme activity, constant traveling between Europe, Turkey and America, plus artistic management, solo performance, creative activities, and the cultivation of family life and friends, all of it by myself, were not easy. Being new on the spiritual path, I had to learn to insert the worshipping activities, self-observation, and the great inner struggle into my busy life. But again, this external speed of an all-day routine enabled me, perhaps, to make rapid progress, but God knows best. It certainly meant a great challenge for me. Life-school is love-school! The only way of learning is a profound descent into daily life!

During those years in the middle of touring around the cities, whenever I decided to visit my beloved teacher, my whole inner state began to change. I felt a mysterious presence enveloping me, like a cloud closing in around my body. Once flying in the airplane towards Istanbul, my heart started beating quickly. In the taxi on the way to finally meet him again, I felt very nervous. Entering into the building where I would actually encounter and greet him, I began to sweat. But once seeing him, kissing his hand, all anxiousness disappeared immediately.

Real masters give so much love to you that one worries for nothing. Living our daily lives in this world and visiting a holy man is as if you fill your tank with petrol. After refilling one's containers with their bounties, tenderness and loving care, we can drive further with our vehicles along the road towards the truth. The joy we receive, the blessings, the nourishment, and the wisdom give us the energy to travel in a lonely world. These highly fulfilling visits made these four years of hard work much easier.

At the time when I first came to Turkey, my dance performances were becoming less and less successful in western cities. It was not because of the quality, because I was at the height of my career, but because the cultural market was totally saturated. The competition destroyed the morale of most artists. Being a successful artist meant also to be a successful marketing entrepreneur.

At this moment, God opened a door to the east, where everything was the same as when I began my career in Switzerland. In Turkey, the fresh, new, and exciting atmosphere helped me to be fully creative. Again, God put me in the right place at the right time for the right thing, to flourish in what I love to do.

I will never forget the night at the Atatürk Cultural Opera House, which was sold out completely. I had just finished my performance and left backstage through the crowd wanting my autograph. I signed in a hurry, because I eagerly wanted to catch the last part of the evening with my beloved master, who was holding a ceremony on the same night I was performing. I jumped into a taxi, and put on a scarf in order to be able to catch the last moments where I could sit in his presence.

Up until that day, I was always able to work in my profession in Turkey. I either performed or taught, and it was very satisfying. Turkish people are very warm-hearted, either as spectators or as students. So after an exhausting life of four years traveling and working between Basel, Istanbul, and New York, my spiritual master told me to move to Istanbul. I had become very tired, not knowing where in the world I should stay. I was everywhere for short periods of time, which gave me the feeling of being nowhere. In short, I felt rootless. Therefore, I felt the need to build up some solid friendships with people I felt close to. Once my master pronounced his wish for me to move near him, I became quiet and felt very peaceful.

To comment on my new life in Turkey and my professional and economic concerns, I can say that it was, and it is, very easy for me in all aspects. First, Turkish people love foreigners. On top of that, they are crazy about modern dance, because Turkey in this respect was in the first stages of development.

From the beginning of my life here, I performed, taught, and gave lectures in theatres, universities, schools, and art galleries. But most importantly, I did not come empty-handed! I came with the savings of the success I had achieved in Europe and America.

Of course, having the privilege to sit in my beloved master's presence every week for many hours helped me enormously! I did not understand Turkish, but I learned to drink from his presence, and he quenched my thirst so well! He nourished me so well!

Staying in Istanbul for two years, I got married, and after one year I gave birth to a boy. Getting married, and becoming immediately pregnant and a mother, was the spiritual experience 'par excellence.' As I wrote, the perfection of a human being culminates in servanthood. Being a loving, caring mother teaches one real servanthood. If I had known the value and joy of motherhood before, I would have wished for many more children. I was in my forties when I gave birth to my son.

May God the Most Merciful nourish the mothers all over the world with the knowledge of the essence of motherhood. May our beloved Lord guide us mothers to bring up our children in goodness and sincerity! After the pure love towards one's spiritual master and towards our noble Prophet Muhammad, peace and blessings be unto him, it is the love from the mothers to their children that represents absolute fulfillment. As our blessed Prophet, peace and blessings be unto him, said in a holy tradition:

> *Paradise is under the feet of the mother.*

This statement represents the station of motherhood in God's eyes. The tradition shows that mothers are valued in the highest ranks. God's supreme qualities of mercy and compassion are of the same quality that feed the relationship from the mother to the child.

Throughout the years living in Istanbul, there were no notable changes in my life until the passing away of my dear teacher into the realm of eternal beauty. To lose one's master marks the beginning of a new spiritual life. It is comparable to the second chapter of a book.

During the last years of his life, he was often sick. We could not see him very much. We wore him down until he was walking around almost like a ghost, but with a brilliant radiance in his face. His community was very large and he took the fullest responsibility over all our lives. It is a sign of a true master that his body and functions deteriorate from the enormous weight of the spiritual responsibilities of his followers. The more his body weakened, the more he beamed in luminous brightness!

Over seven years, I had the privilege to learn from him, receive his help, protection, love and guidance. He gave me the taste of eternal beauty, and the joy of being an obedient servant. I can never thank God enough that I knew him and loved him. As I write in my reflections that the love for a spiritual teacher stretches to infinity, this writing—I like to call it a work of adoration—is intended to be a token of my gratitude and of my love towards him.

At the same time, I wish to express my contentment and thankfulness to God Himself, the One and Only, who invited me to walk along His path of truth. I pray to God the Almighty and ask that He allows me to live in constant contemplation and admiration towards Him, about Him, and with Him for the rest of my life. This is the prayer I say everyday: *"Oh my Lord, lead me to the places where I can please You."*

God let me find and taste His divine beauty and wisdom. Especially, in the last few years, I have tried to do nothing else other than thank Him in my actions.

Additionally I wish to communicate to the reader how well my spiritual teacher trained me. These contemplations are an expression of his teachings, of his nourishment, of his spiritual guidance. Insh'Allah, God willing, it will help and enlighten the reader in the same way that he helped and enlightened me. His life was pure servanthood; he showed us the art of living for others. He was truly submerged into the nature of our beloved of hearts, our Prophet Muhammad, peace and blessings be upon him. He was living his noble character; he was living his humbleness; and he was living his wisdom.

Being in love with him gave birth to my love for the prince of the universe, the reason for creation, Muhammad Mustafa, peace and blessings be unto him. Starting to write about my spiritual experiences for the first time in my life, I could do nothing else but express my intoxication with the perfection and beauty of pure servanthood which my master represented in such clarity! To receive a true taste of the essence of servanthood through my teacher gave birth to the need to write about the jewel of servants, our beloved Prophet Muhammad, peace and blessings be unto him. This is how this work of adoration came to be written.

Here is what happened to me after his death. It was not a very big shock, considering his severe illness. I immediately went to our Sufi center because I knew that his body would be brought there overnight. A few people came to be with him, and we stayed the whole night. His body was wrapped in a white shroud. This night will probably never leave my memory. In the room where he rested was a very powerful, intense atmosphere. One could feel a mysterious presence.

In the morning, I went home to get my son off to school and to get some sleep. As soon as I fell asleep, my master appeared in my dream. He was in the same room where the mourners were with him during the night, but in the dream, he sat on his death-bed and when he saw me, he rushed towards me. We then talked together intimately, like real friends.

Another incident pleased my broken heart, especially in the first weeks of his passing away. During the last week of his life, I wrote a letter to him. I felt this great urge to do so, because so many spiritually important things were happening to me, most of all very beautiful dreams and experiences in Medina al-Munawwara. Not being able to communicate with him was unbearable, but because of his health, I could rarely see him in person, so I wrote to him. But underneath there was another more powerful force which drew me to write to him. I must have known subconsciously of his departure, having felt such a great urge to communicate. Only after his death did I begin to understand fully my need to reach him.

I gave the letter with a framed picture of Medina al-Munawwara and a glass bowl with beautiful designs that I had bought in Medina to the people who would see him that night. This happened two days before his passing away. Of course, learning of his death, I wondered if he had read the letter or got the presents before he left us.

In the following weeks, I decided to visit his family to give my condolences and share my sadness with them. I entered the living room, kissed the hand of his mourning wife, and sat down—and right next to her, on one shelf, was the picture of Medina, and behind me was the glass bowl on another. I broke out in streaming tears, saying to myself: *"He read the letter, he read the letter!"* This was the other meaning of the dream, where he showed me his love and profound friendship, and at the same time, he showed me his contentment about the contents of the letter.

From the moment of his departure from this world, I felt not just comfort and friendship, but eternal richness coming from his soul nourishing me, sometimes more than when he was alive. I will never forget the moment on the funeral day, when the power of his soul began to be fully effective. They had just buried him and all mourners did the afternoon prayer. As soon as I entered into the prayer, saying *'Allahhu Akbar!'* a spiritual power hit me with such impact that I started to tremble, my tears flowing like a stream. Now that his body was buried, his soul was free to reach the ones who loved him. The light of the soul of a perfect man knows no time and no space. This eternal light communicates in the language of purity.

From the day of his burial up until today, I try to do everything possible not to lose his love, the closeness to his soul. I do not think that I could bear to feel separated. The brothers and sisters who share this path with me also know this feeling. Saints do not die; they just pass from one realm to another. They truly can influence us even more strongly because they are free from the limitations of their bodies. All my efforts go into trying to fulfill the duties and responsibilities which God and my teacher desire from me.

These efforts are voluntary acts and, as I said earlier in the writing, if they are executed with sincerity, they will embrace the whole of our lives. The only way to reach closeness to the Only One is to please Him! And the way to reach His contentment is with servanthood. It is a divine rule of our Creator to love us, once we serve Him wholeheartedly! And once He loves us, He will become the tongues with which we speak, the eyes with which we see, the ears with which we hear, and the hands with which we hold.

LIVING IN TURKEY

The reader might wonder how a famous solo-dance artist from a country like Switzerland, with its high economic standard of living, perfect functioning order, security, and cleanliness could come to live in a country like Turkey which is less fortunate in terms of social and economic stability. When asked by Turkish people where I come from, for example, taxi drivers, they become perplexed by the answer that I come from 'the paradise of Switzerland.' How could I decide to live in an economically and politically run-down country? Many of them have the great dream to go there, and I left it by my own free will!

But as I wrote explicitly, Turkey became paradise for me, and Switzerland makes me feel, in many respects, restricted, empty and low, because of its materialistic way of life. It is true that in moving to Istanbul, I came to far distant opposites, but every situation has two sides. What I could not get in Switzerland, I can get in Turkey—and what I cannot get in Turkey, I can get in Switzerland. Being economically secure has had enormous advantages, because I had the material base to quietly build my spiritual life, whereas the reverse situation of having a spiritual life and having to build a material base would have been very difficult.

Now, I have lived here for over ten years and looking back, the only real problem I can think of is the constant struggle with uncertainty. But this fact is the best opportunity to train oneself in the school of life! One needs, at all times, flexibility, endurance and awareness. If one is able to succeed, especially in Istanbul, where all of life's problems are very condensed, one can make it anywhere.

To be a pilgrim means visiting a sacred place. I came to Istanbul for spiritual reasons. Therefore, to live here represents a small pilgrimage for me. To be outwardly as well as inwardly on a spiritual travel is such of enormous advantage, when one is able to use it. I try not to forget, but everyday life weighs heavily on one's shoulders. Istanbul is a truly holy city, maybe the most holy city after Mecca and Medina. The divine treasures to be discovered, the spiritual blessings from thousands of graves of saints, the most exquisite mosques, museums and libraries—not to forget the hundreds of spiritual gatherings throughout the week of all the lovers who are living here. All these bounties can be of immeasurable value to every citizen. I have profited countless times from the pouring of blessings and grace.

The same is true for the whole country. Turkey's soil produces such enormously rich crops of fruit and vegetables, corn and wheat, minerals and oil, and so on. All of God's bounties are given to this country in the greatest measure. At the present time, unfortunately, modern life, with stress factors such as inflation, traffic, air pollution, political instability, corruption and so on. In short, life has become very unbalanced. Therefore, it seems to me Turkish people has become ungrateful and forgotten the beauties and blessings that surround them.

Like me, many people in the west have become overwhelmed by materialism and capitalism. We began to feel great discomfort and went in search for some spiritual realities, which were only available in the east. Of course, this was only a minor movement and still is a small percentage of people who opened up to the east.

But, unfortunately, now I discover that the east has become westernized as well.

Modern life ideals have penetrated the populations of eastern countries, and many of them have become consumers. This is sometimes sad for me. I ran away from the material world, and now I have to watch them becoming consumers of the latest western technological innovations. They are overjoyed to get new cars, the latest cellular phones, computers, televisions, refrigerators, and so on. It is a tragedy that they do not recognize and appreciate the richness and beauty of God's bounties that surrounds them. This fact certainly appears to be the same all over the world.

Every human being has to decide if he wishes to participate in the modern way of life. Never before have people had so many choices in a modern society. This is a very sensitive point for everyone. We can choose from thousands of lifestyles. We see a danger, especially in the West, that the free will of man will grow to monstrous proportions. Within the high-tech life, which gives great comfort to people's lives, we think we own the world—but at the same time, we have become insensitive to the true purpose of existence.

I conclude, if the east would learn from the west—not just accumulate wealth—and the west would learn from the east—not just exploiting and profiting economically—there would be much more unity in the world.

In the problematic world of today, in order to function well, we must train the capacity for reflection and analysis. Especially, my country Switzerland is an excellent example of using the mind efficiently to organize all levels of modern life. On the material level, it is perhaps the best-organized country in the world.

On the other hand, the east has many riches to offer to the west, such as an exemplary family life! Additionally, moral values like respect, hospitality, devotion, shame, endurance, submission, receptivity, simplicity, modesty, fear and so on, still persist. But the most important of all characteristics seems to me to be the inborn capacity for belief! In the west, we need absolute rational proof; whereas to know with the certainty of the heart and, consequently, submit to the unseen, is the favored capacity eastern people possess along with rational conviction.

This is what touches me so profoundly since my life took a spiritual direction—qualities such as submission, stillness, contemplation, secrecy, concealment, surrender, respect, receptivity, and especially, silence—which are mostly missing in Western culture. It is love that encompasses all of them. Love is our true origin, the wealth of human goodness.

Western culture is based on consumerism, effect, noise, high-tech-comfort, entertainment, palaver, talk shows, intoxication, superficiality, and so on. People's minds are bombarded, and the ability to truly hear, observe, listen, receive have degenerated. This material heaviness stops any reflection, any sublime sensitivity. Right up until today, I suffer from the constant materialistic turmoil that modern society inflicts upon us all. The more I grow into spiritual maturity, the more I experience the state of the words of our beloved saint, Mevlana Jalal al-Din Rumi, who says:

Your noise is my silence.

Additionally, in this modern life, we have to redefine terms like free will, destiny, love, freedom, eternity, soul, spirit, heart, and so on. These words are overused and, therefore, have become meaningless. For people who are interested in the inner realities of life, there is an absolute necessity to rediscover their true meanings and to try to incorporate them into our daily lives. These concerns are of immense importance to both eastern and western people, especially in religious communities where they use these words loosely and take the meanings for granted. In the past, Sufism was a reality without a name—and later, it become a name without a reality.

A very long time ago, a good friend of mine asked me if it was possible for a western person to adopt an eastern lifestyle and be inwardly, as well as outwardly, completely assimilated. He was an outsider and knew about my involvement in spirituality. I was aware then, and I know today, that the answer is certainly, "Yes!" I feel extremely comfortable in my 'new clothes.'

Of course, I did not simply take off my western dresses and put on my eastern dresses. When one internally submerges into the truth of any religion, when one is assimilating heavenly qualities within oneself, the outer life takes naturally the appropriate form. In other words, when one's inner spiritual work is sincere, all things fall into place. The external appearance of each person is certainly an expression of his or her mentality. I never felt the slightest problem about adopting outward behavior or making external adjustments, not even in going to Saudi Arabia on pilgrimage.

Each believer who is growing spiritually will automatically feel more ashamed, humble and respectful. These qualities appear naturally, like a tree bearing fruit, having grown through the years, from the sunshine, the rain and the soil. This means one takes much more care about covering one's body with appropriate clothes—whereas a shameless person will expose her body very willingly.

When one goes to Mecca, one covers much more. Being there in constant prayer, I felt so beautiful, so right in those pilgrim clothes, because it is the divine atmosphere, composed of perfection and beauty, which makes one feel like an angel! I am not exaggerating! I dressed like a nun and felt totally at ease!

All the Prophets called humanity to love, unity, equality and brotherhood. We always should remember that our blessed Prophet Muhammad, peace and blessings be unto him, was the most natural and most humble man. They say he resembled a man in a row. Is not his appearance the highest example for all humankind?

Everything in nature grows naturally according to its inherent laws, without having a choice. There are no mistakes, imperfections or disharmonies in the mineral, vegetable and animal world. Even seemingly 'malfunctioning,' the imperfection of animals represents God's perfection. In the book written by Ramazanoglu Mahmud Sami, the author gives wonderful examples about 'imperfections' within creation:

> *The bat does not show himself during the day because he thinks he is the most beautiful, and the evil eye might hit him because of his beauty, if anyone were to see him during daylight.*
>
> *Again there is a kind of bird which lives on rivers and over watery places, but drinks very little water, cannot satisfy his need for water and dies of thirst.*
>
> *There is an insect in Taberistan. It is alight at night and is shiny; it does not fly during the day but flies at night and it is seen with charming green wings. Whereas in reality, it does not have*

any wings. It eats soil. It is scared that the soil will be finished, so he eats very little and perishes from hunger.

And Sami Ramazanoglu comments:

"Both this bird and this insect point to the fact that they are subjected to poverty whilst being in wealth because they are misers to themselves and they cannot eat a meal in peace; and even though their posses- sions are plentiful, they fear that what they have will be finished."

Only man can live against his nature, because God Most High has given us a limited free will. If used wrongly, in the worst case, we degenerate into creatures worse than animals. Man should listen to God's guidance, to God's orders, and live accordingly. Living in unity with the divine order, we grow into discreet, simple, shame- ful, humble, modest and natural people. Our internal goodness will radiate natural beauty. The beauty of a human character manifests itself in kindness, gentleness and generosity.

A true saint never demonstrates what he knows or who he is. He keeps all and everything secret because his life belongs to God. He has no will of his own. How could he proclaim any authority?

Here is another proof of how each western person can assimi- late Islam. God let me find peace, contentment within myself. Finding inner peace is the absolute sign of accomplishing assimila- tion into the truth of all religions! Now I admire, respect, and love the Prophet Jesus, blessings be unto him, much more than when I was a Christian. I understand his life and messages much clearer through studying all the other Prophets and, especially, through contemplating our blessed master, the Prophet Muhammad, peace and blessings be unto him. The Prophet Jesus said that the kingdom of heaven is within us. Is this not the hidden treasure that God speaks about? He also said, *"I am the way,"* which indicates that all Prophets God sends us are perfect examples for humankind.

But only in the East we can find the specialists for the com- plexity of the soul, the heart, the mind and the psyche, because these specialists of the soul are all connected to the law of the religion. That is why 'spiritual growing' works.

Let me give an example of how form, time, place, distance and closeness dissolve. If we truly absorb ourselves in the ritual prayer, time and place do not exist anymore. When one prays, one leaves this temporal existence and submerges into the eternal existence. During worship, I sometimes feel like I am breathing in the divine scent of the hereafter. At other times, confronted with the impact of the holy verses of the Qur'an, I am often pierced through with a spear to the core of my being. The verses are in the Arabic language. I do not understand or speak Arabic. How is this possible? Again, the knowledge of the heart takes one into the divine realms where there is no time, place, distance, closeness or form. The Sufi saint, Sidi Hamza al-Qadiri al-Butchichi, comments:

> *Knowledge is not acquired through books. It would be too easy to bend down and collect all of the books dealing with Sufism to acquire it. The science of truth will come to you from inside, from your heart. Only the heart understands. It understands that nothing is outside of God.*

Let me conclude that when one has understood the universal messages of all the Prophets, one understands that there is just one God, one truth, one religion and one message. Recognizing the truth of the revelations, one sees that spiritual realization is the purpose of our lives! At the origins of human existence, there are no Jews, Muslims, Christians, or Buddhists. There is no east-west, past-future, time-place, ancient-new. When spiritual experience becomes grounded, we are dealing with eternal values. God's religion is a religion of love and a religion of transmission and light. All souls are one, all existence shares with all existence; all nature celebrates the oneness of being. The desired state of every true believer is to leave this plane of existence, to break out of these earthly limitations. If he is successful, his way of life becomes the way of life of the hereafter.

I always had this longing, which is why I became a dancer. The performances brought a kind of trance, where I could freely express my growing need for poetry. How satisfying it was to express one's deepest feelings in music and movement! From the beginning of my dance career up until now, God has given me constant opportunities to feed my profound longings for spiritual contentment.

Once we have broken out, we cannot return. God's power of attraction is irresistible and overwhelming for every living soul. Even if we just get a glimpse of His paradise of intimacy, we will wish to reside there forever.

CONVERSION

At the point of changing my religion, I did not feel that I converted from the Catholic religion to the religion of Islam. With this extremely important fact, I wish to highlight what happens to a person who encounters "the Truth"—meaning the truth about religion; the truth about God; the truth about the Prophets and saints; the truth about human beings; and the truth about the hereafter:

I did not convert;
I simply discovered the hidden treasures inside of me.
I did not change my belief;
I came from a misguided, meaningless life to a life of eternal richness.
I did not travel from the west to the east;
I only came from my own unawareness
And encountered the reality of my own being.
I came from the life of this world,
And discovered that everything one looks for
Is on the other side.
I came from drought
Into an infinite ocean of love.

It is 'heart-knowledge,' the direct vision of eternity, which reveals the truth to us. The fact that I experienced a so-called 'reawakening' in the middle of my life is an immeasurable grace. It represents certainly an enormous advantage for spiritual growth. The more I advance on the path of truth, the more I profit truly from the 'raining' blessings I received as a so-called 'convert.' I was given the opportunity to newly discover the true meaning of life;

that is to say, I felt surprised, astonished, amazed, and bewildered. In short, I felt a positive 'shock'—maybe something like a spiritual electric shock. In other words, I felt hit by the light of the religion! This fundamental experience is comparable to the sensitivity of a newborn baby. One perceives reality in an undistorted, fresh and unconditioned way. That is why it is comparable to a 'rebirth' in its higher meaning, and in its lesser meaning, to an 'awakening'—depending upon a person's efforts.

Especially for people who are born as Muslims, it would be good if they could experience a 'rebirth,' that is to say, re-discover the true value and meaning of their own religion. Many of them live in a mechanical day-to-day routine. Most of all, they do not feel the necessity to reflect or question anything of spiritual nature, taking all religious matters for granted. This state of heedlessness can be called spiritual degeneration. Religious concerns have to be our daily bread, otherwise our whole lives become worthless and meaningless.

Without God's loving care, the world would vanish in one moment. We live in His infinite gifts and bounties. Without gaining the proper awareness and respect for our most kind and generous Creator, we live a life without grace and beauty. He teaches His Closeness to us. He is closer to us than our jugular vein. His place is our existence. He does not fit into the entire universe, but He fits into the heart of man.

Yet without thinking, we lose the meaning of life; we become disconnected from our true origin, which is love. The source of all existence is love. Every dutiful believer has to be alert every moment not to sink into ignorance and darkness. It is the hearts that are blind, not the eyes. Everything is a question of love. We have an experiential relationship with God, the Everlasting and Self-Sufficient! When we taste the beauty of this relationship of the lover to the Beloved, and the slave to the Lord, we will reach the highest stage of contentment with Him and in Him.

May God give us the opportunity to become aware of Him every moment of our lives, up to the point of the most vital fundamental function, our own breath! If we breathe out and He does not allow us to breathe in again, that will be the very moment of our death. Through this state of complete 'alertness,' a believer's heart regains the capacity to cry, to feel ashamed, to be bewildered and perplexed, and to truly feel sorrowful and compassionate. Whereas a heart that is not softened cannot feel love. It has lost God's most precious gift! But for the heart of a believer that is woken up to the perfect consciousness of God, destiny will bring joy, and religious duties will bring pleasure.

I feel attached with the profoundest admiration to the jewel of servants, our Prophet Muhammad, peace and blessings be unto him, and for this reason, I feel attached to his family and companions, because they all radiate his exalted beauty, goodness and nobility of character. There are thousands of reasons for any believer, and me, to be enslaved to their supreme enlightened examples of divine love. Our blessed master and his family and companions were constantly confronted with terrible hostilities throughout their whole lives! The never-ending tyranny grew into real war and threats against their lives. In fact, all of them died as martyrs. This is the reason why I wrote that we actually owe them our lives!

But what did I do to deserve the greatest gift from God, the gift of faith? All divine treasures were given to me without having to pay a great price. God made it very easy for me. First, without looking consciously, He let me find Him. Second, without any real hardship, sacrifice, hostility or discomfort, He let me realize my new belief from the beginning of my path up to this day.

And why did all the Prophets go through so much hardship? The only reason is to convey the meaning and value of a human being to humankind, living the beauty of the human character. They demonstrated how extremely valuable we are in God's eyes. The people who will come in later times can receive the fullness of God's perfected religion due to the readiness of the Prophet's family and companions to sacrifice their lives for the sake of the truth. In other words, through their supreme example, we are able to understand and learn how to live in true belief, sincerity and goodness.

SPIRITUAL EDUCATION

As the theme of my life story states, '*I was nourished so well*'—I did not write that I was educated or trained so well. Along my path, I did not receive a spiritual education comparable to a student going to university. All religions are designed to reach peace, love and goodness within ourselves. These qualities are precisely the nourishment for our souls. The intensity of the search for love, divine knowledge and internal peace creates need, hunger and a profound longing. It happened to me because I was eager for knowledge and love and, consequently, such seeking nourished me well! When we knock on the door with true need, the gates of paradise will be opened with certainty, and God will satisfy our profoundest yearnings.

Most of all, my own beloved master fed my soul, as well as my psyche, my heart and my body. It was extremely comforting to sit in his presence. I felt healed from the cares and worries of the world. The body relaxes, the mind gets quiet, and the heart feels warmth and closeness. He fed all of his followers with the meaning and value of a human being. He was full of compassion, embracing all of his followers with his loving concern. A perfect master feeds our need for God, because he represents the source of eternal life. If we drink, we will learn. Spiritual education happens through nourishment!

Whenever there was a gathering, it always started in the evening and lasted well past midnight. The doors of the spiritual center were, and are, open up unto this day, for all kinds of people coming from all over the world. After the ceremonies of remembrance, we would sit around our beloved master like moths around a flame. However, his regular students would all stay at the back of the room as he made the visitors, the tourists, and the foreigners the centre of attention. He took good care of them the whole evening, and fed them with whatever spiritual nourishment they needed. This is divine hospitality.

Many times drunkards, unbelievers and crazy people visited. They were all treated with higher respect than his own students, because of their state of helplessness. He made all people into one big family. The evenings were extremely joyful. True masters know perfectly how to deal with people—when to make them laugh, when to make them listen, when to make them feel light, when to confront them, when to give them sweetness, when to give them bitterness, when to charge them with weight, and so on. Most of all, they know how to lead inspiring conversations on the divine.

Still, it is never about the mind. It is the business of the heart. That is why one feels like part of a family, although one does not know all of the others. Going to these gatherings for over ten years, I experienced so many of these heartfelt relationships, where I felt a kind of unity, although some of us were strangers.

The true religion is a religion of taste. When we drink the same drink, we become one with each other; we become brothers and sisters on the path of truth. There is nothing more precious than the brotherhood of milk, which means divine companionship! The delight of higher friendship is immeasurable, because it unites those who drink. True companions nourish themselves with the same knowledge, which is the eternal divine wisdom of God Most High! We become lovers of the lovers, who are the lovers of the lovers, until we reach the Sultan of all the lovers, our beloved prince of the universe, the Prophet Muhammad, peace and blessings be unto him!

The divine love one feels for our blessed master is of an eternal nature. It is the love for God's sake. The divine love felt in a believer's heart will extend throughout the entire universe, embracing the whole of humankind with deep affection—whatever religion, race or status they belong to. The truth of the religion is spoken in the language of purity. It is through the nourishment of

God's Light that the truth uncovers its face and God's wisdom can be attained.

The revelations of the holy Qur'an are light descending into the purest heart of our blessed Prophet. It is the eternal light, God's divine manifestation, communicating in the language of purity to all humanity. For this reason, the knower sees with the light of God. Caliph Umar, blessings be unto him, said:

My heart sees my Lord with the light of my Lord.

The ignorant person lives in darkness and blindness, whereas the believer lives in light. Once the material, low attributes covering the purity of heart and soul are lifted, light will shine through all the regions of one's being. This is why we say of a spiritual master that he is an enlightened and an enlightening man. Thanks be to God that I could be nourished with this pure light. He was a true friend of God!

Another nourishment for the soul is the divine scent. Divine realities can bring us a gentle breeze of sweet scent. The great saint, Muhyiddin Ibn Arabi, talks about the 'perfume of existence.' The wise men say that the saints are the perfume of this world. If one has the nose to smell it, one will constantly search for this sweetness as if one is looking for lost property. I have had the good fortune of tasting this miraculous scent countless times. It is the grace from heaven that God bestows on His lovers to sweeten from time-to-time their long, enduring struggle on this earthly plane. Whoever has visited the Ka'ba, God's house, knows the profound sweet odor coming from its stones. Breathing this divine scent brings a state of trance in the pilgrim. What an excellent description is the term 'the perfume of existence,' for this exalted experience; it represents the inner purity of a perfect man. When pure lovers inhale and exhale, they are living the perfume of remembrance.

Dreams are also nourishment. A lover's soul feels the greatest pleasure in receiving dreams, because they are news from God the All-Merciful. To hear from our beloved Lord gives profound excitement to our hearts. Isn't one very happy to receive a letter from one's beloved? The sweet taste of dreams has always been given to my longing heart, especially in times of great need, when there was much turbulence without and within me. They are similar to tranquillizers, like a divine touch, they comfort you and give you a certainty of mind and heart.

True dreams have a visionary character, they resemble revelations. These divine messages are a direct and pure communication from and with our beloved Lord, He never leaves a sincere believer by himself.

SPIRITUAL GROWTH

How did I experience spiritual growth during all those years? It was very difficult, and yet it was very easy! About the difficult part—we have to undergo trials and great hardships. Only through great internal struggles do we reach human perfection. Spiritual growth takes place in the 'school of love.' The knowledge to be learned is the knowledge of the soul. There are two divine descriptions given to the traveler on his voyage to the truth:

If you know yourself, you know your Lord.

Die before you die.

The more I advance, the more these two statements become real and valuable instructions for the daily, twenty-four hour routine. The internal work is a co-production with one's master. He is the surgeon operating constantly within us. We are patients in a hospital to be treated. He gives us medicine and it tastes bitter. The healing processes can be painful. The work of the surgeon is to cut the attachments to the world. Our egos do not want to give up their pleasures. They want continuous satisfaction. To say, "No," hurts. Waking up from the sleep of unconsciousness is painful.

I saw constantly that most of my behavior was wrong. Great incapacities and insufficiencies were staring at me. A lot of the time, I felt depressed when faced with my weaknesses. But this is again the crucial point. Only where difficulties arise can one win true faith and strengthen one's good character features. If one listens to and obeys one's master, if one also loves and fears him, then rapid and great progress can be accomplished.

The greatest difficulty one encounters on the path is the body. This is where true internal struggle takes place. The body is the obstacle between God and ourselves. This is the place of our self-hood, our ego. In other words, the root of our animalistic nature sits in our organs, senses and faculties. One of the first efforts to be taken is to reduce sleeping, to reduce eating, to reduce talking, and to make good usage of one's time, and thousands of things more.

Now for the western reader, I say that the mind has very little to do with spiritual maturity and the process of self-realization. As we see, spiritual growth is intense internal work, a constant struggle leading into the dimensions of height and depth. Once we reach the height of human evolution, aiming towards the purity of heart and soul, we arrive at the place of true love. The fulfillment is achieved through cleaning the heart from the filth of this world, and replacing one's lower qualities with one's higher qualities. This work is the work that lasts twenty-four hours.

A useful method to grow towards spiritual maturity is to work with opposites and try to assimilate them. Only a blind person knows the value of seeing. Only a hungry person knows the value of food. Only an angry person knows the value of peace. Only a sick person knows the value of health. To experience consciously these losses and difficulties, and thus recognize their true value, brings enormous benefit to one's state. The cup has to be emptied to be filled again. We have to go to the bottom of suffering, failure, imperfection, and distress in order to regain the values of God's bounties and blessings given to humanity.

Poverty is the best teacher, which means becoming poor to the world, like reducing all of our needs, emotions, satisfactions, comforts, and the appetite we have for worldly things. It means replacing temporary values with eternal values. It will help us to find internal peace and harmony.

I wish to mention the supreme help, the miraculous effect, which the sacred duties of the religion can provide for a spiritual traveler, if they are performed with sincerity. All of existence—the universe, our planet, and our bodies—is made out of the same substance matter: the four elements of earth, water, fire, and air. They are all in constant movement. The miraculous activities of our bodies are chaos making thousands of changes in one second. We have to oppose these heavy transactions with a divine substance of light, in order to cut the material attachments to our bodies. That is why in the religion of Islam, the body is most involved in completing sacred duties.

The most important of the obligations is the ritual prayer. Performed five times a day, it is highly body-oriented and it will help us to tear off our dependence on the material plane. The fast of Ramadan, lasting one month, is exquisite training to reduce activities like eating, drinking, smoking, as well as encouraging us to try to fast with our senses, like our eyes, ears, and tongues. And the pilgrimage represents a most profound physical struggle, of turning one's back to the world and becoming more aware of the hereafter. Giving alms to the poor is also an excellent method to cut off the attachments to personal possessions, status, fame and wealth. In summary, the spiritual evolution of a human being can only be realized if one follows divine orders. Educating the body is nothing else than making matter subtle, making what is heavy, light—and striving towards cleanliness, innocence and purity. In short, the body has to become refined by our own efforts up to the point of transforming it into a holy instrument. This work is called the holy struggle, 'jihad.'

On the other side, the soul has to be translated into the body. One's spirituality can only be perfected in daily life. Sainthood manifests itself exclusively on the earthly plane. The hidden treasure has to be discovered here and now.

Body and soul are opposed to each other, and in the process of personal growth, the body loses the element of opposition if the body-members obey the command of the intellect. This is why the struggle of the lower with the higher nature in man is called the holy struggle—in other words, the struggle of the angelic realms against the animalistic nature. Again, with the application of the description, "Die before you die," we reach spiritual maturity. This is how we will gain closeness to our Supreme Creator. We can say that the body represents the ego, whereas the soul represents the divine names and attributes of our beloved Lord.

Needless to say, besides the education of our bodies, the concentration on worship is as important. A practicing believer knows that all religious duties are charged with prayers, especially Ramadan and the pilgrimage. If we fail to feed religious duties with worship, these will degenerate into a purely physical, selfish manifestation. Ramadan would come to be exclusively about the stomach. And sacrificing an animal would come to be strictly about the meat. The pilgrimage would become something done for personal benefit. The act of charity would give us the illusion that we are the donors. And the ritual prayer would become a mechanical routine.

Instead, Ramadan is the month of light, because the Qur'an first descended during this time; and, additionally, we have the opportunity to become aware of our Creator's infinite bounties! Praying means being engaged in divine, sublime discourse with one's beloved Lord. It represents a moving sequence of loving surrender in front of our great Lord—that is to say, by the nature of the ritual prayer, the spiritual and physical level feed each other. Sacrificing an animal is about getting closer to God, because it means self-sacrifice. By giving alms, one feels compassion and wishes truly to help and love one's fellow beings. In turn, pilgrimage is the spiritual journey of a believer's lifetime, a self-sacrifice of body and soul designed to change the pilgrim's life.

Having experienced some years of this holy struggle, I wish to mention a beautiful fact which impressed me profoundly and brought the greatest pleasure to my longing heart. The sacred duties helped enormously to increase the capacities of mutual sharing between people! They are precisely given to bring the believers closer to each other. This is the benefit of a struggling soul. In return, God feeds us with nothing else than love, and this love draws people to each other like moths to a flame. Isn't giving charity to poor people a sign of complete sharing? For a true believer, the idea of loving each other for God's sake makes the world into a paradise.

At the beginning of one's spiritual journey, apart from the never-ending twenty-four-hour business, the most important thing to resolve is the relationship with our parents! I worked very hard and, thanks to God, peace and harmony now exist between my mother, father and me. Applying compassion is the key to the healing energy between human beings!

The next step is to deal with one's nationality! Every person has deep imprints of his homeland engraved on his soul. Of course, not everyone has had the negative influences of one's parents or country, but it might be true for the majority. I know by experience that some people with good parent relationships have more difficulty making progress in their spiritual path, because they are not used to dealing with imperfections in their lives. When God heaps on us calamities, it represents certainly a favor to someone aspiring to spiritual maturity. Even for ordinary people, all problems are only given to them for personal salvation.

Once one has mastered the basic problems and one becomes used to dealing with them, the next step is the truly difficult one! The struggle is not so much to remove bad traits, bad habits, sins, mistakes and so on. It is to train oneself, in whatever happens, to answer with goodness, with patience and with love. This is the essential operating principle of all religions: when people treat you badly, or when misery or war happen, you should answer with compassion and mercy.

Moreover, we have to train ourselves to become indifferent to both praise and blame. We usually wish to win in order to feel happy, and we usually fear to lose in order to avoid feeling bad. Only with the strenuous efforts of a believer will one be able to remove these conditions on our personalities and attain the desired state. These are the noble character features of all the Prophets and saints. May God help us to reach some humble imitation of their praiseworthy goodness and beauty!

With regard to the easy part, on the way towards God within the hardship, there was, at the same time, abundant grace and beauty pouring on me. As I wrote before, most of all I felt these joyful moments through my master! One gets a taste of paradise in this world if one shows sincerity. Again, the result is not important; it is the purity of intention and the true need to grow towards spiritual maturity which brings us close to the Only One.

When we love, we are helped so much. This is the secret. I could drink with the greatest pleasure from the fountain of my beloved master. Sitting in the presence of a perfect man, the sweet taste of inner meanings was given to me, and the sweet taste of eternity was given to me. In my personal experience, the secret rested in learning through the richness of a perfect believer! Entering the spiritual path in the beginning, I was completely overwhelmed, because we are all like newborn babies being fed with bottles of milk, loving the master like a father. In time, learning to walk on one's own feet, one's master becomes gradually a teacher and, further along the path, he can become our true friend, but this is a rare case. The fulfillment of a real devotee, the end of this kind of path, lies naturally in becoming a master, too.

The other blessed source of grace happened to me on pilgrimage. God rewards every pilgrim endlessly who is visiting His Holy House, the Ka'ba, and visiting His most beloved Prophet Muhammad, peace and blessings be unto him, in Medina. I had just finished the circumambulation of the Ka'ba several times, praying extensively in front of it, when this thought came into my head: 'I have taken God's bath, I have bathed in His mercy, grace and blessings. The Ka'ba is the root of God's circle of infinite radiation, and the root of God's infinite attraction. Through it, He gives us His nearness, the greatest satisfaction for a believer's soul. One encounters here divine Perfection, a synthesis of His divine qualities of Majesty and Beauty. And one is drenched in His unconditional divine Hospitality.'

Visiting Medina al-Munawwara means to visit the city, the illuminated. A pilgrim there finds himself in the presence of the 'source of light.' I just wish to refer to the Part One in this book dedicated to our beloved Prophet, the honor of the universe. It might give the reader some idea of the profound affection I have felt during the nine visits as a pilgrim with which I have been blessed. May God Most High allow me and all the followers of his community to continuously be honored to give salutations before his resting place and pray in his Sacred Mosque, which gives the pilgrim one of the highest and most blissful experiences in his life.

In the city of Mecca, one has to actually reside in the sacred area of the Ka'ba itself in order to feel spiritually connected. On the contrary, in the city of Medina, wherever you are, there is a penetrating effect on your body and soul from the most holy presence of our beloved Prophet Muhammad, peace and blessings be unto him. Of all the cities in the whole world, only in the city of Medina al-Munawwara, does one have such a mysterious feeling. At the airport, in the streets, going shopping, or visiting people in their homes, it is he—the reason for creation, the prince of the universe ,who touches his lovers with the merciful presence of his soul. An unseen power from his resting place spreads through the entire city. It is not easy for a pilgrim to digest this supreme source of light.

When I first visited, I was devastated by his holy presence. As a human being, I felt a heavy burden of responsibility, next to the honor of the universe. I could literally see my 'dirty' existence, my lowness, my insufficiencies. In short, I felt terrible. After long streaming tears, his tender help came from his holy grave, and it comforted and enriched me to such exalted heights that I had never known before. In the following visits, over the next few years, the joy my heart received became indescribable!

Once, a newly returned pilgrim came from the visit to the Prophet's holy grave and was asked how he felt. He was unable to give an answer. Speechless, he simply broke out in flowing tears and wept for a long time.

As I mentioned, spiritual education happens miraculously through the nourishment of love. Spiritual masters are submerged into the nature of Muhammad, peace and blessings be unto him. They offer their whole being to the honor of the universe, like poor loving slaves. They live the reality of the greatest miracle, our Prophet Muhammad, in their noble character, imitating his supreme qualities and wisdom for they have been annihilated in the source of light. This is the highest illumination a human being can reach! This is precisely the richness we call love.

In other words, my love for my own master is composed of my master's abundant deliverance and slavehood towards our most beloved Prophet Muhammad, peace and blessings be upon him. God enabled me to taste a glimpse of this truest of all illuminations which a perfect man possesses. Even if I would be given thousands of lives, I would never be able to thank our Creator sufficiently. The same is true for the immeasurable favors which God bestows on the followers of the Prophet Muhammad's community! To be honored, to belong to our beloved Prophet's community, is the biggest gift a human being can receive.

In fact, I believe that it is impossible to realize the honor which God bestows on his servants in blessing them with a true master. So I try to do everything that is within my capacity to grow constantly in the divine love I feel towards him.

THE ONENESS OF BEING

Let me tell you what I found so extremely attractive when I encountered the religion of Islam for the first time, entering into that place in downtown New York. I felt total acceptance! I came as a sophisticated modern-type looking woman, an artist, unknowing and misbehaving, but I felt such a warm welcome from the people and the atmosphere in that place. There was such a heat! It was as if the air was thick, containing a lot of richness. In short, I felt as if I was in another world. Everything was naturally flowing in peace and harmony. I could recognize myself in everything, as a part of the whole; and likewise, the whole was part of me.

The same was true for my two best friends, and I am sure that it does happen to most people. How else, then, could these downtown New York actors, playing bad guys in movies, have gotten involved in mysticism?

All existence celebrates the oneness of being. The world, human beings, and the cosmos are all made of the same fundamental substance, and everything co-exists. The universe is created in unity. All forms of the world receive divine grace. All existence shares with all existence! This is the essential concept of God's creation.

In all places of worship, like mosques or remembrance circles, this is what one feels—the harmony of all existence. The human being in prayer tries to leave his individuality, his ego, behind, in order to surrender in front of his great Lord and reach the divine realms of everlastingness. The happiness one feels during the prayers or remembrance ceremonies is exactly this 'melting' of one's personality into the ocean of oneness. This is the heat! This is the power! This is true love! This is why I had such a red flushed face!

Islam stresses the fact that there is no separation between the mystical and the ordinary earthly life. Only in living the fullness of this earthly life on all levels can we reach the spiritual realms; taste the divine realities; and accomplish nearness to our Creator. One exercises spiritual growth in trying to be a good husband or wife; father or mother; student or teacher; good neighbor or friend; merchant or secretary; doctor or nurse; and so on. This is the message our blessed Prophet Muhammad, peace and blessings be unto him, brought to humanity so perfectly. The illumination takes place within our worldly lives! God Most High desires this state for all human beings, whatever religion they adhere to. The perfection of a human being culminates in servanthood. God wants to show us that true love reveals itself through being useful to each other. Becoming a true servant is superior than becoming a saint.

Our most beloved of hearts brought a universal religion, whereas previous Prophets were restricted to a certain community, time and place. Our beloved Prophet Jesus, upon him be peace, did not marry, nor enter into a commercial life, nor participate in wars. This is why he is called Ruhullah, the Spirit of God. Therefore, one could say that full guidance for the perfection of a human being in everyday life was not given to mankind until the prophethood of Muhammad. In addition, spiritual perfection in some religious denominations is exercised only for a select few. This fact is very important, for they exclude their spiritual life from their worldly life. Yet when one sees the sacredness of all life, one understands that all human beings must be given the chance for spiritual growth.

Thus, spiritual movements in the east are pulsating within domestic life! For this reason, I can more easily encounter and then get involved in a spiritual activity here, whereas in the west few similar mystical gatherings were happening, and I could find an enlightened teacher there only with difficulty.

Some so-called Sufi centres in the West are not connected to the law of the religion, they sometimes create their own 'free-style love gatherings,' which do not bring any transformation, spiritual benefit, or attainment of the truth, except temporary relief of a psychological or physical nature. God reveals Himself to humanity through His prophetic books—the Torah, the Psalms, the Gospel, and the Qur'an—and through the basic obligations for believers, like praying, fasting, charity and so on. Without form, there is no way; without the way, there is no work; and without work, there is no becoming. Without submission to God's Revelations, there is no spiritual growth. This is the crucial point.

For all human beings are only created for spiritual realization. Islam revealed the full truth of the religion and the fulfillment of each human being as a potential saint. For this reason, the messages of the holy Qur'an embrace every level of human life. All directions and guidance for human perfection are available. This means that God has given us higher responsibilities, and he has given them to everyone! As we mentioned before, it is our duty to recognize that we are part of everything and that everything is part of us. This is the essence of God's teaching to humanity. Consequently, nothing stays only with us, as our blessed master says in a holy tradition:

> *If we murder one human being, it is as if we killed the whole of humanity.*
>
> *If you give true guidance to a human being, it is as if you give eternal life to the whole of humanity.*

It means that if we hurt or damage someone or something, we will hurt the whole of the cosmos; and if we do good acts for the sake of God, we will do well for the whole of humanity. In this way, we will please our beloved Lord. The greatest fulfillment which a believer can attain is to reach His contentment. Everyone is responsible and will be required to account for his behavior and his actions. Becoming aware of the sacredness of all life changes our whole attitude, our intentions, our sensitivity, and our respect towards all of existence—from the mineral world, to the plant world, to the animal world, and up to our fellow human beings.

All life is divine and "Sacred things have the right to ask for the whole of man," as Martin Lings says.

In Islam, everyone is his own priest, his own shepherd, responsible for his own life and his own flock, meaning himself, his family, his neighbors, work colleagues, his friends and so on.

Again we have to stress that in Islam, all human beings carry the fullest responsibility over all the matters of their lives. In a tradition the Prophet Muhammad, peace and blessings be unto him said: *"Classification is not written down for us."* There is no categorization amongst human beings. Everybody possesses the same value before God. Thus, everyone carries, potentially, the seed of a saint in himself or herself.

In reality all forms of monotheism are one. All believe in the One and Only God. It is the human being in his ignorance, arrogance, and egotism, who split the original unity of all religions. The words from God transmitted to all of the Prophets came directly from the realm of His own Essence, His Eternal Light, His Oneness, His Infinity, His absolute transcendent Truth. It is necessary to go back to the origin of all existence, the home of all and everything, where there is not the slightest diminishing or deviation from the glorious Unity of His all-encompassing Truth. It is through the diversity of beliefs and human communities that the original oneness of the religion gets distorted.

Quoting from Martin Ling's book, *What is Sufism*:

In the tenth century, some three hundred years after the Prophet, peace and blessings be unto him, Abu 'l-Hasan Fushanji commented: *"Today Sufism (tasawwuf), is a name without a reality. It was once a reality without a name."*

Commenting on this in the following century, Hujwiri added:

> *"In the time of the Companions of the Prophet and their immediate successors, this name did not exist, but its reality was in everyone. Now the name exists without the reality."*

Shortly after our blessed master, the Prophet Muhammad, peace and blessings be unto him, left this world, the unity became distorted. For this reason, it is our duty to shed light on the inexhaustible everlasting treasures within ourselves. The mysticism of all religions speaks about the wisdom of the hereafter and the eternal values within human beings. Our Lord the All Merciful says to His most beloved creatures :

I was a hidden treasure; I wanted to be known, so I created creation.

The truth of the religion is based on this statement. This divine revelation is the foundation for the spiritual realization of every human being. It is the secret prescription for unlocking all the gates to eternal happiness. Now, every human being in this world has to realize the purpose of creation and search within himself or herself, and with God's help, discover the real meaning of this earthly existence. May we pray to our Creator to provide divine guidance for His needy creatures, so that we may be able to plant seeds of goodness in our hearts. May He give us the opportunity to nourish these seeds with good behavior and actions, so they may grow into a tree of loving beauty and harmony.

ON THE WAY TOWARDS GOD

O n the path of personal growth, I discovered a truly valuable piece of wisdom, that whatever we think is good for ourselves, in reality can be bad—and whatever we consider bad for ourselves in reality can be beneficial:

> *It may be that you dislike a thing, and God brings about through it a great deal of good. (4:19)*

On all levels of spiritual life, this pattern is bound to reveal itself. Why does this happen? Once we have set out on the way towards God, once we walk on the path of truth and try to live according to God's will, we will change the way we look at the world and ourselves in a reversed manner.

Within our human lives, we have to realize that there are two planes of existence—the physical and the spiritual, or external and internal realities. For travelers on the path of truth, the world seems to have a shallow appearance, because beneath it, they discover an ocean of unimaginable beauty. This sea of astonishing realities is, in its nature, not just amazingly wonderful, but at the same time, endless and inexhaustible—like an ocean with no shore and no bottom. Consequently, what appears to be real, what we take for granted, becomes, in fact, an illusion—false and artificial; but the non-existent, the unseen worlds, become the centre of our attention.

In achieving this, there is an organ that must be discovered and developed: it is *the eye of our hearts!*

This means that we have to seek the inner meaning of what we see. Once we have set out on the way towards God, we have to shift our perception from the outer appearance, the external reality, into the unseen world, the inner divine realms. This marks the crucial point where a human being turns into a believer, because he is now one who "believes in the unseen" (2:3)! True faith starts with the opening of the eye of our hearts. From this moment on, the seed of faith starts growing in the depths of our being. For example, Prophet Moses, upon him be peace, found true faith after he fell unconscious. When he awoke from his own darkness of unconsciousness, he saw that he could not see. That is where true faith begins!

When we see with the eye of our hearts, the world becomes a jail and the hereafter becomes the only desired place to be! It is not viewed only as a garden of paradise in which to dwell, but as a place that reveals divine inspiration, eternal richness and beauty to our inner being. Our soul, living in the body, feels like it is living in a cage. Only the lover becomes aware of the imprisonment of his soul. Once he closes the eyes of the world and opens the eyes of the hereafter to the fullest, his soul will find the greatest joy at the moment of death—where, finally released from its cage of the body, he flies directly to unite with his Well Beloved, the Lord of Majesty and Bounty.

Sharpening our perception for the reality of the divine realms, we begin to see that we are, in fact, asleep when we think we are awake—meaning we are asleep in this earthly life because we have not yet awakened the eyes of our hearts. However, as soon as we learn to perceive our lives in the reverse way, which means in the way of God, we will be awakened to a new consciousness, we will experience a rebirth, and we will become eternally alive.

It is a sad fact that most people do not wake up before they die. Once they are in their graves, God will instantly reveal to them how heedless and ignorant they have lived in their earthly lives. The Holy Qur'an says, speaking about the majority:

It is not the eyes that are blind but the heart. (22:46)

Jalal al-Din Rumi says that the world is a veil over reality:

> *If everything that appears to us were just as it appears, the Prophet*
> *who was endowed with such penetrating vision, both illuminated*
> *and illuminating, would never have cried out, "Oh Lord, show us*
> *things as they are!"*

In order to attain what we might call 'heart-wakefulness,' we
have to make difficult what is easy for ourselves; and what
appears to be difficult, we have to learn to let go. In other words,
when we consider ourselves as healthy, we actually need treatment; and when we seem to be sick, we are in a state of spiritual
well-being.

When we are in love with this world, we become very excited
about winning; but in reality, we descend to the level of being a
loser. However, for a true lover, losing in this world means spiritual success in the eyes of God. Consequently, whatever feels pleasant and satisfying for someone of this world feels bad, distasteful
and disagreeable for the lover of God. Looking with the inner eye,
making true spiritual progress, does not mean climbing up the ladder of success. Real spiritual maturity goes backwards to the roots
of one's being!

In the west, one expects to achieve success through accumula-
tion; but within the human personality, decreasing, building downwards, and diminishing, will bring true progress for the flourishing
of our true human nature. To properly develop our personality,
then, we must go back to the root of our being. There is the home
of our origin, the place where we came from, the essential reality of
our being, the beginning of our earthly existence. It is a sacred area.
This place is a place of total harmony and contentment. At the root
of our being, purity and illumination will reveal itself, whatever was
hidden will manifest, and whatever was closed will open. In short,
our salvation does not lie in going forwards; rather, it lies in going
backwards!

When we look with the inner eye, the state of poverty represents our greatest riches! Especially, Prophet Jesus and our Prophet Muhammad, upon them both be peace and blessings, demonstrated with their enlightened example of living in true poverty, how beautiful it is to live in God's riches! As our beloved master said:

My poverty is my pride!

In Sufism, they call an aspirant, *'al-faqir,'* the poor. Once one sets out on the way to God, one wishes to become poor, poor of the worldly. The state of poverty is tightly connected to the state of purity, which again means cleanliness from the filth of the world.

This state of poverty explains perfectly the real meaning of life. God only created human beings for self-realization; that is to say, we are in this world for the sole purpose of finding Him, getting to know Him, realizing Him, and finally annihilating in Him, signaling the extinction of the created into the Creator. Through our disappearance in Him, we gain the state of poverty, which means non-existence. This is the work.

As Muhyiddin Ibn Arabi says:

Oh Lord, let me dive into the infinite ocean of Your Oneness.

Looking with the inner eye, I wish to give some examples that profoundly influenced my life, and which reveal the reality of the reversed way of perception of worldly and spiritual realities. I know a place with hundreds of people, a kind of rest home. God took from them all the things of this world, their belongings, clothes, houses, money and family. Not only that, God took away their health, their sight, their capacity to move, their speech, and their hearing. The only thing left that could be taken is their lives! They are in this place, patiently waiting to die. Now I went there with the intention of comforting them, helping them, and loving them. However, this is not what happened. They helped me! They gave me so much love that I could never have received from anyone else in this world. I experienced such unimaginable beauty and love from within this great outward misery.

All through my spiritual path, when I visited the tombs of great saints, an unexpected experience happened to me in an almost shocking way. You make a visit to a dead corpse and you encounter more power than you ever experienced before in your life! The illuminated power of their unburdened soul hits you and, to your great astonishment, your body trembles and your eyes stream with tears. Eternal life hits you! For the friends of God, when their soul leaves the body at the moment of death, it is like pulling a sword from its sheath, only now revealing its splendid power to be fully effective. The beloved of God never die; they just exchange the realm of the worldly for the realm of eternal existence.

The same overwhelming experience for a believer happens when he or she is standing in Mecca as a pilgrim in front of the house of God, the Ka'ba! How can the house of God, a house made of stones, affect millions of hearts in the profoundest way? Again, eternal life hits you. His Majesty and Grace, His Power and Mercy are pouring over the believers circumambulating it.

The Ka'ba is the place of God's manifestation, and when we consider the whole world, God's house represents what we might call "point zero." For this reason, from this infinite source, thousands of secrets gush forth! May God Most High give us a taste of the truth of His Holy Sanctuary!

Just recently, I experienced the death of my father. When the news of my father's passing away came, I naturally had a small shock, but right away, God's grace started pouring upon me. There was a release of such tremendous love within my family and relatives! Only the unavoidable event of 'death' can generate such love and beauty between people. Now that his soul was free from the sicknesses, strains and limits of his body, I could really feel and love my father as never before. It was as if our two souls embraced each other.

As another example, my own mother called me one day; she was desperate and pleading, crying on the telephone, "*What can we do now? What a terrible state the world is in! Where will these wars (Iraq) lead us?*" Before, she had never cried about a war and never before did millions of people go onto the streets to demonstrate for peace, whatever race, religion or country they belonged to. The tears of my mother, and the profound sadness and worry of humanity about the Iraq war, are a clear sign of true love waking up in people's hearts. Again, not just myself, but human beings all over the world, are beginning to be able to experience within the outward misery of war the opening and sharing for love and peace.

I have concluded that there is an essential truth of God manifesting itself in our lives, especially at the present time, in the twenty-first century. The world is smitten unceasingly with miseries, catastrophes and wars. It is exactly these 'dark' events that enables us to see the truth, and enables us to wake up from our sleep of heedlessness. I have never witnessed such love, goodness, belief and conviction between people, especially with these ongoing wars and human catastrophes.

I have never experienced so much of God's grace, His eternal light, and His infinite beauty as in the last few years, going through the greatest hardships of earthquakes, September 11th, and the Middle East wars! What I have felt is God Himself, His Holy Presence! As our great saint Muhyiddin Ibn Arabi said:

> *Everything that God has arranged is in His loving concern.*

God is All-Just, All-Knowing, All-Good, All-Merciful, All-Providing, but all human beings have to undergo certain examinations before they learn to see and hear His divine realities. Only a sick person knows the value of health! Whatever tragedy and suffering befalls us, it is certain that we deserve it, because all destinies come from God Most High. The examinations will help us to find our personal salvation.

In a holy tradition, God says:

The more God loves a servant, the more He heaps on him calamities.

The Prophets were the most tested because they were the most beloved of God and then down the scale, His beloved friends, His saints and His righteous servants have also been tested. The most desired by God experienced the biggest difficulties in their lives, so they were able to represent the most enlightened examples to all humanity. The afflictions that God gives us are not His punishments but His gifts! Again, we have to see with the eyes of the heart. It is the reverse of the picture that presents the divine realities and the essential truth to us.

We have to answer everything with hunger! In a holy tradition, our blessed master said, *"Die before you die."* That is to say, we have to knock on the door of paradise with hunger, meaning real need. The secret prescription for spiritual perfection has now finally been given through the religion of Islam. The Prophet Jesus, blessings be upon him, said that man has to be born twice.

The very fact that I found surgeons, instructors, advocates, artists, alchemists and physicians of the soul changed my whole life! I believe that this shows the immense importance of finding a master who is able to operate inside the greatest complexity of the soul. Our great saint, Muhyiddin Ibn Arabi, said that "It is relatively easy to find God, but it is not easy to find a man who has found God"—meaning a man who can bring you close to God through his own annihilation in Him.

God does not change anything unless we change it for ourselves:

God will never change the grace which He has bestowed on a people until they change what is in their (own) souls; and verily God is He Who hears and knows (all things). (8:53)

If God sees the growing need for Him, the sincerity of search for Him, He will immediately place true guidance in front of us. There is no spiritual growth without divine guidance and instruction. It is absolutely necessary to have a spiritual guide in order to advance on the way to God.

I ALWAYS WISHED TO REVEAL
THE BEAUTY IN MY LIFE!

Here is our God. He invites me to the religion of beauty and adoration. I am a full-blooded artist, and He pulled me towards His divine realms of everlasting beauty. How could I not fall in love? Like no other religion, Islam is the religion of adoration. Trees, herbs, mountains, and all of nature adores God. God's adoration towards His most beloved Prophet became the reason for all of His creation. The richness of true adoration and wonderment is the inner wealth of God's religion. If all artists could know and experience what happened to me, they would run to apply for scholarships in the school of love, and they would wait impatiently to be let in.

When I started to write the first part in this book about our beloved Prophet, I melted when I came across the sentence uttered by our prince of the universe:

O Lord, increase me at marveling at You!

So his prayer of adoration became the source of inspiration for this writing. What is an artist? My answer is that he or she has a need to communicate how he or she feels! Artists cannot help expressing themselves with their works of art because they are hungry for beauty, perfection and love, which are God's attributes. Now, I increasingly begin to know the real meaning of art, because I study God's creativity. Needless to say, God is the greatest and, in fact, the only Artist existing.

The cosmos, the world and mankind are created substance and God is its Maker. By its existence, the whole of creation points to its Creator. When the believer is able to discriminate between himself and God, his human nature and God's Essence, adoration and profound longing towards his most Beloved will arise in his heart. We can call it divine inspiration, which the true artist and the lover of God share.

In the past, I thought I was a real artist, but now I am discovering that the work one has to do is to become a channel. One must create the sensitivity and the situation where God can act through you! This is real 'creativity!'

We live in a creative relationship with God. One has to increase one's sensitivity to receive from His divine realms. The divine eye, the divine ear—which are those of the heart— are the essential organs allowing us to become aware of the truth. We have to develop the art of true hearing and seeing, the art of divine inspiration, the art of receiving His divine bounties and His gifts. In every aspect of life, heightened attention, care and respect is demanded, most of all for our fellow human beings. It is the art of living for others—it is the art of giving!

The perfect man or woman, the true believer, masters all of these divisions and subdivisions of human life. The believer's body will become a sacred channel where God acts through him or her. He will become the master of the moment, and the moment will be His Breath. I wish to convey that the highest form an artist can aspire to is to become a believer. In other words, the highest form of life is belief!

For a seeker, it is a duty to contemplate God's creation. The world is a mirror where God's wisdom and secrets are reflected for the one who looks with the eye of his heart. He is able to see the hidden divine realities. If we search with the eye from our need to know the Only One, He will reveal Himself to us. In this way, we become seekers of His infinite plane of existence. In fact, we cannot help to fall in love with the complexity of His manifestations.

I, myself, have become aware that the miracle of creation is the essence of all religions. For example, when we look at the infinite multiplicity of the cosmos, this seemingly never-ending space, and the incomprehensible realities of heavenly bodies, all swimming in space and following a perfect order, we are in awe of the immensity of light coming from the stars suspended in such boundless space. This marvelous sight compels us to fall in love with its Maker. The same is true with the infinite treasures of the ocean, the fascinating worlds of deep sea creatures and plants. Even more astonishing is the perfect functioning complexity of our physical bodies. Is there a greater miracle within all existence, starting from an atomic particle up to a living entity, than the human being? We all stay alive because millions of cells work miraculously together.

If we learn to see the beauty and perfection of God's creation, we will automatically turn into profound admirers and believers.

THE LIGHT OF THE PRAYERS

When the fire of love for the All Merciful has stricken one's being, one wishes to become intimate with Him. One yearns constantly to communicate. This profoundest of all loves, the love for God, will transport one to the level of real friendship with Him. In this state, one wishes to express constantly one's love, admiration and longing towards the Only One. It is the desire to get close to Him, the longing to see, hear and talk with Him. This is the crucial point where real worship starts, where the door of divine communication and contemplation from the believer to his Creator begins, and where the flame of the true realization of the nature of the human being in relation to his greatest Lord becomes enlightened.

In fact, the worship modes in the Christian religion that I belonged to, have degenerated in everyday life. There is plenty of moral education, plenty of advice and great philosophies, but no practical way to translate the theories into daily behavior. On the other hand, the Shariah is either missing or diminished, like praying, fasting, pilgrimage and giving alms. Every human being needs a balance: one wing is worship, and the other is good conduct and action.

At first, when I entered the path, nothing helped me so much as praying to God, because worshipping helps to establish a relationship with the Only One. Comparing my old life to my new one, this is exactly what was missing; and comparing my new life to my old one, this is exactly what was enriching. In my present life, I can say with conviction that praying changed my life!

Praying is like a divine infusion in the blood veins of the body. Praying is food for the soul! Those who turn themselves every day to their Creator with love and submission will attain the wisdom of how things really are. They will discover the divine realities, and they will see and taste paradise within themselves.

The benefit of prayers is immeasurable. When we pray to God with sincerity, we strengthen our relationship with him and increase our desire for Him. When we turn towards Him, He always answers! His response covers everything. As we desire Him, He desires us. This is the secret of the mutual relationship, because as far as we are in Him, He is in us. The substance of prayers is the greatest power generated in the universe. If a perfect man's heart prays, it can change the destiny of all mankind.

All worship-modes, the ritual prayer, pilgrimage, and activities like remembrance and the whirling (*Sama*), and so on, have pre-described patterns, which the worshipper has to follow, with the exception of the personal supplication, the *dua*. Here, the believer expresses his profound wishes and exposes his most private needs in front of his supreme Lord. The height of divine communication with one's Beloved is experienced in its fullest sense. It is true love-talk, or *muhabbet*. The worshipper is alone, in deepest intimacy. It is only him and Him. He raises his hands in utter humility to be completely receptive towards the infinity of God's outpouring of grace and blessings. Nowhere else than in our most private moments of conversing with the Only One is true creativity and inspiration is needed, because within the personal supplication, there is the total freedom of our soul. What is in our hearts? What will we plead for? What do we wish to be changed? What do we have to offer? What do we ask from Him? What do we hope to be forgiven for?

We live in the end of times. It is more virtuous to pray for our fellow beings than for ourselves; that is to say, we have to pray for each other. For this reason, the personal supplication is an excellent opportunity to think, to feel, and to plead for other people—and when we learn the art of living for others, we learn the art of giving!

As I mentioned, for a believer, there is nothing more desirable than to arrive at the door of intimacy with one's Lord. Having traveled all the channels to God the Merciful, the door will open and pure love will extend from Him to us. In offering ourselves with sincerity within the *dua*, we will enter into the circle of His irresistible power of attraction. Our Creator will respond in loving friendship and embrace. There is a verse in the holy Qur'an about offering *dua*, where God has told us:

> *Therefore, when you are free (from one task), resume (another task); And seek and strive to please your Lord. (94:7-8)*

Abd al-Qadir al-Jilani interprets:

> *As soon as you have finished performing the ritual act of worship,* ibada, *you must set to work on the prayer of supplication, the* dua.

And the Prophet himself, God bless him and give him peace, is reported as having said:

> *As soon as the prayer leader, the* imam, *is standing at his niche, and the ranks of the congregation are properly aligned, the merciful blessing of God will descend upon the assembled worshippers.*
>
> *An angel will then call out: "So-and-so has gained a benefit, and so-and-so has suffered a loss!" The beneficiary will be anyone who lifts up his hands in offering the supplication to God, as soon he has finished performing his prescribed ritual prayer. The loser will be anyone who leaves the mosque without having offered a supplication. If someone does leave without having offered a prayer of supplication, the angels will say: "O, so-and-so, how can you manage without God? Do you have no need of anything that God has at His disposal?"*

BEAUTY WITHIN MISERY

I first observed the radiating beauty of my teacher and later, having drunk so much of his harmonious being, I learned to see and feel these qualities in other human beings, whatever mentality, and whatever nationality they belonged to. Much later, I started to perceive God's beauty in animals, plants and the universe as well. Now I can sometimes see beauty in outward miseries, in dirty street corners, in overfilled buses, and especially in the crying pictures of poverty, particularly in the recent years. The more people are stripped of wealth, status, clothes and health, the more people are reduced to the minimum of existence, and the more they shrink to pure poverty, the more they become radiant with something 'other-worldly!'

Thus, I have wondrously come from perceiving beauty within beauty to perceiving beauty within misery. In miseries, wars, tragic catastrophes, and in painful pictures of poverty, one can feel God's Presence and God's grace more than other times. This is His place, His manifestation, and His source of flowing mercy, and these experiences have become my real reason for writing!

For example, I felt shattered to see the state of the people after the earthquake near Istanbul. They had lost everything, even their relatives, and they were sitting in a field, in poor quality tents, devastated and in shock. The grace I received in embracing them, in trying to comfort them, was indescribable. I felt this even more so in the hospitals, where whole families were lying in rows with injuries to different parts of their bodies. I will never forget a woman, lifting her nightdress slightly to indicate that this poor cloth was all that remained of her life. But she was so warm and loving with me, as if I was her daughter. Although we had met one another for only a few moments, it was as if we had known each other forever. When people are helpless and needy, their hearts soften and they turn to gentleness.

After many years of experiencing this infinite mercy and compassion overwhelming me during these visits, I not only realized the inexhaustible treasures of such graceful relationships, but I came to the conclusion that these people were the only true friends I have in this world. In our present time, it is a tragic fact that people are veiled from each other through ambition, greed, ulterior motives, luxury, and selfishness; and for this reason, I am grateful to find warmth, closeness and purity with people who have nothing, such as the needy, the poor and the lonely.

It is mostly through streaming tears that I become able to experience divine reality! Unfortunately, it seems that such awareness requires a tragic event, such as an earthquake, to be precipitated. This is the crucial point. All the dark events the world is experiencing should shake us up and purify our inner being, like a heavy storm. These catastrophes are like a wake-up call from God Himself to all humanity. *Insh'Allah,* God willing, we will find our original state again, our lost purity, which will enable us to celebrate human relationships again.

The loneliness of people in modern life is great. How else could it be that I embraced a young woman from Sudan with streaming tears and great affection and she did, too, in the *Masjid al-Nabawi,* the Prophet's Mosque, after having known her only for ten minutes. May God guide us towards mutual sharing, towards the true closeness of hearts, towards the lost unity. Separation among human beings is like a virus, a disease, spreading from a man to his family, neighbors, working colleagues, friends and communities, through his city and his country. We can never put enough value and take enough care for inner peace, especially in the world today, where human life, on all levels—socially, politically, economically and religiously—has become very fragmented.

In our present 21st century, instead of being brothers and sisters of the hereafter, human beings have lost their closeness to each other. The separation of hearts is the real catastrophe! What we see happening in the world is the mirror of the present state of humanity. We have lost divine harmony internally and for this reason, nature and the cosmos have lost it, too.

Thus, these experiences have become the real source for writing, reading, sharing, and learning, in order to rediscover, and to revive the lost property within our hearts. May we experience beauty within beauty, if God wills, so that we do not have to undergo wars and misery in order to find each other again.

Slowly the world is being emptied out of the radiance of His saints, of the goodness of His friends, of the teachings of His supreme masters, of the purity of His representatives, of the authenticity of His gnostics, and of the humbleness of His true servants. This is the state of our world today. True believers are hidden or very rare. As it appears in the present world, most saints with the noblest of characters and exquisite knowledge have gone to the hereafter. However, their graves do not separate them from people who are still alive. Their spiritual influence works for those who have the capacity to receive. Only higher awareness can grasp divine existence, and only true faith survives in the jungle of the world's confusion and darkness. Real saints operate from their graves even more effectively than when they were alive.

THE CRISIS IN THE MODERN WORLD

The Prophet Muhammad, peace and blessings be unto him, said in a holy tradition:

Man is the enemy of what he does not know.

All religious traditions call human beings to direct their attention towards the inner selves, instead of blaming all misfortunes on factors outside of themselves. In order to resolve any problems humanity faces today, we have to research what caused them. We have to find the root of our sicknesses. To remove the symptoms will only multiply the dark events that confront the present world. Only knowledge that is the common ground for all cultures, religions, and countries can lead to a deeper understanding of what is needed. Only mutual sharing between the east and the west will bring peace.

Today, the necessity to link the confused and disoriented modern mind with the deeply rooted, solid ground of true eternal human values is most urgent. It happened to me; I lived a meaningless and empty life until I discovered the source of beauty and goodness. Stepping beyond form, looking beyond external events, becomes absolutely essential in our present world. Humanity is faced with great tragedies! It has never been so urgent to obtain a broader and deeper awareness about human life on this planet. Profound care, generous insights, loving, and mutual sharing can bring salvation to all human beings.

I feel a compulsion to write about these problems because we have no time to lose. God most High wakes us up with catastrophes, such as the destruction of nature, resulting in floods, fire, earthquakes and typhoons and, additionally, at the present time, the great war on terror. I believe and experience that the whole world's consciousness has changed. The whole planet is faced with a powerful movement of globalization. We should take this opportunity to rediscover the truth about human life and to find common values which will unify us again, instead of heading faster and deeper into our own ruin.

Especially the West, with its highly industrialized societies and highly developed capitalism, possesses a great potential for destruction and, therefore, it grows into the greatest power, dominating the whole world. Since the beginning of history, this is the endless problem humanity has faced on this planet—that of wealth against poverty, the strong against weak. Most wars between peoples arise from a few power-hungry ignorant men, misled by their own devils.

I wish to say that we do not need to stop fighting on the battlefields in order to find peace. We do not need a mosque in order to pray. We do not need to circumambulate the Ka'ba in order to fully surrender. We do not need to fast in order to fully abstain from the satisfaction of our egos. And we do not need to give alms in order to become truly generous. For when the heart is woken up to perfect consciousness, true worship, true peace, true generosity, true thankfulness, and true fasting will arise from the core of our being. These are eternal qualities which emanate from God's beautiful names and attributes. In a pure heart, nothing can be destroyed and nothing can be demolished. The only real thing in man is his soul, and the soul belongs entirely to God! All souls want nothing but Him, consciously or unconsciously.

I read an article recently about the Mosque Al-Aqsa (in Jerusalem). The author is in grief, describing the sublime temple, which appeared to him to be sorrowful and exhausted. It was once the source of thousands of holy experiences. Now it feels like it is bleeding internally and can no longer breathe. This honored pulpit now looks like a candle that has been blown out, a skeleton about to collapse. He goes on to say that from now on, faithful hearts will not be able to meet and hug each other with love amongst the walls of this place in which Adam's voice still echoes, the Prophet Abraham's breaths are still felt, the Prophet David's and Solomon's cries are still heard, and the Prophet Muhammad's journey to unite with his Beloved is still known. Yet if we feed ourselves with negativity in the present state of the world, if we mourn extensively about catastrophes, tragedies, and dark demonic events, we will only add to the forces of destruction that face humanity.

At the present moment of history, it has never been more urgent to realize the universality of the truth, to offer a true vision of the meaning and value of a human being. We have to oppose the crisis in the modern world with a strong, substantial positive energy. We need to know that the water is one. We have to look from the station of absolute eternity, where the original oneness of being is unaffected. We have to take directly from the source.

I believe, and I wish to say, that a pure believer's heart is still able to hear the echoes of Adam's voice amongst the walls of the Al-Aqsa Mosque, is able to feel the breath of the Prophet Abraham, and is able to know the ascension of the Prophet Muhammad to infinity, to unite with his Beloved, even though the world is smitten with tragic wars, especially in the Middle East. The Prophet Muhammad, peace and blessings be unto him, after returning from a bloody battlefield where he lost a great number of human lives, would immediately plant a seed in the earth for a tree to grow.

Only with a creative dialogue between east and west based on the universal truth inherent in all religious traditions, will we be able to work for a better unifying future. The holy Qur'an says:

> *In the Name of God, the Beneficent, the Merciful,*
> *Praise be to God, Lord of all the Worlds. (1:1-2)*

These are the very first lines of the opening chapter of the Holy Qur'an. God addresses the whole of humankind. It is the essence of His message to the human race. He embraces every single soul living on this planet, and everyone should embrace the One and Only God, too. He has delivered a universal message, and He has provided divine guidance for all nations. He brought His beloved Prophet Muhammad as a mercy for the whole world. The holy Qur'an says:

We have made you a middle-way community. (2:143)

Only respecting the eternal values, the universal messages, can save us from selfishness, arrogance, and our hunger for power. Especially in our present time, the answer to everything is divine compassion. Muhyiddin Ibn Arabi says:

There is no misfortune. For the divine Mystery pervades the entirety of the world, and there is no misfortune. All of what God has arranged is the domain of His loving concern, because it is in the grasp of the Real. What is in His grasp is near Him, and what is near God is good and preserved; misfortune is evil and there is no evil in Him.

RITUALS

The western world praises individuality. Egocentric styles of life create separation and encourage competition and fighting. People are mainly concerned with achieving success in their own work fields. We have lost the human values that will generate love in our hearts, the most precious gift that we possess. Additionally, we miss true rituals and ceremonies that enrich our lives and will be able to bring peace and unity to civilization. Festivities such as Christmas, Easter, marriage, death, and harvest, have degenerated into mere public holidays which have become excessively commercialized. Because of this void, a great spiritual need has arisen in the west and has been answered mainly by eastern philosophies and practices.

In short, the essential element of 'celebration' has vanished from our western lives. This is the crucial point! When I entered into the life of a believer, this is what impressed me most of all, the capacity for mutual sharing for a good cause, for the sake of God. The ceremonies in the east occurring throughout the year have a truly unifying effect on everyone. These rituals give true respect to the fact that all things are sacred and all life is divine and, at the same time, express profound thankfulness to our Creator through their nature. Ceremonies in the eastern traditions bring people together, eliminating differences, undermining status, wealth, education, and so on. Thus, the danger of people getting lost in their own lives, becomes very small.

In this way, rituals become, in a full sense, a prayer, and in a full sense, a thanksgiving to our Creator. If, within ceremonies, respect towards the sacred and thanks and praise to the Lord is missing, the services become invalid and meaningless for the participants. Thus, because true rituals are not practiced in the west, human beings have lost their inner harmony. This is why there is so much restlessness in our modern world. One does not want to have time for oneself or to face the other. In other words, people hide from their responsibilities towards their Creator.

One of the greatest rituals which human beings experience is the pilgrimage to Mecca. Pilgrims become God's guests. He invites them to enjoy in His nearness. For example, within the ritual prayer, a million or more people freeze, stay motionless at the same time, or prostrate at the same time. What a miracle! Nowhere else in the world can we witness such a miraculous discipline of the thousands upon thousands of people celebrating the sacredness of the moment!

Throughout the entire Islamic calendar, there are so many other beautiful celebrations, too, such as the Night of Ascension, the Night of Absolution, the Prophet's holy birth, the Night of Power, Ramadan, and especially, every Friday, God opens up the gates of heaven to pour special blessings and grace upon all believers. The Friday ceremony is the peak of experience, the essence of celebration for a worshipping heart.

The same is true for Ramadan. It represents the greatest festival for humankind. For thirty days, millions of people all over the world do not drink or eat for the whole day. The splendid power which is generated every day and every night during the holy month is immeasurable! After the fast breaks, profound and excellent voluntary worship, and unceasing tearful supplications to our Lord, are performed. What a great purification for a believer's body and soul! My blessed master said that if we knew the true value of the holy month of Ramadan, we would wish it never to end for the rest of our lives.

In truth, the eternal richness of eastern rites can never be described with words. If only people could know what they are missing. Only the ones who taste, know. . .

However, to truly pray, to truly give thanks, and to truly celebrate, has now, unfortunately, become rare in the East as well.
This inner tragedy, the inner darkness of the human heart, is the
essential problem. If our lives are not based on God's wisdom, we
will decay morally. We are created for eternity. This is the message. The only salvation of the human being lies in eternal peace.
This means we have to find inner peace before we can establish
outer peace. A true believer who is aware of the richness within
and without him will celebrate each moment, will celebrate each
breath, because he knows that he lives in the blessings and the
bounties of God Most High.

TEARS

Sheikh Abd al-Qadir al-Jilani gives us the most exquisite imagery about the precious values of human tears:

If you do not place your forehead of urgent need upon the soil of admitted incapacity, and if the tears of sorrow do not rain down from the clouds of your eyes, the plants of your delight will not become verdant in the orchard of daily life. The gardens of men will not become fecundated to suit your purpose. The branches of patience will not put forth the leaves of contentment and the fragrant perfumes of intimate friendship, nor will they bear the fruits of the nearness.

If we truly wish to seek, to taste, to see, to love, to know, the whole of our lives has to be accompanied by tears. Tears are our best companions. Tears become our tool. The more we weep, the more we are able to grow towards spiritual maturity. Tears are a token of divine love for our Great Lord of all the worlds. They are our most precious divine capital. Only when we feel affection for our beloved Lord will streaming tears will be able to flow abundantly. Weeping without expecting any result, weeping for the sake of weeping—what great bliss for our souls! The great saint, Jalal al-Din Rumi expresses this point in his exalted poetry:

God has afflicted you from every direction in order to pull you back to Directionless.
Whatever makes you tremble, know that you are worth just that!
This is why the lover's heart is greater than God's Throne.

When we are truly lost, perplexed and in a state of helplessness, that is when tears flow, and that is how we can reach the Lord of Majesty and Bounty. If we let go all of our attachments to this world and become truly incapacitated, we will be extremely successful. In the face of divine beauty which brings us in a state of wonderment, fascination, amazement, and astonishment, streaming tears will be our companions. To get lost in God's Infinity is the believer's work. As Jalal al-Din Rumi says *"The lover's profession is to drown in the ocean,"and Muhyiddin Ibn Arabi wishes "To dive into the infinite ocean of oneness."*

If a believer does not realize his incapacities, his nothingness, in the Presence of God's All-Embracing Power, how could he ever shed tears? If a believer is not in a state of deep sorrow, insufficiency, sadness, humility and shame, how could he ever shed tears? If a believer does not feel eager desire, burning longing, intense yearning, ceaselessly pleading and ask for help, how could he ever shed tears?

If a believer does not possess pure joy, the highest bliss melting into the divine Truth, how could he ever shed tears? If a believer does not feel wonderment, amazement, and bewilderment in the face of divine Beauty, how could he ever shed tears?

When witnessing divine beauty, our hearts will become soft from shedding tears, and we will begin to tremble. This state is most desired by God. This is man in his original form, the ideal as he was created—shameful, soft, tender, humble, helpless, fearful and kind. A true lover will lower his head often, because of fear and abundant humility towards his Lord. As Abd al-Qadir al-Jilani reports, humming sounds, like the simmering of a cooking pot, could be heard coming from the blessed breast of our Prophet Muhammad, peace and blessings be unto him, during his prayers, due to the intensity of his fear, the vision of the Majesty of his Lord, and the divine sublimity that was revealed. A pure heart, like that of the Prophet, can be hit with such a mighty impact that the effect becomes apparent in the physical body.

A young man once came to Sheikh Semnun and asked him what love is. At that moment, a bird bit his finger and he cried. A tear dropped on his finger. The sheikh pointed at the tear on his finger and said: *"That is what love is."* The love in the heart of the young man represents the pain due to separation from God. Because the human being is originally created from a drop of water, tears represent a return to the state of purity and innocence.

Most tears are shed when a believer feels pain due to separation from God. He is in a state of deep sorrow, insufficiency, and sadness. The believer also sheds tears when he realizes his incapacities, his nothingness, and his imperfections in the Presence of God's All-Embracing Power. He also sheds tears of sadness when he witnesses the miserable conditions of human tragedies, like crying images of poverty, and the devastating pictures of terror and war.

A spiritual path deprived of tears will degenerate into a life philosophy. But tears bring you beyond time and space. ; in other words, through tears, we can experience and participate in a historical event, such as Karbala, as it were today. For through tears, the veils on the spiritual path can be removed and the glorious truth can be revealed. Consequently, the weeping heart of a true lover participates with his whole being in the reality of all events in terms of their spiritual nature, whenever and wherever they happen. Junayd al-Baghdadi, may God be pleased with him, said:

Neither praying nor fasting save us, but the tears that we shed at dawn.

According to another report:

Tears for the sake of God can extinguish the believer's fire of hell.

And Jalal al-Din Rumi said:

I wonder at this tiny infant who cries, and its mother giving milk. If it should think, 'What profit is there in crying? What is it that causes milk to come?' then it would not receive any milk. But we see that it receives milk because of its crying. How should the infant know the effect its cries have upon hearts? So weep, even if you do not know the result! The everlasting gardens and rivers of paradise will be born from your tears.

PART THREE

The Sacredness of the Human Being

Of all the terms, love is probably not only the most misunderstood but the most important word in existence. God's creating man is an act of intimacy, because His love for human beings is the motivating force for creation. The creation of the universe and man is based on a relationship of lover and Beloved. God made man in His image of unity and grace. And God loves that which He created in His image (Muslim, *Birr*, 115; *Jannah*, 28).

The Qur'anic verse proves the fulfillment of humankind:

> *He loves them and they love Him. (5:54)*

Using the attribute of love does the Qur'an speak of the relationship between God and man. In the concept of creation, there is an equal balance of divine love and human love, which proves that God's love for human beings is absolutely unique. God says:

> *I created everything for you and I created you for Myself. (hadith kudsi)*

God, the All-Compeller, is always mentioned in the Holy Qur'an with His attributes of absolute Dominion, Power, Greatness, Exaltation and Majesty. As creatures towards our Creator, we are always under the influence of the attributes of weakness, incapacity, helplessness, insufficiency, ignorance, disobedience, abasement, mortality, dependence, and so on. However, in terms of love, God most High affirms mutual love for us as He affirms love for Himself. Love made Him create the universe and all that it contains. Thus we can say that we exist because of the love God has for us.

The Sufi Saint Ahmad Sam'ani comments:

> *The angels said: "What, will You place therein one who will work corruption there, and shed blood?" And God said: "I know what you*

do not know." In other words, "I know that I will forgive them. You know their disobedience, but I know My forgiveness. In your glorification, you make manifest your own activity, but in My forgiveness I make manifest My own bounty and generosity. I know what you do not know, which is My love for them and the purity of their belief in loving Me. Although outwardly, their good works are barefoot, inwardly their love for Me is pure. I know what you do not know, which is My love for them. No matter what they are, I love them."

Baha Walad enlightens us about the intimate relationship to our Creator with an excellent description:

If existence is not at rest with the giving of existence, with what will it be at rest? Since My desire, My act, My attribute, My creating, and My mercy are connected to the creatures, if they are not intimate with Me, with whom will they be intimate? Intimacy is My act. All the words between lovers, their whispered secrets, their touching, and their intercourse–I bring all this into existence. With whom does it want intimacy to last if not with Me?

The All-Merciful says:

My Love, My Existence is their love for Me.

And according to Jalal al-Din Rumi, in the realm of the souls before man entered into the world, a significant conversation took place:

God said, "I have hurried to you, I have made you for Myself, I will not sell what I have made for Myself at auction."
I said "Who are You?"
He said "The Desire of all."
I said "Who am I?"
He said, "The desire of the Desire."

Our supreme Creator never holds back to reveal constantly His infinite love for His most honored and desired creatures. He never ceases to pour His favors, bounties, gifts, and blessings on humankind. He is of such gentleness and kindness that He forgives before His creatures ask forgiveness from Him. And the All-Wise, the All-

Compassionate gives great news to His servants, for He nurtures His most honored and beloved creation, the human being, with the brilliance of His light, with supreme pearls of wisdom:

- *I am his secret and he is My secret.*
- *Neither the heavens nor the earth contain Me, but the heart of My faithful servant contains Me.*
- *My place that is your existence.*
- *If you know yourself, you know your Lord.*

And in the Qur'an:

And We are nearer to him than the jugular vein. (50:16)

The One and Only, with His loving concern, with His merciful guidance, is teaching His closeness to us! Each one of these inspiring lines carries an inner wealth of infinite richness. They reveal nothing else than the wonder and treasury of the relationship between God and man. It means that the divine favor towards humankind is immense! God the most Merciful gave all and everything to man, so that we might know Him.

These magnificent lines prove that God is closer to us than we are to ourselves. We are eternally rooted in Him. The deep-seated relationship between God and His creatures becomes the most mysterious, most perfect, most unique, most sublime, most holy, most precious and, therefore, most intimate of all relationships.

And there are beautiful words of the Prophet Muhammad, upon him be peace and blessings, which prove a creative relationship and deepest intimacy between God and His creatures, and which are reported as a *hadith qudsi*:

- *My servant can only approach Me with something which pleases Me more than that which I impose on him. My servant approaches Me ceaselessly by free acts until I love him; and when I love him, I am the hearing by which he hears, the sight by which he sees, the hand with which he takes holds, and the foot with which he walks. If he prays to Me, I give to him certainly, and if he looks for My help, I help him certainly.*

- *I witness the invocation of he who invokes Me.*
- *Remember Me, and I will remember you. (Or "Name Me, and I will name you.")*
- *God says: "I am to My servant as he expects of Me, and I am with him when he remembers Me. If he remembers Me in his heart, I remember him to Myself; and if he remembers me in an assembly, I mention him in an assembly better than his; and if he draws nearer to Me a hand's span; I draw nearer to him an arm's length; and if he draws nearer to Me an arm's length, I draw nearer to him a fathom length; and if he comes to me walking, I rush to him at great speed."*

And there are divine verses which give further proof of God's all-embracing love for His creatures:

And He is with you wherever you are. (2:115)

God is well-pleased with them – and they are well-pleased with Him. (5:119)

As we see, our most beloved Lord of all the worlds never lets us out of His Sight! He is always watching over us. His love and desire for His servants is infinite. The highest form of love is the love of God for His creatures.

The Almighty has made man in His Image and He has breathed into man from His Own Spirit, and He has created man from the beauty of Muhammad's light. This love is the love for the best of His creation, the human being! For this reason, God asked the angels to prostrate themselves before His first created man, Adam, upon him be peace. God's love for His creatures is the reason for creation, expressed in His saying:

I was a hidden treasure and I loved to be known, so I created creation. (hadith qudsi)

So His love manifests itself in His desire to be known. Loving God means knowing God, which means that man's awareness of God is the highest form of love, the ultimate spiritual fulfillment a human being is able to experience.

God wishes that we participate in His love for humankind. At the time of creation of man, the Almighty planted divine love in his deepest interior. In other words, real love is the love for the Divine in one's own self. The renowned poet, Jalal al-Din Rumi, describes God's nature of kindness and mercy towards His beloved servants:

> *With God, two I's cannot find room. You say "I," and He says "I." Either you die before Him, or let Him die before you; then duality will not remain. But it is impossible for Him to die, either subjectively or objectively, since He is The Living God, the Undying. He possesses such Gentleness that if it was possible, He would die for you so that duality might vanish. But since it is impossible for Him to die, you die, so that He may manifest Himself to you and duality may vanish.*

The Sufi Saint Ahmad Sam'ani also talks about the reality of intimacy with such an exaltation:

> *God most High addresses His creatures: "O Ridwan, paradise belongs to you! O Malik, hell belongs to you! O cherubim, the Throne belongs to you! O you with the burnt heart, you who carry the seal of My love! You belong to Me, and I belong to you. O accursed one, are you proud of fire? You belong to fire, and fire belongs to you. O Pharaoh, are you proud of the Nile? You belong to the Nile, and the Nile belongs to you! O you who declares My unity* (tawhid), *are you proud of Me? You belong to Me, and I belong to you."*
>
> *God created every creature in keeping with the demand of power, but He created Adam and his children in keeping with the demand of love. He created other things in respect of being the Strong, but He created you in respect of being the Friend.*
>
> *God most High addresses His disobedient creatures as His servants: "On the Day of Resurrection, you will say, 'My body, My body!' Muhammad will say, 'My community, my community!' Paradise will say, 'My share, my share!' Hell will say, 'My portion, portion!' And the Lord of Exaltation will say, 'My servant, My servant!'"*

May God allow us to enter into deep intimacy with Him. May He allow us to arrive at the door of intimate conversations. May He allow us to actualize the divine synthesis with Him in our daily lives. May He allow us to return His endless divine favors by showing thankfulness in our behavior and actions.

Baha Walad gives us a beautiful advice how to love God:

> *So look upon the meanings, how God constantly keeps you in the palm of His hand and His breast. Belong to your Lord and be His companion! Be a stranger to other things and other states. Keep your gaze upon your Sovereign. Whatever you want, ask it from Him. Rub yourself against Him. Mix with Him like milk with honey. Then you will find all the houris, palaces, and sweetnesses of paradise in ready coin. You will find God. Your felicity is for this door to be opened to you, for you to know that' He is with you wherever you are'.*

Life on this planet is a very serious business, because we are of divine origin. In the Holy Qur'an, God most High said to the angels at the time of creation of man:

> *I am creating a mortal of clay. When I have shaped him and breathed My Spirit into him, fall you down, prostrating yourselves to him. (38:72)*

The only real thing in man is his soul, and the soul belongs entirely to God; that is to say, we are created for eternity, meaning that we are created for spiritual realization. Man carries the title of "chosen." We carry great responsibility because we carry God's trust. The Trust was imposed on man in the realm of the souls before entering the world. God most High made us testify about ourselves and all the souls responded after being asked, *"Am I not your Lord?"* with, *"Yea! We testify."* So man agreed the carry the Trust with the responsibility involved, which is nothing else than becoming secure in the knowledge of God. The Qur'anic verse gives the following description:

> *We offered the Trust to the heavens and the earth and the mountains, but they refused to carry it and were afraid of it; and man carried it....(33:72)*

This means that for each individual, the life-span from his birth to his death means learning, education, and evolution, because the ultimate fulfillment of a human being is to represent God on earth as the perfect man. For this reason, each human being has to become a professional seeker in his life. Spiritual evolution is a gradual growing of one's personality towards spiritual maturity. It is not acquiring knowledge; rather, it is a becoming. The way of life will be a never-ending evolution towards the roots of our being, meaning homecoming. We will find ourselves on a spiritual journey as travelers continuously in motion, because the final destination is our beloved Lord. The great poet, Jalal al-Din Rumi, gives us the following advice about the spiritual combat:

> *Bounty for the body makes you unripe, but the body's affliction matures you. Until you undergo the affliction of religion, you will not win the good fortune of faith.*

I wish to say that it is our essential duty to study the nature of the human being. If we do not become researchers of the complexity of our soul, we automatically degenerate in our values. Through the cultivation of our souls, we will reach the marvelous heights of our existence. We will discover some of the mysteries of human nature, and we will be able to establish the true relationship to our Creator, to man and the universe.

For this reason, all human beings through the descent onto this earthly plane, find themselves consciously or unconsciously, willingly or unwillingly, in the school of life. God most High puts us at the time of our birth in a workshop. Our life represents a training-camp for becoming true human beings.

Moreover, with God giving us life, He invites us to the path of love, which is the path of transformation. For each individual, the goal is to become immersed in His divine beauty. A true lover offers his whole being unconditionally towards his beloved Lord. He is immersed in true servanthood. He will be consumed by the love he has for God, up to his own extinction. Annihilation of man in the Divinity represents the fullness of being; that is to say, we have to shape ourselves in a state of nothingness so we will be able to live in His eternal richness. In other words, love is only given by our All-Merciful Lord to be realized. Love exists to become eternally alive. Love is existence in God.

I was invited to the school of life. In other words, God let me become aware that our earthly lives represent a school. Additionally, I was invited to join the path of light, meaning the path of God's divine wisdom, the sweet taste of inner meanings. I call it the school of love.

In the first stage we will wake up! Being awake means awareness of the One and the Only. We will learn to see, hear, feel, taste, know Him. We will wake up from a misguided, meaningless life, and we will discover the reality of our own being, a life of eternal richness, the hidden treasure inside of ourselves. If we take the task to learn seriously, we will be thankful for each given difficulty in life, because it brings us closer to our Beloved. The world is a testing ground for the believers. Whatever God has spread before us will be an examination, a lesson to pass, though the greatest examination is ourselves. We are the key and the door for personal salvation; but at the same time, we are the hindrance, its obstacle. The cage of existence, our body, prevents us from spiritual evolution; but in the same time it is our means to reach the One and the Only. The leader of the gnostics, Ali ibn Abu Talib, may God be pleased with him, said:

> *Your cure is within you, but you do not know; your illness is from you, but you do not see. You are the 'Clarifying Book' through whose letters becomes manifest the hidden. You suppose that you're a small body, but the greatest world unfolds within you. You would not need what is outside yourself if you would reflect upon yourself, but you do not reflect.*

In the second stage, we will lose our existence in God and be eradicated in pure love. The end of man's spiritual evolution is, paradoxically, non-existence. The ultimate level is reached through the self-extinction of the lover into the Beloved.

Human beings are the only creatures which can be dispossessed of themselves, which can transcend themselves to reach the state of non-existence. In the spiritual realm, there is no death without a res-urrection. Self-annihilation will lead into a rebirth. Whoever dies before death will receive new life. The ultimate fulfillment of man is to become alive in the Existence of our supreme Divinity. This is our true self. Therefore, if we reach our true self, we will become younger whilst our bodies are aging. In other words, whilst grow-ing old, we will get younger in spirit. In that way, the voluntary death will become our greatest gain; it is a re-birth!

Furthermore, only the human being can smell the scent of the words. No other being is given the sweet scent of awareness. The joy of being human is to be a seeker of the infinite plane of exis-tence.

This world is a workshop for seeking the divine mysteries of life. Yearning to know is yearning for love. The true search is the search for the divine taste! To the degree of the heat of our search, we will find the hidden divine satisfaction. Baha Walad enlightens us with his clear-cut statement:

> *If not for the taste of seeking, I would be dead.*

It means that there is nothing more fulfilling for the believer than working in God's garden and, at the same time, seeking the Gardener.

PROPHET ADAM, UPON HIM BE PEACE

The whole secret of human existence is rooted in the first human being, Adam, upon him be peace, the father of mankind. The All-Glorious created the first human being in the most unique and noble manner, in limitless purity, in order to demonstrate that all his descendants, the whole of mankind, will be able to take a perfect example for imitation; that is to say, all human beings will be able to read their own selves whilst studying Adam's life.

No one else other than Adam, upon him be peace, due to his fall from paradise to earth, reveals the essential features of human nature in a perfect way. Whatever experiences humanity goes through in the life of this world, we can trace these back to Adam himself.

The secret meaning of God saying, *"I wanted to be known so I created creation,"* manifests itself through man's descent into the world. The whole drama of human existence is played out on the worldly stage. In God's judgment, each individual has to play his role perfectly in order to gain meaning and value as His creatures.

God created the first man, Adam, upon him be peace, in His form, that is to say, He has a vision of Himself in the perfect man, meaning, it is Himself that He desires. And God taught Adam, upon him be peace, and God taught him His knowledge. He divulged the true names of things to Adam, upon him be peace, as mentioned in the divine Qur'anic verse:

He taught Adam the names, all of them. (2:31)

At the time of creation, God breathed into Adam His divine Breath of mercy. As the Qur'anic word of God states:

*And when I have unfolded his form, and I have breathed into him
of My Spirit...* (38:72)

By the act of blowing the divine Breath, the essential nature of
man was made manifest. Through the infusion of the breath of
mercy and the knowledge of the divine attributes, Adam, upon him
be peace, becomes a Caliph, the representative of God on earth.

Besides, God most High created man in 40 days with His
Own Hands, whereas the entire creation of the universe and all it
contains took only 6 days. The Almighty says to Iblis:

*What is it that prevents you from prostrating yourself before that
which I have created with My two hands?* (38:75)

Sheikh Muhyiddin Ibn Arabi formulates with great ability the
caring way of God, lovingly fashioning the most honorable creation, the human being:

*At first He created man as an atom in the shape of a beautiful
jewel, upon which He gazed with love and compassion. When His
Sight fell upon it the jewel melted into water, and each drop of this
water burst with divine Knowledge. Then He poured this water
upon the roots of a young tree made out of Divine Harmony, which
gave it the life of Knowledge and Beauty. He named the tree
human being...*

*And God kept man's secrets within His Secrets, and hid his origin
and nature within His Beautiful Names; the Gentle and the
Mighty One...*

*Man tried to escape from his Creator in fear of His fire, His awe-
inspiring Grandeur, and His Wrath. But God caught him gently,
without his even feeling it, and dipped him time after time into the
waters of the azure ocean of hope. Thus the divine Power revived in
man again, and found its right place within him......*

By virtue of receiving a sacred form, the human being possesses the highest rank within the entire creation. He becomes the
jewel of creation, because the human being is the goal and the reason for God creating the universe and all it contains.

God's greatest miracle of creation culminates in the mystery of man. The universe is an outward manifestation of man's inward divine reality. The physical world is just a reflection of the spiritual world. Form is the microcosm and meaning is the macrocosm. Man is the centre of existence, the universe and the world, and what it contains serves him. Everything exists for the sake of man and man exists for the sake of God. Within the evolutionary stages of God's creation, the human being came last, because he represents the crown and the fulfillment within all existence. The great saint Jalal al-Din Rumi wrote:

> *Although the fruit comes last into existence, it is the first because it was the goal! If there had been no desire and hope for the fruit, why did the gardener plant the tree? It therefore means that the fruit gave existence to the tree, even if in form the tree gave birth to the fruit.*
>
> *Man is the substance, and the heavens are secondary. All things are branches and steps - he is the goal.*

Through man, the existence of the world is completed. Man becomes a divine mirror through which God contemplates His creation and dispenses His mercy.

So Adam, upon him be peace, became the mirror of God's names and He became the light of this mirror. So Adam, upon him be peace, reflects the light and the beauty of the perfection of God most High. Jalal al-Din Rumi writes:

> *All knowledge and all things were to be found within Adam's breast. The father of mankind, who is the Master of 'He taught the names,' has hundreds of thousands of sciences in every vein.*

Within the breast of Adam, upon him be peace, there were hidden secrets over secrets, God's infinite treasures of knowledge stored within it because his heart embraced endless diversity. At the time of creation of the first human being Adam, upon him be peace, God fashioned the heart as the most exalted place within the whole of His creation. The Almighty says:

Neither the heavens nor the earth contain Me, but the heart of My faithful servant contains Me.

God made the heart of man into a macro-cosmos, because He made it into a divine mirror where the beauty of His divine light and His divine secrets are reflected. As the great Islamic writer, Jalal al-Din Rumi, comments:

Since Adam saw with the Pure Light, the spirit and mystery of the names appeared to him.

God most High says in the holy Qur'an:

God has made faith lovable to you and He has made it beautiful within our hearts. (49:7)

Ahmad Sam'ani writes:

Look at the Throne to see tremendousness, look at the Footstool to see capaciousness, look at the Tablet to see inscriptions, look at the heavens to see elevation, look at the heart to see love, and look at love to see the Beloved.

When one looks at the human essence, it is tainted and distracted. It is muddiness, a dark water, a clay. But the site of love is the heart and the heart is pure gold, the pearl of the breast's ocean, the ruby of the inmost mystery's mine. The hand of no one else has touched it, and the eye of no one who is not a confidant has fallen upon it. The witnessing of God's Majesty has polished it. And the burnisher of the Unseen has placed its seal upon it, making it bright and limpid. Since the heart is all of this, the Presence of Exaltation has love for it.....

Man is made in God's image means that man is the greatest mirror to God's names, that is to say, he has knowledge of his Creator. The whole of man's make up is rooted in the divine attributes of the Almighty, which means, that he is created in the concept of the perfect man, *al-insan al-kamil*. Therefore all levels of human evolution depend on realizing, tasting, and respectively living the divine attributes, making the hidden treasure manifest. So man will become the true representative of God on earth.

Adam, upon him be peace, who was created as the prototype of human perfection, demonstrates that he accepted to carry the divine Trust. Respectively, he accepted to take responsibility for the knowledge of the divine names that God told him. In this sense, carrying the burden of the divine Trust shows love for God.

Paradise is the manifestation of God's names of Beauty, Jamal. But human beings can only truly taste the reality of love if they experience the names of God's Majesty, Might, Wrath, Jalal, as well as the names of God's Beauty, Gentleness, Love, and Generosity. In order to realize the full capacity of our hearts, in order to measure our own worth, human beings have to embrace all of the names and go down to earth, mix with their fellow beings and undergo heartache, turbulence, yearning, struggling.

This is what is meant with God most High creating the human being with His two Own Hands. Man finds himself between His beauty, Jamal, and His majesty, Jalal. He is in awe before the Might and all-compelling Greatness of His Lord, and he finds himself in loving intimacy in the Gentleness and beauty of His Lord. He constantly slides between fear and hope, because he can receive God's anger as well as His mercy.

Ahmad Sam'ani comments:

> Come into this world, which is the workshop of seeking. The teacher, who is poverty, will write out for you the alphabet of love.
>
> Before Adam was brought into existence, there was a world full of existent things, creatures, formed things, determined things—but all of it was a tasteless stew. The salt of pain was missing. When that great man walked out from the hiding-place of nonexistence into the spacious desert of existence, the star of love began to shine in the heaven of the breast of Adam's clay. The sun of lovehood began to burn in the sky of his inmost mystery.

To conclude, in the concept of creation, Adam's station reflects the perfection and beauty of God most High. So God gave Adam, upon him be peace, the most supreme place within all creation. He honored him to guard His trust, to safekeep His divine treasures.

He created him as a prophet. He chose him to become His representative on earth. Moreover, God fashioned Adam, upon him be peace, as a perfect lover, so he would turn his whole attention towards his beloved Creator. Adam, upon him be peace, becomes the jewel of creation. That is to say, Adam, upon him be peace, was chosen for the perfection of prophethood, sainthood, servanthood, lovehood, vicegerency. He was made for endless worship; he was made for the exaltation of prostration; he was made for abundant servanthood; he was made for loving submissiveness; he was made for tearful repentance; he was made for the highest ethics of humility and shame; he was made for utter joy of obedience; he was made for unconditional love and need; he was made for the inside into divine realities; and he was made for infinite contemplation. As a result, Adam, upon him be peace, becomes the prototype of human perfection.

That is to say, in the divine concept, the human being is pure soul, a saint forever receptive towards divine qualities, infused with God's divine breath of mercy. Therefore, the universe is based on sainthood. The divine qualities are holding the architectural structure of the cosmos together. If he lives human nature in its fullest sense, he becomes *hazreti insan*, a holy human being. In other words, as his descendants, Adam, upon him be peace, comprises in his essential nature all that we need for human perfection. He is the father of mankind and he suffices all of our needs.

Our great Adam, upon him be peace, sat on the throne of tremendousness in paradise. All angels prostrated to his exalted station. He was offered all the riches of heaven, but his heart did not conform to the marvels in paradise. It was designed for poverty and need. Adam, upon him be peace, lived the marvel of glorifying unity with his Lord. But his heavenly exaltation had no value for him. The make up of his heart was pure love. He smelt these mysteries within his breast. He was drawn to loving intimacy with his beloved Lord. He was drawn to loving slavehood.

Adam, upon him be peace, had to leave paradise due to a lapse. For a grain of wheat he was expelled from paradise and had to descend to earth. That is to say, in the concept of creation, Adam, upon him be peace, was made to exchange the official paradise for the paradise of intimacy, the intimacy of divine discourse with his Creator. He left the official kingship of heaven and became the king of hearts. He left his crown, thrown, palaces, gardens, and his honored station in exchange for love. For this reason, Adam, upon him be peace, represents the top model of all lovers. Through him, the path of love got established; sainthood got established in the world. He became the first humble student, the first needy creature, the first tearful admirer, the first truthful searcher, and the first divine intimate converser towards his Almighty Creator.

In other words, God most High created a disobedient act for Adam, upon him be peace—the eating of the fruit from the forbidden tree—so he would have to leave paradise and go down to the world in order to learn, in order to become a learning slave. No one else than his supreme Creator became his teacher. Therefore, the eternal relationship of God and man is based on Adam as the first student and God as his teacher. In consequence, all human beings have to relate to their Creator as pleading creatures, in utter need to be guided, nurtured, protected and taught by His glorious wisdom and power.

Ahmad Sam'ani comments:

> *Aloes (the Aloe Vera plant) has a mystery. If you smell it for a thousand years, it will never give off an aroma. It wants fire to show its mystery. Its face is black and its color is dark. Its taste is bitter, and it is a kind of wood. It wants a sharp fire to make plain the secret of its heart. There was a fire of searching in Adam's breast, and its sparks looked upon all the acts of worship and obedience and all the capital goods of the angels of the sovereignty as nothing. He was an incense that had to be thrown into the fire. From that incense a breeze became manifest. What was it? "He loves them, and they love Him."*

Being expelled from paradise by God gives man the pain of separation. With this act, God wants to make evident the reality of love to the human being. Because God wants to become the object of desire, He separates the human being at the time of his birth from Himself, and this separation hurts man. There is no bigger pain than the pain of separation from Him. And there is no bigger happiness than the joy of union with Him. Being expelled from paradise does not mean punishment. On the contrary, God wants to train the human being and bring him into places of elevation, honor, perfection and true love. That is to say, being expelled from paradise is precisely the starting point of need.

Human existence on this planet is truly educational, because we are entering the world of spiritual growth. The pain of separation will nourish the seed of love in our hearts. It will make grow the aspiration towards the One and Only. We will go restlessly on in search for Him. We will realize our total need and our total dependence towards the One and Only. Through realizing our nothingness, impotence and insufficiency, we will be overpowered by His Glory Power and Greatness.

The Sufi Saint, Ahmad Sam'ani, comments:

> *From the Throne down to the earth, no love whatsoever is sold except in the house of human grief and joy. Many sinless and pure angels were in the Court, but only this handful of dust was able to carry the burden of this body-melting, heart-burning verse: He loves them, and they love Him.*
>
> *In the world of love, paradise and hell are not worth a speck of dust. They gave the eight paradises to Adam, the chosen. He sold them for one grain of wheat. He placed the wares of aspiration on the camel of good fortune and came down to the world of heartache.*
>
> *That great man was adorned with auspiciousness, bounty, and the lights of perfection and beauty, and then he was sent into paradise. Adam, upon him be peace, wandered around in paradise, but he found nothing that stuck to him. He reached the tree that is called the tree of "affliction" (bala), but in fact is the tree of "affection" (wala). He saw it as a road-worthy steed. He did not hesitate a moment. When he reached it, he gave it a kick. That nasty kick*

was called "Adam disobeyed" (20:121). He had good sight, and he saw in it the mystery of a companion for the journey. And the tree also lifted the veil from its face and showed itself to him: "You can't travel this road without me."...

Munificence and generosity sent Adam into paradise, where he was put on the pillow of exaltation. The whole of paradise was put under his command. He looked it over, but he did not see a speck of grief or of love's reality. He said, "Oil and water don't mix."

And Jalal al-Din Rumi gives us the analogy of the fish being thrown on dry land from the waters of the ocean:

Like fish, we say to the Ocean of Life; "Why did You send up waves and throw us onto the dryness of water and clay? You possess such mercy, why did You give us such torment? Oh, Your mercilessness is sweeter than the mercy of all the merciful creatures of the world!

The Ocean replies: I was a hidden Treasure, so I wanted to be known. I was a treasure concealed behind the curtain of the Unseen, hidden in the retreat of No-place. I wanted My Beauty and Majesty to be known through the veils of existence. I wanted everyone to see what sort of Water of Life and Alchemy of Happiness I am. Oh fish! True enough, a fish knows the water's worth, loves the sea and clings to union with it. But his love is not of the same kind, so hot and burning with self-abandonment, with such lamentation and weeping of blood, and with such roasting of the liver, as the love of that fish who has been thrown upon dry land by the waves and for a long time struggles and tosses upon the hot earth and burning sand. Separation from the Ocean allows him no taste of life's sweetness, after all, that separation from the Ocean of Life. How should someone who has seen that Ocean find joy in this life?"

In the concept of God's creation, Adam, upon him be peace, was not meant to reside in paradise. Ibn Abbas, may God be pleased with him, said the following:

God has taken him out of the Garden before putting him into it.

And Ahmad Sam'ani tells us:

*Adam has two existences—the first and the second. The first exis-
tence belongs to this world, not to paradise; and the second belongs
to paradise.*

*Tomorrow, Adam will go into paradise with his children. A cry
will rise up from all the articles of paradise because of the crowding.
The angels of the World of Sovereignty will look with wonder and
say, "Is this that same man who moved out of paradise a few days
ago in poverty and indigence?"*

As we see, the beginning is, in reality, the glorious end.
Human existence starts with the worldly life and ends with the fulfillment of eternal happiness, which is the life of everlastingness,
the eternal bliss of paradise. God wants to show humankind that
we will enter paradise with a much greater excellence than the way
Adam, upon him be peace, has left it.

Through Adam, upon him be peace, residing in paradise before
entering the world, God wants to demonstrate in what great esteem
and honor the human being is held in His Eyes. His exalted station
in paradise shows man's chosenness, man's elevation, man as the
ultimate goal, and man as the jewel of God's creation.

The great scholar, Jalal al-Din Rumi, comments:

*When man receives light from God, he becomes the object of the
angel's prostration, since he was chosen...*

Furthermore, there was no function, no responsibility, no duty,
no goal for Adam, upon him be peace, in paradise, so he was made
to leave the spheres of angels and was honored with the glorious
duty of vicegerency, namely he was given the highest privilege, to
represent the Lord of all the worlds on earth.

Additionally, Adam, upon him be peace, paved the way to
truthful regret, shame, repentance and modesty towards his supreme
Creator. Jalal al-Din Rumi says:

*Whatever makes you tremble, know that you are worth just that!
This is why the lover's heart is greater than God's Throne.*

Fear, hope, forgetfulness, weeping, weakness, brokenness, shame, shortcomings, humbleness, insufficiency, surrender, these are all essential attributes of being human. The first condition for a human being is to feel ashamed. When we look at ourselves, we must look with embarrassment. This is the true nature of our father of mankind, the prophet Adam, upon him be peace. The crucial point of his descent into the world shows the beginning of the most noble human features of shame, humility and need; it shows the luminous brightness of abundant servanthood in the desert of existence; and it shows the beginning of true-felt, sincere repentance. Adam, upon him be peace, having committed a sin and being expelled from paradise, felt utter shame before God and repented at once.

The whole drama of human existence staged by God most High is primarily, to make Himself known to His creatures and secondarily, to draw them towards His endless ocean of mercy, kindness, gentleness, forgiveness and love. If we play our part on the worldly stage as humble servants in a pleasing manner to Him, we will earn His infinite bounties, favors, gifts.

Humankind is only and only brought into this world in order to become aware of God. If we actualize the goal of creation, which is to make the hidden treasure manifest, we will receive His inexhaustible blessings and mercy. There is no greater joy than the joy of knowing Him; and there is nothing sweeter than the taste of awareness of Him. Divine awareness will give birth to need. Human consciousness is inseparably linked with need. Knowing Him will increase the need for Him which will bring us to the everlasting realms of His nearness.

So what sort of Adam do we know, the first human being ever created? Here again we have an excellent description from Jalal al-Din Rumi about the true nature of Adam, upon him be peace, the prototype of human perfection, the man of purity and honor:

> *When Adam lapsed, God exiled him from paradise. God said to him, "Oh Adam! Since I have held you responsible and punished you for that error you committed, why did you not dispute with Me?*

After all, you had an argument. You could have said, 'All is from You, and You makest all. Whatever You desirest in the world comes to pass, and whatever You do not desire will never come to pass.' After all, you had such a clear, correct and patent argument. Why did you not give expression to it?

Adam replied, "I knew that, but I did not abandon courtesy in Your Presence; love for You did not allow me to reproach You."

What sort of Adam do we know? It is the Adam of love! He is the possessor of true shame and humility, which are the highest ethical qualities of a human being. We can see how precious the features of humility and modesty are when we compare his character with the devil, the accursed. Also in the words of Jalal al-Din Rumi:

Adam's lapse was a borrowed thing, so he repented at once. But Iblis' sin was innate, so he could not find the way to precious repentance. Hence Adam quickly asked forgiveness, but that accursed one was too proud to repent.

And that great poet, Jalal al-Din Rumi, gives humankind, the children of Adam, upon him be peace, the following advice:

Those who are the elect of Adam's children breathe the breath of "We have wronged ourselves."

Display your need before God – do not argue like the impudent and accursed Iblis.

With the attributes of shame and modesty, the human being earns God's gentleness, kindness, generosity and, especially, mercy and forgiveness. There is a lesson here, for without the human beings disobedience, failures, insufficiencies like sinning, mistakes, wrong-doings, going astray, how could God be the Forgiver, the Merciful? Through the human state of weakness and imperfection, God most High becomes the object of desire, the object of hope and salvation. Adam, upon him be peace, had to sin so God could show His mercy and forgiveness to him.

The Prophet Muhammad, upon him be peace and blessings, said:

Surely there is no sin too great for God to forgive.

And Ahmad Sam'ani comments:

O angels of the celestial dominion! Although you are obedient, you have no appetite in your selves, nor do you have any darkness in your makeup. If human beings disobey, they have appetite in their selves and darkness in their makeup. Your obedience, along with all your force, is not worth a dustmote before My majesty and tremendousness. And their disobedience, along with all their brokenness and dejection, does not diminish the perfection of My realm. You hold fast to your own sinlessness, but they hold fast to My mercy. Through your obedience, you make evident your own sinlessness and greatness, but through their disobedience, they make apparent My bounty and mercy.

The further people are away from God's gentleness, the more they become disharmonious, irritated, impatient, and ill-mannered. Adam, upon him be peace, the father of mankind, is perfectly opposed to the nature of the devil. Adam, upon him be peace, represents the attribute of love, while the devil represents the attribute of envy and arrogance. His power is his cleverness. He can twist the truth to the utmost extreme, and alter reality in such a way that its opposite appears to be the truth. Iblis, the accursed, is the master of deception and falseness. Corrupting peoples' minds and hearts, he transforms the believers of God most High into believers of his evil policies. But cleverness can only be applied in the worldly domain. It is opposed to divine intelligence, the supreme Intellect, or Universal Intellect. In the divine realms of everlastingness, cleverness turns into stupidity. This is the crucial point of the devil's eternal failure, which brought him from the supreme heights of angelic existence downwards to the lowest level of the accursed devil. With his wordly logic, driven by base desires, he was unable to perceive the divine nature of the human being. He only saw Adam's form, his exterior, his body, his material nature. As Jalal al-Din Rumi puts it, Iblis saw Adam, upon him be peace, "as an imprint in clay!"

His incompetence, his ignorance, and his refusal to see things as they really are, resembles exactly the modern man who is full of himself, arrogant, calculating, greedy, envious and, therefore, spiritually blind. The devil's refusal to see the treasury of the divine wisdom, the beauty of the divine light, the infusion of the divine breath of mercy of Adam, upon him be peace, can be compared with man's heedlessness in modern societies, not having the slightest idea about his own existence. Again, Jalal al-Din Rumi gives us an excellent description:

- *Though Iblis had knowledge, he had nothing of religion's love, so he saw naught in Adam but an imprint in clay.*
- *Sell your cleverness and buy bewilderment! Cleverness is opinion, and bewilderment is vision.*
- *He that is fortunate and a confidant of the mysteries knows that cleverness is from Iblis and love is from Adam.*

The devil was envious of the purity, wisdom, beauty and elevated station of Adam, upon him be peace. We can observe that envy is one of the most powerful negations of human goodness and love. Envy represents one of the lowest, most animalistic human qualities, and its effect is like fire, consuming and burning up all goodness of the human heart. As Jalal-al-Din Rumi describes it:

Oh God, envy is such a veil between two friends! Yesterday they were like a single spirit, and today they are headstrong wolves.

Envy is an innate attribute of the devil. He was envious of the beautiful attributes of Adam, upon him be peace, of his illuminated nature and the light of his soul, namely his righteousness, his generosity, his humility, his devotion, and his love. The root of envy comes from Iblis' feeling of being deprived of God's divine favour, as given to Adam, upon him be peace. This means when people are envious of each other's houses, cars, children, status, wealth, in fact, they are envious of each other's divine beauty, the goodness of human qualities.

Again, Jalal al-Din Rumi comments about the devil's envy:

He is destitute of the bread and provisions of the heaven; God has not thrown him a single bone....

The devil's deep-seated attribute of envy gave birth to selfishness and arrogance. It gave rise to the thought: "I am better than you; I am more worthy than you; I possess more than you; I am more beautiful than you."

Moreover, envy creates competition and hate between human beings. In other words, it negates human love, and it creates arrogance, ambition. It is one of the worst sicknesses of the heart. An arrogant person pretends to be better than everyone and everything in this world.

Furthermore, envy causes spiritual blindness. Misinterpretation of reality is extremely dangerous. Iblis was a jinn in paradise and his spiritual blindness degraded him into an ugly and accursed creature, the devil. Spiritual blindness is nothing else than the darkness of unconsciousness, which will give rise to insecurity. And insecurity is nothing else than not knowing the truth, not knowing how things really are. Within the make-up of the human being, we should never underestimate the psychological state of insecurity. Insecure people become restless, disharmonious, irritated and chaotic, leading to aggression, power-hunger, and envy, like the devil himself. Insecurity is directly opposed to belief, because true belief is equal to absolute certainty. It is the certainty of belief which gives peace of heart. Belief is the only security which the human being possesses; it is security in God. The divine knowledge of God makes you firm in yourself. To summarize, only true belief gives you certainty. Insecurity is from the devil and the ego.

Envy also generates disobedience, the complete refusal to accept God's Existence and His messages. The devil refused to prostrate to Adam, upon him be peace, although it was commanded by God most High. Through his disobedience, he was expelled from paradise and became Iblis, the accursed. He made claims, became arrogant, and refused to prostrate and repent. But Adam, upon him be peace, repented at once and became a loving slave. In Jalal al-Din Rumi's words:

Close your Iblis-like eye for a moment. After all, how long will you gaze upon form? How long? How long?

To summarize, without an earthly life, Adam, upon him be peace, could not understand the value and meaning of the divine names that God taught him. How could he taste God's beauty and perfection, without acknowledging his shortcomings, baseness, and inadequacy? How would he ever know the infinity of God's attributes without tasting his own limits, restrictions, determinations? How could he receive God's generosity, kindness, mercy and forgiveness without his disobedience?

Moreover, he could not have achieved the secret of love without having executed servanthood. He could not have tasted the secret of love without the attribute of distance. He could not have become aware of love without weeping, pleading and pain. He could not have known the reality of love without need. He could not have realized the reality of love without living the divine attributes of beauty and majesty. That is to say, if the human being does not taste loneliness and separation, it will not know union with Him. If the human being does not experience hunger, it cannot appreciate God's bounties. If the human being does not experience poverty, it cannot appreciate the value of God's richness.

There is wisdom here. The other creatures, like the animals and angels, do not taste both the exalted joy of nearness and the burning heartache of separation and distance. Therefore, they cannot know spiritual evolution. The sweet taste of awareness is not given to them. What makes the human being so unique is the reality of spiritual growth to infinity. In other words, man has endless levels of evolution in his makeup. He can degenerate downwards to the lowest of the low, spiritual decay; and he can ascend upwards to the highest of the high, spiritual evolution. What distinguishes the human being from other creatures is that he is distant to his own home, the roots of his being. Therefore, there is a task waiting for man—it is the task of sainthood! He has to return to his source, the home of his soul, the home of exalted bliss and contentment.

As we see, the fall from paradise of Adam, upon him be peace, reveals that there is a respectable trade between God and man happening. If we offer ourselves completely towards our Lord of Majesty and Bounty in sincere need, true regret, shame, and poverty, He will answer immediately with His endless grace. He will reward us with the beneficence of His beautiful attributes. When we wake up from our own darkness of unconsciousness and see that we can not see, His divine bounty will be instantly executed. That is to say, God rewards our loneliness with union, our weakness with strength, our poverty with richness, our helplessness with support, our nothingness with true faith, our brokenness with wholeness, and our imperfection with perfection. In other words, we should realize that loss is our gain! Only through loss and poverty we will be able to truly love. And, even more important, a true lover will finally be given the eternal bliss to meet with his beloved Lord.

Adam, upon him be peace, opened up the wisdom that poverty is our pride; that crying is our capital; that weakness is our jewel; that pain brings remedy; that mistakes are our good; that humility, shame and embarrassment are our wealth; that slavery is our honor; that incapacity, shortcomings, and forgetfulness are our salvation; and that nothingness is our elevation. In short, human imperfection leads to the perfection of love. As we see, the human being needs failures, disobedience and imperfection in order to grow towards spiritual maturity. In other words, man has to eat the fruit from the forbidden tree of paradise to be able to reach human perfection.

And Ahmad Sam'ani comments:

> There is a mystery hidden here, for the angels saw that they were pure, but Adam saw that he was indigent. The angels were saying, "We call you holy, that is, we keep our own selves pure for Your sake," while Adam said, "Our Lord, we have wronged ourselves." God

showed Adam that the slip of him who sees the slip is better in His eyes than the purity of him who sees the purity. That is why He gave Adam the honor of being the object before which prostration was made, while He gave the angels the attribute of being the prostrators.

What is more, Adam, upon him be peace, opened up the exalted gates for the 124,000 prophets to come, to honor the world below with God's all-embracing wisdom. In addition, Adam, upon him be peace, opened the way for the best of all good fortune, namely that the light of the universe, the Prophet Muhammad, upon him be peace and blessings, would honor the world with his holy appearance.

Adam, upon him be peace, demonstrates that if love has captured our hearts, we will be able to achieve the ultimate fulfillment of spiritual life. This is the concept of God's creation.

Thus, I would like to conclude by saying that Adam, upon him be peace, the first man created in God's image, shows us how to live up to our own potential as human beings.

ETERNAL FRESHNESS

There is eternal freshness at the source! The path of love is the path of return. If we go back to the roots of our being, if we find the source of all existence, we will experience the full nature of being human, the true meaning of who we are. True lovers are immersed in eternal freshness every moment. This is why when you sit in their presence, it means drinking from the fountain of life. Especially in our present world of deep degeneration, people feel their lives have become meaningless, worthless, tasteless, and aimless, which makes them feel low, empty, weak, bored, heavy, and so on. Looking for some way out of their frustration, they find shallow satisfactions, which give them a 'kick' for some moments, a kind of new experience. But it will have no effect on their state; it will not help them to remove their dissatisfactions.

There is a source of eternal life. There is a treasury of divine beauty. There is a home of our origin, the place where we come from, the essential reality of our being. It is a sacred area. This place is a place of total harmony and contentment. At the root of our being, purity and illumination will reveal itself; whatever was hidden will manifest; and whatever was closed will open. At the source, there is the beauty of the divine light shining in endless brightness through all created realities. At the source, there is the inexhaustible treasury of love. There is no time or place, no subject or object, no setting or rising, no beginning or end, no day or night, and no letters or sounds.

Jalal al-Din Rumi comments:

When the water of knowledge bubbles up from the breast, it will never become stagnant, old, or discolored.

True change for the human being is possible if we return to the root of our being! Man in his daily life needs the experience of revival, which is true nourishment of his soul. He has to remind himself of his true self, the state of innocence and purity, which means he will gain new life; that is to say, he will be born twice. In other words, we have to restore the saintly nature within ourselves, to restore our original unity, and to regain our lost purity. It is becoming who we truly are. This possibility is inherent in everyone; this is true spiritual evolution.

Man's true existence is paradoxically non-existence. We find our originality in self-extinction, nothingness. We will have to undergo a voluntary death. We have to die before we die! We negate ourselves and we reaffirm our existence in Him. God makes us die away from ourselves and live in Him. When we are reborn to a new consciousness, the way of life in this world will become the way of life of the hereafter.

The people who taste death before dying become the real representatives of God; they mirror Him in the world below, because they truly live in Him. This is the price we have to pay. Then we will live our lives in the way God meant us to. We will become the pillar of heaven, and the pupil of God's eye.

Once we will arrive at the roots of our being, inexhaustible treasures will reveal themselves. When we drink from the fountainhead, God's gifts, bounties, and favors will gush forth infinitely. Within every breath, we will be able to give witness to God's Oneness. We will be able to discover the sacredness of all life and celebrate every moment, the blessedness of all things. The end of spiritual evolution is purity, purity of the divine mirror where the everlasting secrets of the One and Only will be reflected.

The speech of the saints comes directly from the source! When they speak, we hear them as theirs were the fresh words from the lips of our beloved master, the Prophet Muhammad, upon him be peace and blessings. The friends of God are such true inheritors of our beloved messenger that they are completely immersed in his merciful presence and they take you way back in time to make you sit with the most noble of all men.

On a public, worldwide level, I feel that it has never been more urgent to speak of the origin! We have no time to lose. Our present world of instability, disasters, terror, and catastrophes is in desperate need of freshness, naivety, clarity, tranquility, easiness, unconventionality, and innocence. We have to make transparent the purity and the oneness of all creation. The Holy Qur'an was sent at a time of human distortion and darkness in order to give peace, clarity, truth and righteousness. The revelations stress the source of all creation, and they are a restoration, a revival, of the very beginning of existence. Modern society has lost touch with its origins, the true purpose of life. It is necessary to go back to the home of all and everything, where there is not the slightest diminishing or deviation from the glorious unity of the all-compassing Truth of God Most High.

At the present moment of history, it is never more urgent to realize the universality of the truth, and to answer with a substantial positive energy. We have to offer a vision of the true purpose of life, the meaning and value of a human being. Know that the water is one. We have to look from the station of absolute eternity, where the original oneness is unaffected. We have to oppose the crisis in the modern world and take directly from the source. Today, the necessity to link the confused and disoriented modern mind with the deeply rooted, solid ground of true eternal human values is most urgent. It happened to me; I lived a meaningless and empty life until I discovered the source of beauty and goodness.

THE SECRET OF LOVE

I wish to say that it is our essential duty to discover the secret of love, because we exist due to the love which God has for us. The source of all existence is love. The purpose of life is consciousness of our innermost selves, which means achieving lover-hood. The seed of eternal love is born in the deepest interior of man. It represents our divine origin; it is the wealth of human goodness. It is God in the heart of the believer who is loving:

> The secret of love is not to fear hell and not to wish for paradise;
> The secret of love is to become part of the Breath of the Merciful;
> The secret of love is homecoming;
> The secret of love is to feel impotent towards the overwhelming power and perfection of our Creator;
> The secret of love is the treasury of pure modesty;
> The secret of love is knock on the door of a hunger;
> The secret of love is being born twice;
> The secret of love is to see and feel the beauty of the Prophet Muhammad, upon him be peace and blessings;
> The secret of love is die before dying;
> The secret of love is gaining the fruit of awareness;
> The secret of love is to experience the perfume of existence;
> The secret of love is selflessness;
> The secret of love is learning through God's Beauty;
> The secret of love is to have no fear and no worry;
> The secret of love is looking for thirst instead of looking for water;
> The secret of love is to discover our nothingness and God's Greatness;
> The secret of love is to see and hear with eyes of our hearts;

The secret of love is to wish to escape in eager desire from the limitations of our earthly existence to the realm of limitless divine beauty;

The secret of love is to see oneself as nothing;

The secret of love is when hunger becomes our food;

The secret of love is to buy from God the nearness of God;

The secret of love is to transform the way of life of this world into the way of life of the hereafter;

The secret of love is the recognition of our imperfection;

The secret of love is to know that we exist due to the love that God has for us;

The secret of love is to be in continuous admiration;

The secret of love is to experience that the underlying cause of existence is love;

The secret of love is seeing with the light of God;

The secret of love is to know that love's remedy is pain;

The secret of love is to satisfy the needs of others and be indifferent to one's own needs;

The secret of love is to be both, lover and Beloved;

The secret of love is weeping before God's door of intimacy;

The secret of love is to clean oneself of all ulterior motives;

The secret of love is to know that the best of lovers is God.

Through going hungry to the world, we reach real love. Through deprivation, we can know the worth of the endless bounties of paradise. Through starving, we get aware of limitless divine beauty. Through fasting from the world, we reach the hidden treasure within ourselves. Wherever there is hunger, reality can appear. Hunger peels off falsehood; hunger removes veils; hunger burns away indigestion, boredom, and anxieties; hunger enforces sharing; hunger shows the world's images in a naked way. If we are wealthy, we become indifferent, irresponsible. If our head and stomach are full, need cannot grow. Selfhood enforces conformity, while hunger enforces opposition.

In order to reach the secret of love, we have to see things as they really are. We have to develop a true vision of the universe, the world and man. The divine perception will reveal our human inadequacy, imperfections, and impurities. If we do not clean our-selves of our base desires and egotistical motives, there will be no clarity in the divine mirror, where divine secrets can be reflected on the mirror's pure surface.

I believe that one of the true inheritors of the noble character of our Prophet Muhammad, peace and blessings be upon him, is Seyyid Ahmed El-Kebir Er-Rufai. His humility reached exalted heights, and the tails of his life reveal the sweet scent of pure love and the treasury of pure modesty. In one of his speeches he said:

> *In order to be received in God's Presence, I wondered before all the doors of paradise. The ones of fasting, praying, pilgrimage, and charity, were filled with people. Heavy crowds were gathered in front of them and I couldn't find any entrance. I saw only one door empty, and I immediately entered and became honored to be in God's divine Presence. This door is the door of degradation, helpless-ness, humiliation, poverty and modesty.*

Rabia Al-Adawiyya expresses in her famous prayer:

> *O God, if I worship You for fear of hell, and if I worship You in hope of paradise, forbid it to me. But if I worship You for You, do not hold back from me the Everlasting Beauty.*

Our great lover, Seyyid Ahmed Rufai, and our supreme woman saint, Rabia Al-Adawiyya, are representing the secret of love in the purest exaltation.

I would like to conclude with a statement from Jalal al-Din Rumi on this subject:

> *If the head is not full of love, that head is behind the tail.*

BETWEEN LIGHT AND CLAY

Man is made of the most exquisite poetry. At the time of man's creation, God showed loving tender care. Our Creator knitted the human being with His Own two Hands. Furthermore, God blew into man the soul from His Merciful Breath; that is to say, man's soul belongs entirely to God. Man's divine nature is God's pure love towards him. With his illuminated nature, man becomes the jewel of creation.

But man is born with a duality in his breast! This place represents the borderline of light and clay, spirit and matter, soul and body. In other words, the birth of the human being into this world means nothing else than the soul getting link to the matter of the body. Man's refined nature meets the limits of the earth. His limitless purity hits the borders of determined selfhood. That is what makes the human being such a fascinating, elevated, sensitive and interesting creature, the meeting place of light and clay. This place can give birth to awareness, resurrection, new life, and rebirth, which will generate true union with the Almighty Creator. That is to say, man becomes extremely precious in his earthly existence, because he is able to give birth to the glorifying unity, the splendor of his purified soul. In other words, his duality represents his salvation.

So the task of man is, therefore, to overcome the limits of his body and strive for the divine everlasting values of his soul. We show a tendency, and God most High creates the action. We remember Him, and He gives us life. We learn His attributes, and He gives us being. This possibility is inherent in man.

God manifests Himself towards His creatures with two opposite attributes of Might and Forgiveness, Power and Grace, Glory and Compassion, Wrath and Kindness. In other words, His Perfection is always paired with His Beauty; His Severity is paired with His Gentleness. Therefore, a believer finds himself between the two attributes of His all-Encompassing Power and His loving Beneficence. Besides, God created everything in pairs, of opposites, from the mineral, vegetable, animals, cosmos, up the man, such as man–woman, expansion–contraction, day–night, east–west, beginning–end, lost–found, clean–dirty, poverty–wealth, good–evil, active–passive, etc.

Through these opposite attributes that are inherent in human nature, man finds himself in an existential dilemma, like two persons who are constantly at war. These two opposite forces, positive and negative, are symbolized by the angels and the devil. Therefore, man will shift between good and bad, humanity and animality, happiness and suffering, laughter and tears, intellect and sensuality, and so on. God created suffering and disease so that we might know happiness and health. God created confusion and imperfection so that we might know clarity and perfection. God created rebellion and multiplicity so that we might know righteousness and union. God created the lion and aggression so that we might know sheep and humility. God created hate and bitterness, so that we might know love and sweetness.

But man's struggle does not exclusively take place on a moral level; his principle work has to take place on the ontological level—he has to be concerned with the discrimination between his true self and his false self. Man is shifting between the pure being, which is light, and the relative existence, which is clay, matter. His task is to combine the external realities with the internal realities, respectively, form with meaning. Man's appearance is form, but there is a mysterious presence of meaning within him. He possesses an outward reality pointing towards temporality and an inward reality pointing towards eternity.

The lesson is this: the human being needs evil and severity in order to reach to complete his spiritual nature. He needs the struggle with the negative forces so that within this struggle he can accomplish spiritual maturity. He has to advance backwards to the roots of his self. On the way, he will encounter the darkness of his own ego-substance. If he shows firm faith, he will conquer his base desires and arrive at the paradise of innocence and purity; there, he will display the hidden treasure in its totality.

Jalal al-Din Rumi comments:

> *Without doubt, man is compounded of a body that is base, base; a spirit that is noble, noble, noble. God the Exalted brought these two together through His perfect Power. A hundred thousand wisdoms are manifested from that noble spirit, and a hundred thousand darknesses from this gross body. He connected the body to dark clay and the spirit to the breath of His own Spirit, so that the light and divine Breath would make this dark clay its instrument for righteousness, justice and guarding God's Trust; so that it might be a means of salvation, elevation and high degrees. The purpose was not that the dark clay, through its greed for the light of, 'I breathed My spirit into him,' should make the lamp its instrument for treachery and theft. On the contrary, the lamp and candle of the Breath-Spirit should illuminate the clay of the body with the light of the religion and hold back from its greed for clay, ignorance and heaviness. So he whose intellect dominates his sensuality is higher than the angels, and he whose sensuality dominates his intellect is lower than the beasts.*
>
> *The angel was delivered through knowledge and the beast through ignorance. The sons of men remain struggling in between. Some men have followed the intellect to such an extent that they have become totally angels and sheer light. They are the prophets and saints. In some men sensuality has dominated their intellects, so that they have totally assumed the properties of animals.*

For a believer who has mastered his duality, there are no opposites any more, as the great saint, Jalal al-Din Rumi, said:

Every light has a fire,
Every rose a thorn,
A serpent watches over every treasure hidden in the ruins.
Oh, Thy Rose garden has no thorns!
Thy pure Light has no fire!
Around Thy Treasure is no serpent, no blow, no teeth!

Again, the saint Ahmad Sam'ani gives us an excellent description of man's duality:

> *If a palace does not have a garbage pit next to it, it is incomplete. There must be a garbage pit next to a lofty palace so that all the refuse and filth that gather in the palace can be thrown there. In the same way, whenever God formed a heart by means of the light of purity, He placed this vile self next to it as a dustbin. The black spot of ignorance flies on the same wings as the jewel of purity. There needs to be a bit of corruption so that purity can be built upon it. A straight arrow needs a crooked bow. O heart, you be like a straight arrow! O self, you take the shape of a crooked bow!*

> *When they put the dress of purity on the heart, they show the heart that black spot of wrongdoing and ignorance so that it will remember itself and know who it is. When a peacock spreads out all its feathers, it gains a different joy from each feather. But as soon as it looks down at its own feet, it becomes embarrassed. That black spot of ignorance is the peacock's foot that always stays with you.*

It has to be mentioned that, although man is created with a duality, he is also given the possibility to overcome it. Man's nature carries immaturity, but he is also equipped with the possibility of evolution towards spiritual maturity. He is put in the physical realm of the lowest of the low, but he is given the ultimate level of spiritual fulfillment, light upon light. He carries an animalistic nature, but he carries, at the same time, a vertical nature which gives him the possibility of the ascension of his soul. He lives a separate existence from his Creator, but he is given the possibility of the gift of reunion with Him. He is covered by 70,000 veils from his beloved Lord, but he is given the possibility of eventually removing them. He is put in a world of deception, illusions, shadows, dreams—but he is given truth, awareness, power of discrimination. He is brought into the realms of temporality, profanity, and restrictions—but he is given transcendence, eternity and light. He is the fallen man expelled from paradise, but he is given spiritual elevation to the infinity of God's attributes.

Looking from another perspective, due to man's inborn state of immaturity, as caused by his fall from paradise, man is veiled from his Creator, meaning that he is separated from the truth. He is the fallen man, expelled from paradise, living in exile. He left the state of oneness with his Creator and descended into the state of multiplicity within creatures. The holy Qur'an says:

> *Then we make him descend to the lowest of the low. (95:5)*

Man is brought onto this planet like a tree with no fruit, like a plant with no flower, like an infant with no speech. Therefore, man has the duty to develop the full potential of his human nature. He has to regain his lost purity. He has to earn the portions of the hereafter in the same way that he earns his livelihood. He has to rip off his being from falseness and indifference. He has to remove the veils of darkness and ignorance in order to perceive the light of his soul. He has to leave his temporal, limited self and recognize and encounter the eternal Presence of divine beauty, his glorious Lord of Everlastingness. In other words, the goal is to make manifest the secret of the human substance.

Furthermore, there is another lesson. God most High does not reveal Himself to humankind without a believer's intense wish and efforts to see Him. This is divine policy: God makes Himself secret so we might strive towards Him, and go in search for Him. That is to say, He wants His creatures to be aware of Him.

The Almighty is hiding the soul of man in the depths of man's innermost being. The face of beauty is veiled from the eyes of man. The pearls are hidden in the deep sea. The secrets are kept under the earth. He says:

I am a hidden treasure. I wanted to be known, so I created creation.

God reveals Himself through what He hides from us. His nearness is His distance. He is hidden through being closer to us than we are to ourselves. He manifests Himself through making Himself a mysterious Presence. God hides Himself in the darkness of our bodies—that is to say, the road to God is hidden. But it can be found in the heart. This is divine policy: the greater the treasure, the thicker the wall—the greater is the lock for safe-keeping.

Consequently, there is nothing more hidden within the whole of created realities than our supreme Divinity, the Lord of Majesty and Bounty. This is the wisdom for mankind: He is hidden and we have to make Him apparent!

As we see, man is not only born with a duality as well as an immaturity; he is also separated from his Creator through his fall from paradise. He is brought from the highest station in proximity with God, to the lowest of the low, the earthly existence. Additionally, there are 70,000 veils of darkness and light between God and man. This means that man is born in a state of spiritual blindness. In his earthly life, he finds himself in the darkness of unconsciousness and is not aware of God, living in a sort of forgetfulness and heedlessness.

All of these above-mentioned conditions that man finds himself in his earthly life demonstrate that there is a great gap between man and God. Therefore, God created man with the wish for Him, the desire for union with Him. Man becomes a creature of total need! We are born with this treasury of need and love within our breast. In other words, we are born with the aspiration to meet our Creator. Man is knitted with the earth of need by God most High. It is precisely the fall from paradise where need was born. Only true need brings you to God. The heart can only be satisfied with God.

God created the human being homeless, impure, disoriented, and unstable, so he would go on search for his original home, the lost purity, the root of his being.

God created the human being forgetful, unconscious, ignorant, so he would try to remember, to wake up, and to see.

God created the human being with thirst and hunger, so he would go on search to quench his thirst with the water of life.

God created the human being with baseness, weakness, sin, and mistakes, so he would ask for forgiveness and help.

God created the human being with illness and injuries, so he would seek salvation, health, and remedy.

God created the human being blind and deaf, so he would strive to see and hear with the eyes of his heart.

God created the human being poor and limited, so he would reach out for His richness and infinity.

God created the human being insufficient and incomplete, so he would strive to grow towards perfection, satisfaction, and fulfillment.

God created the human being with the fire of love, with the pain of separation, so he would long and yearn endlessly for union with Him and seek the everlasting values of paradise, the beauty of His Face.

God created the human being insecure, helpless, confused, so he would long for peace, certainty and resolution.

Moreover, God wants to see our obedience as original; our intention as firm; our works as unique; our love as everlasting and unconditional; our generosity as heroic; our striving as continuous; our search as sincere; our efforts as enduring; our longing as elevated; our pleading as tearful; our thankfulness as infinite; and our service as noble. That is to say, God wishes to see love within all our daily acts. He wishes to see true sincerity in our intentions and actions. He wishes to see true servanthood.

Our earthly life represents the greatest honor, the most exalted station among creation, because we are able to gain the fruit of awareness; we are able to gain the station of loverhood; and we are given the station of vicegerent, to represent our Lord on earth.

The true human state is a state of utter need and search for the One and Only. This is how God intends us to be. Mevlana Rumi says:

What is love? Perfect thirst.

Prophet Muhammad, upon him be peace and blessings, said:

Knock on the door of hunger, meaning real need.

True need is the root of everything. Need is more important than love. All need comes first. It is the basic quality of a human being. We have to search with the eye of need. Then love can grow, and wisdom can grow. Therefore, the true seeker is looking for thirst not for water. The holy Qur'an says:

Then every soul shall be repaid in full what it has earned (while in the world), and they will not be wronged. (3:161)

Sahl ibn Abdullah Tustari said:

I gazed at the path and I set the eye of insight on the realities. I saw no path that takes nearer than need, and no veil thicker than making claims.

And Ahmad Sam'ani comments:

Look at the path of Iblis, and you will see nothing but making claims. Then look at the path of Adam, and you will see nothing but need. O Iblis, what do you say? 'I am better than he.' (7:12) O Adam, what do you say? 'Our Lord, we have wronged ourselves.' (7:23)

To finalize, everything is determined by the sincerity of the search for Him!

Moreover, a needy creature, a sincere believer, is the one who wishes to fill the needs of other people. He is utterly sensitive towards the hunger and thirst of his fellow beings. He has the utmost concern to be available for any kind of urgent call, so he forgets even his own needs. Whenever crying need appears, he cannot help but answer instantly, because he feels an irresistible attraction to help. It is his way of life. It is called servanthood. The true need is the need for the search for God!

I wish to conclude that the greatest mystery in this world is the human being. It needs the fire of love to make plain the secret of human existence. It needs intense longing and deep affection to reveal the mysteries of human nature; that is to say, it needs love to explain the secret of life. Within the heat of our search, we can find the truth, which is the hidden treasure in its totality.

THE SCIENCE OF UNITY

O f all the sciences there is a science called the science of unity. They gave it a name, *tasawwuf*, or sufism. At present, a division has been made between the science of religion and the science of unity. This is a paradox. Especially, the modern world has made this distinction, because humanity experiences a total lack of understanding of the true purpose of human life. We have lost our roots. Additionally, we experience a great lack of divine thirst, need and love. We have forgotten that every single soul is created in the concept of the perfect man. We carry potentially the seed of sainthood in ourselves. The human being is, in its nature, a mystical being.

We are drenched in misconceptions about religion. The original oneness of the religion has become distorted. Spiritual growth is a contradictory concept in modern society. In Prophet Muhammad's time, spiritual reality was fully present in everyone, and the name, *tasawwuf*, did not exist. Sainthood was a way of life. Today, this reality has vanished to a tragic degree and there is no other reason why I write. In other words, the lack of the awareness of the divine reality within man is the root of all problems. The true religion is a religion of unity, a religion of light, a religion of mercy, a religion of the heart, and a religion of oneness.

The word "Islam" translates into submission, peace, and balance. The meaning derived from its name shows the perfect proof of unity. If we submit to the Will of God, we will achieve inner peace and harmony, and we will be drawn to loving union with our Creator. Islam reveals God's wisdom in its totality, which is the science of unity.

Nowhere else than in Islam, the perfected religion of the heart, in its doctrine and method, is the mind so eternally linked with the heart; the heavens with the earth; the body with the soul; the vertical with the horizontal; the inner with the outer; the world with the hereafter. It is precisely the science of unity which teaches the fusion of the material with the spiritual reality. The religion of Islam teaches divine perfection in revealing the prescription for sainthood and giving to mankind the ultimate spiritual fulfillment for life on earth. So the path of truth is a path of awareness leading into loving union, the annihilation of the lover into the Beloved.

The gradual stages of spiritual evolution are very well-defined in the science of unity, *tasawwuf,* as the following three degrees of consciousness:

– The "Lore of Certainty," *ilm al-yaqin*
– The "Eye of Certainty," *ayn al-yaqin*
– The "Truth of Certainty," *haqq al-yaqin*

First we know, then we see, and then we become. At the last stage, knowledge and love unite. This is the beauty and strength of the religion of the heart: the lover can be raised to the same level as the Beloved and share a secret identity. So the "Lore" means knowing with the certainty of belief; the "Eye" means having vision with the certainty of the heart; and the "Truth" means total self-extinction into the Supreme Divinity. One loses one's existence in the Existence of God.

God most High says with the coming of His beloved Prophet Muhammad into this world:

> *Today I have perfected your religion, I have perfected My favors, I have perfected My light, I told you knowledge from My Presence, I have perfected My blessings, I have sent my beloved Prophet to perfect good behavior.*

Therefore, the truth of the religion reveals itself in full splendor in Islam, because it is the completion of all revelations ever given by God to humankind. It dissolves the polarities of object and subject; gives prescriptions for sainthood; looks at the ideal of man as he was created; gives the agency to man to carry out God's will on earth; reveals the hidden treasure; gives witness to God's Oneness; gives the key to the inner meanings; brings sacredness to our lives; and gives answers to all questions.

Prophet Muhammad, upon him be peace and blessings, was the "living Qur'an." For this reason, the truth of Muhammad manifested itself in his noble character features. His whole life gave witness to the glorious unity of being; that is to say, the reality of Muhammad found expression in the deepest regions of his earthly existence, which is servanthood. In other words, the truth of Muhammad reveals his noble character features and vice-versa. The noble character of Muhammad, upon him be peace and blessings, is God's most excellent and dignified creation; it represents the inner treasury of the religion of Islam. His noble character is a direct expression of the divine eternal Truth; that is to say, God's Words are his existence.

This means that for the believers, the most excellent way of life, the highest station they can achieve in their life on earth, is the Prophet's most noble character (*ahlaki Muhammedi*).

I see religion as pure joy, as a celebration of life, because we are celebrating the reunion of the created with the Creator:

> Doesn't religion look at the ideal of man as he was created?
> Doesn't religion teach the art of life?
> Doesn't religion give prescription for sainthood?
> Doesn't religion give answers to all questions?
> Doesn't religion resolve all problems?
> Doesn't religion reveal the sacredness of all existence?
> Doesn't religion reveal the inner wealth of the human being?
> Doesn't religion give the honor for the agency to carry out God's will on earth?
> Doesn't religion teach the art of living for others?
> Doesn't religion give the power of awareness?
> Doesn't religion reveal intimacy with our great Lord?

The Sufi saint, Sidi Hamza al-Qadiri al-Butchichi comments:

> *We all came out of the same light. There is no distinction, there is only union. We make the distinction between one another, but in reality we are united in One. We cannot attain this view unless we pass through every step of the path.*

The problem is in the description. Especially, man in the present societies does not know what context to place religion in, what significance to give to religion, or how to deal with religion in his own life. Whereas, in reality, religion is equal to human life. Nothing exists outside of God; therefore, nothing exists outside of the truth of the religion. The life on earth of man is a divine act of our Supreme Divinity. Man is the expression of His Will. Therefore, human beings have to acknowledge the fact that religion has to be the guiding principle in everyone's life. In that sense, the highest form of life is belief.

Since the beginning of entering the religion of Islam, I have studied the greatest of all mysteries, the science of unity, *Tasawwuf* or Sufism. All existence is based on it. What is unity? How can we perceive it? How can we experience it? Where can we find it? How can we study it? How can we accomplish it?

Wishing for God means wishing for unity. Realizing God in oneself means realizing unity. It represents the ultimate fulfillment of a human being in his earthly life. Within all existence, only man can declare unity; and within all existence, only man can realize God. But there is a divine condition; it needs love to focus on God as it needs love to focus on unity. Love is such a power; it can overcome, transcend, dissolve, and surpass the limitations, the temporal, the restrictions, and transitory creation to realize unity, the eternal realms of our supreme Creator. Love reaches far beyond the dimensions of time, space, object, and subject. The lover must focus on God to the exclusion of everything else and tear off the attachments to the world—that is to say, completely move beyond the limits in which he exists. This way, the light of unity can prevail. There is no greater bliss for each single soul than diving into the infinite ocean of oneness.

In this present world, in the midst of all the confusion, disturbance, chaos, and distress, I became a "unity declarer." I became a searcher for the underlying oneness of all things. Especially, in our present societies of confusing multiplicity, we need to hold onto the cord of our beloved Lord. The heat of our aspirations will lead us to climb up to the realm of His nearness.

God is infinite; God's realms are realms of infinity, the infinity of His holy attributes. There is no end to love, to beauty, to knowledge, to perfection, or to His mercy and compassion. Through embracing His attributes, we will reach the desired union with our All-Compassionate Creator.

All religions teach us the science of unity. This is precisely what religion is there for. A religious person sees himself as a part of creation. The true vision sees that all three levels co-exist—the cosmos, the world and man. Only an ignorant person sees himself as an isolated individual.

The human being, in his arrogance, ignorance, and egotism, split the original unity of all religions. There is just one religion, the religion of truth, which is the religion of Islam. Every human being on this planet belongs to it, either acknowledging or denying. God most High confirms with the verse of the Qur'an (3:85):

> *If anyone desires anything other than Islam as a religion, it will never be accepted of him.(3:85)*

The human being is a spiritual reality. We are of divine origin. Our Lord created us only to bow to the Truth, day and night. We are brought on this planet with the highest divine purpose, namely to reach saintly perfection. Every man is created as a representative of God most High. At the time of our birth, we descend from unity into the world of separation—meaning that from the realm of the souls where we were in proximity with God, we descended into the realm of the world where we are separated from God.

Therefore, our work is unity, looking for the lost togetherness with our beloved Lord. Man becomes the supreme goal of God's creation. The Almighty says:

I created everything for yourself, I created you for Myself.

We exist due to the love God has for us. Therefore, the Creator's desire for His creatures and man's desire for his Creator is inherent in man's nature. The eternal need of the servants for their Lord lies buried in the deepest interior of man. It is the underlying cause of our existence. All molecules of our body are sensitive towards our Creator. All cells are drawn towards Him, wish for Him, and strive for union with Him. This most elevated of all longings for divine union is of such profound power that it dominates our whole being.

It finds its expression in the place of the "Covenant of Alast," (Am I not your Lord?) where all the souls as a disembodied spirit were living in the highest heaven of bliss in proximity with God before entering into the world, and entering into the gross matter of the body. This realm of the souls symbolizes the place of oneness and purity.

After having been born into the world, there are the ones who realize the original state of unity they have lost in the world below; that is to say, they remember where they came from, and they realize their true self. They are the ones who feel an irresistible divine attraction towards the beauty of this place and the Grandeur and Majesty of their beloved Lord. They do not get tied to the world and do not get tied to their bodies. They are the ones who realize the worth of the union they had in the realm of the souls with their Lord. They are able to remember the happiness and sweet taste of their heavenly existence. For this reason, their earthly existence has become a place of lamentation and weeping, a place of exile, a place of painful separation. They see nothing else; they want nothing else than to return to the place where they came from, the paradise of unity with their beloved Lord. Thus, the

"Covenant of Alast" is the place of all places, the desire of all desires, the heaven of all heavens, the treasure of all treasures, the contentment of all contentments, the conscience of all consciences. It is the place of the glorious union with the One and Only.

The science of unity, *Tasawwuf*, means to be in harmony with what we are. In order to live in a peaceful and harmonious way, we need to hold on to the sacred law of the religion, the *Shariah*. The *Shariah* is the foundation of unity. The divine law consists of five pillars, given by our Creator as a religious duty to every believer. *Shariah* symbolizes submission to the will of God. It is the key to inner peace and harmony, because these sacred rites are directly nurturing our souls. We can say that the *Shariah* is our daily bread, whereas *Tasawuf* is to digest it. In other words, conforming to the divine law leads into the fullness of being. If the *Shariah* is not understood correctly and executed properly, all further levels up to the degree of pure unification will be veiled from our eyes. The sacred law has to be understood as the foundation for the spiritual realization for the human being.

Within the sacred laws lies the whole inner wealth of the religion. The All-Glorious One gave us a miraculous prescription to reach the ultimate goal, which is spiritual illumination; sainthood. These are precisely the five pillars of the religion: the testimony of faith; the ritual prayer; alms giving; pilgrimage; and fasting. God gives us the form, because our spiritual evolution is a becoming. So every believer is given the possibility to fill the form with meaning and light according to his capacity. Within the performance of the religious duties, he can either accomplish the ultimate ascent of his soul, the heights of spiritual evolution—that is to say, complete annihilation in his beloved Lord—or he might receive nothing at all.

When he performs the ritual prayer, he can either be blessed with intimate divine discourse, or simply perform a mechanical routine. Within the pilgrimage, he either self-sacrifices his whole being in loving surrender, or he wishes to gain some personal profit. Within fasting, he either has resigned himself to the world with all his senses, mind, feelings, body, will—so that he truly fasts—or he merely experiences only hunger. Within charity, he is either heroically generous and masters the art of giving, or his donation represents an empty gesture. The secret lies in executing the sacred law with the obedience of a loving slave— namely, with pure joy. And then, as God wills, the believer will be given the chance to feel and hear his beloved Lord whilst performing his religious duties.

Nowhere else than in the testimony of faith, the first pillar, can we observe how much all the religious duties represent a means for spiritual growth—how much divine prescriptions generate a spiritual becoming. In order to enter and belong to the religion of Islam, man has to pronounce the testimony of faith, the *Shahadah*, the affirmation of oneness, *tawhid*: *"I testify there is no god but God, and I testify that Muhammad is His Servant and His Messenger."* One bears witness to the oneness and unity of God most High, and then one enters true "believer-hood."

Again within the first pillar, God gives us uncountable levels of personal evolution. "Believer-hood" always involves, at the same time, the first step—the affirmation of oneness—and the last step—the oneness of being. This means that we either pronounce the *Shahadah* exclusively with our tongues, with no consequences whatsoever and, therefore, remain unfortunately at the first step; whereas for a true believer, the testimony of faith means spiritual evolution at every moment, and what he pronounces with his tongue will be a reality within his whole being.

In other words, we may live our lives disinterested, empty, and detached from the divine richness within the form, or we may achieve the heights of true belief, reaching out to the infinity of His attributes. Within the *Shahadah,* God gives us the entry to His nearness, and He gives us the triumph of unity. The essence of belief is to believe in one God. That is to say, the highest form of belief is believing in the oneness and unity of our supreme Divinity.

The *Shahada* is complete awareness that nothing else exist but Him. Nothing else is real but the Real. We negate everything other than God and affirm the absolute Presence of the Mighty One. In other words, we turn away from the world, the created realities, and give ourselves totally towards the Creator. Therefore, the testimony of faith means, in a pure sense, self-annihilation into God. We renounce everything other than God and come to subsist in Him. All love for things, all idols, have to be removed from our hearts so that God Himself can triumph as the All-Glorious divine Presence.

We can conclude by saying that the *Shahadah,* in the ultimate sense, gives witness that nothing other than God exists. This is what it means for all believers living in sincere faith. In order to survive in the jungle of the world's confusion, we have to apply true faith; we need the power of the affirmation of oneness.

Because God gave us the rites of the *Shariah* and filled them with heightened divine symbolic meanings, all religious duties are acts of pure love. Their merits are immeasurable. Let's look at the posture of the prostration within the ritual prayer. It carries precisely the quality of complete submission and intimacy of a servant to its Lord. During the prostration, the worshipper can breathe the sweet scent of nearness.

Especially, the pilgrimage represents, in its deepest sense, the return to the undistorted oneness of all living souls. All pilgrim have one goal, one breath, one dress—leaving their personalities behind, surrendering themselves in the Presence of the All-Merciful Lord on the Plain of Arafat. All hearts of the pilgrims unify with each other.

And Abd al-Qadir al-Jilani writes about the inner worship:

> *The time for inner worship is timeless and endless, for the whole life and in the hereafter. The mosque for this prayer is the heart. The congregation is the inner faculties, which remember and recite the Names of the unity of God in the language of the inner world. The leader of this prayer is the irresistible wish. The direction of the prayer is toward the oneness of God, which is everywhere, His eternal nature and His beauty.*

Only wholehearted surrender towards our Creator can lead to loving union. It is sincere submission that opens up all the channels from the servant to God most High. Then we will get consumed by the love He has for us, and get consumed by the love we have for Him. We have to know that all the prophets and saints did nothing else other than nurturing the rites of the sacred law with their pure soul. During their acts of worship, they constantly felt divine pleasure, the highest affection, pure joy, awe, wonderment, perplexity, and admiration—all of which transported them to the realms of everlasting beauty and perfection. Divine pleasure is the supreme state of the beloveds of God. They take joy in the submission to God's Will, and they take joy in serving that Great Will.

Let's ask ourselves: during the performance of the religious obligations, do we yearn for Him? Do we experience the ascension of our soul towards Him? Do we increase our awareness of Him? Do we heighten our thankfulness and contentment towards Him? Do we remember our divine source? In other words, do we actually remain in his blessed Presence while performing the sacred duties? For if we obey with joy, the sweet taste of heaven will be given. And when human perfection is reached, it will be as though eternity will exist here and now.

To finalize, Ramadan, the ritual prayer, and the *Hajj* are nothing else than celebrations of the religion of unity. The element of celebration is celebrating unity, *tawhid*.

The Holy Qur'an says:

> *Your creation and your resurrection are as but a single soul. (31:28)*

Prophet Muhammad, peace and blessings upon him, said:

> *The believers are brothers, and men of knowledge are like a single soul.*

Jalal al-Din Rumi said:

> *When bodily houses have lost their foundations, the believers become like a single soul.*

Once the believer with a higher vision, with the eye of discernment, removes the veils covering the divine realities, breaks out from the jail of his body, and looks behind the wall of existence, he will see the divine mysteries of the Unseen and realize the oneness of being. He will witness the original unity.

In substance, all things are one; all existent things are pure light. By the fact that all existent things are created by God, all creation feels an irresistible attraction towards its Creator. As the foam gives witness of the immense reality of the infinite ocean, all created realities point to the glorious oneness of their Creator. Further, human souls, emanating directly from God's Essence breathed into bodies through His Merciful Breath, are dominated by the wish to return home, to re-emerge with their origin, to rejoin their lost union with their Creator.

This is the concept of God's creation. All parts feel attracted to the Whole. All creation is under the law of marriage. The attraction of all existent things towards each other is an expression of unity. The macro-cosmos and the micro-cosmos are all subjected to this law. Nature, the universe, the world, and man are all striving to return to the Whole. All creation worships Him, desires Him, proclaims His glory, and strives for union with Him.

Again, in Jalal al-Din Rumi's words:

> *All parts, whether moving or still,*
> *Are reciting "To him we return."*

To live divided, to live a separate existence—that is to say, to live in exile away from one's true home—gives rise to pain, affliction, sickness, and torment. The more one is separated from the whole, the more one is wounded. But it is exactly the pain of separation which brings us to the remedy. The pain of the injury will look for its healing. When a newborn baby feels hungry for milk, it will cry for its mother. When a man is locked up in prison, he will look for freedom. When a woman is sick, she will try to regain her health. The more we are hurt, the more we are separated, and the deeper the cut, the more we will become aware of health, unity, healing, salvation—which amounts to nothing else than becoming aware of the One and Only.

The true existence of being human is to recognize that one is part of the whole creation! Therefore, man's profession is taking refuge in God most High because he belongs to Him, he is inseparably linked with Him, and he totally depends on Him. His duty is to cry for refuge; to plead and supplicate to his Creator; to turn to Him; and to seek His help. No one else other than the human being gives the clear proof of living a 'part-of-the-whole-existence'!

For this reason, a man living in isolation will be completely lost. He will become a miser to himself. His isolation will bring him spiritual illness, and the only cure will be to unite with his fellow beings. Togetherness, embracing, sharing, brotherhood, communal life, are all necessary elements for human survival, because they are food for the soul. It is through the mysteries of firm belief that the beauty of brotherhood, loving embrace, sharing, and unification will occur amongst human beings.

The power of divine unity is needed to advance in the mysteries of life. It is a necessity for man to experience the ascension of his soul if he wishes to inhale the sweet scent of the Hereafter. Only higher awareness can give a voice to the eternal realms of God most High. Only a universal conscience can encompass the secrets of life. Only true vision can explain the hidden meanings of existence. That is to say, the clarity of heart, and the clarity of vision, will embrace the infinity of God's wisdom. It is the clarity of the mirror of the heart.

In this respect, Jalal al-Din Rumi enlightens us with an excellent piece of wisdom regarding the necessity to integrate the science of unity into our lives and to apply the science of unity in order to understand the messages of the holy Qur'an. In other words, to truly be receptive towards the inner teaching of God's revelations, we have to show sincere faith and willing submission:

Many people have gone astray with the Qur'an; with that saving rope, one group fell into the well. The rope has no sin, oh quarrelsome man! But you are unconcerned with traveling upward.

In other words, we have to be utterly careful how we approach and interpret the inner meanings of the Holy Qur'an. Jalal al-Din Rumi gives us another warning:

- *When a stranger enters my door, the women of the harem hide in the veil. But if an intimate friend, free of all noxiousness should enter, these ladies lift their face coverings. Whatever is made good and fine and beautiful, is made so for a seeing eye.*
- *The Qur'an is like a bride. Although you pull the veil away from her face, she does not show herself to you. When you investigate the Qur'an, but receive no joy or mystical unveiling, it is because your pulling at the veil has caused you to be rejected. The Qur'an has deceived you and shown itself as ugly. It says, 'I am not that beautiful bride.' It is able to show itself in any form it desires. But if you stop pulling at its veil and seek its good pleasure, if you water its field, serve it from afar and strive in that which pleases it, then it will show you its face without any need for you to draw aside its veil.*

As we see, with the slightest deviation from the '*sirat al mustaqim,*' the straight path, we will fall into error. Man is an extremely sensitive and precious creature. And the road to God is like the sharp edge of a knife. So man lives in constant danger of slipping. This sliding away from the truth is equal to a misinterpretation of reality. The error is spiritual blindness, the darkness of unconsciousness, which means we will fall into the danger of idol-worshipping. One worships the things one loves most. One's heart is full of love for food, drink, talk, sleep, and children. The holy Qur'an asks:

Have you seen one who takes for his god his own passion? (25:43)

People's eternal problem is idolatry, ascribing partners to Him, because idols are substitutes for God. The mother of all idols is yourself, your selfishness. People are drowned in their own simple-mindedness, narrow-mindedness and forgetfulness. They have a distorted view of reality, and they take their illusions for reality. They stop at the picture of the world.

In contrast, a true believer always finds himself in a delicate balance between idolatry versus unity. He slides back and forth between false existence and true existence. The path of truth needs total submission. Religion teaches the art of giving. It demands the whole of man! If we sacrifice our whole selves, we will receive eternal life. This is the divine plan, the contract between God and man. There is no other trade between God and man existing. We give ourselves, and He gives us eternal life. All other dealings and transactions, are mere calculations created by selfishness and egotistical desires. When man is busy with these calculations, accumulating deeds, property, wealth and status, love will depart from his heart. In the realms of the everlasting, there is no place for selfishness, sensuality, or animality.

The straight path is the path of light leading into the infinity— the beauty and perfection of our noble character features, which stem from the divine attributes of our Almighty God. Deviating from the straight path means neglecting one's divine origin, and effectively being heedless to the divine treasure within oneself. Not acknowledging one's sacred roots is equal to refusing to see the hierarchy of existence, the countless layers of meanings within creation. Man is a manifestation of divine perfection.

In Sheikh Ghalib's words:

> *Look at yourself with joy, for you are the essence of the universe.*
> *You are the Adam, the pupil of the eye of the universe.*

To know the value and meaning of a human being in his earthly existence is equal to knowing the treasury of paradise. More precisely, the task of man in his life is to rediscover and experience paradise. It is the hidden treasure. Therefore the time given to man in his earthly existence represents a rehearsal for the hereafter, because exclusively in his present life, he can seek the hidden treasure. This means that the sweet taste of paradise is given here and now. Man will earn the fruits of the Hereafter in proportion to his good works, the nobility of his character and his good actions in this world.

God's wisdom is eternal. The root of all science is from eternity; therefore, we have to contemplate the eternal rules that shape the universe. The whole of existence is like a book. By contemplating nature and its mysteries, we can read its signs. All existence displays the miracle of creation. It is the infinity as such, the infinity of the incomprehensible created realities which represents the essence of all religions. If we study God's creativity, every moment in this world becomes an absolute miracle. We are nurtured by the delight of God's infinite beauties and blessings. We become intoxicated by the boundless wealth of creation. Abundant riches and uncountable multiplicity flow through the universe. All of creation shows a perfect and harmonious order. Nobody other than our Supreme Creator holds this perfect working organization that shape the universe together. All existence shows evidence of His overwhelming oneness.

When believers celebrate sacred rituals, when they dwell in the bliss of divine awareness, time becomes everlasting. They leave the world and taste the Hereafter. A pure heart can transcend time and place. When the souls ascends towards the realms of nearness with their Creator, beauty within beauty, time within time, space within space, illumination within illumination, bewilderment within bewilderment all reveal themselves.

As we know, Prophet Muhammad, upon him be peace and blessings, was given the honor by his beloved Lord to enter into His eternal Presence in the night of the ascension. A trajectory of this miracle is given in the ritual prayer to sincere believers. It is called the ascension of the believer. He is given the possibility of ascending with his soul towards the eternal Presence as well. This night of the purest elevation symbolizes the fulfillment of the glorious union with our beloved Lord. As Jalal al-Din Rumi interprets this exalted experience of our beloved master:

On the Night of the Ascension, the Prophet in his selflessness trav-eled a 100,000-year journey.

It is the love for our Lord of all the worlds, and the love for our glory of the universe, which lets us transcend the created realities and strive towards the paradise of intimacy. Moreover, it is love that allows us to feel as though we are with the most exalted beings, the prophets and saints, although they have passed away in the realms of eternal beauty. Through love, we can be with them in the same way as when they were alive. This means that when we love wholeheartedly, we can be everywhere at any time. In the world of union, there is no subject and object, time and space, rising and setting, end and beginning, words and sound. The world of union is the world of beauty and love. The light of unity generates beauty and overwhelms the owners of such hearts with infinite love.

Know that the Truth cannot be given for nothing. Unity is the greatest power in the universe. The light of unity holds everything together. Through unity, we reach the enlightenment of our being. It is the highest goal of the true believer. Through the mystery of belief, there is unity. When selfishness vanishes, unity appears. It is pure selflessness that holds the universe together. Unity is the highest form of spiritual education, and it is the most excellent teaching because the light of unity prevails over everything—it breaks through all created realities. This light extinguishes all hypocrisy, superstition, myths, illusions, sensuality, confusion, magic, and the darkness of our unconsciousness.

Unity means obtaining peace of heart; it is the perfect balance of the inner self. Unity is traveling upwards. Unity is to be in admiration with God's beauty and perfection. Unity is dwelling in friendship with God the Merciful. It is truly knowing our Creator where unity will flourish and the secrets will gush forth. Only higher awareness can grasp divine Existence. Unity is when your moment becomes His Breath. Unity requires total submission the All-Glorious One, accepting to carry the responsibility as a representative of God, and accepting to carry His trust. Divine union demands the whole of man. Unity demands self-extinction and annihilation. The science of unity is needed to understand the significance of the human being, nature, the world, the cosmos, the hereafter, the soul, the angels, the devil, and death. Only love finds union. Love always reaches out for union. It draws people together, eliminates all differences, diversities, separations, and divisions. Only with wisdom can we reach unity.

To finalize, unity is never-ending servanthood. Unity could not be better described! Our great saint, Jalal al-Din Rumi, states:

> *Oh, union with You is the root of all joys!*
> *For these are all forms, but that is meaning.*

God most High wishes that all human beings would offer themselves unconditionally and wholeheartedly to Him:

> *Wherever you are, there is the Presence of God. (2:115)*

Does not this verse prove that He is always watching over us, always together with us? We should return willingly His loving concern in complete surrender. We should show gratitude and praise in all our actions. We should feel the utter need for Him and put our total focus on Him. His Gaze should consume us up to our own extinction. This is the state of excellence, true sincerity, *ihsan*. It represents the highest station a believer can achieve. Then we will gain divine acceptance. Only mutual affection finds desired union. This way, the light of unity will prevail. The light of our soul will meet His light. We will live in Him, for Him, with Him, and through Him.

The whole work for the human being is to understand sainthood. To understand sainthood is mastering the science of unity. It means the utmost humility and surrender, and the utmost servanthood. As the Sufi saint, Sidi Hamza al-Qadiri al-Butchichi, comments:

> *True Knowledge can only be acquired through humility. The path*
> *towards this knowledge is like a person's wanting to drink from a*

stream: he has to lower himself to be able to drink. Water seeks the lowest level, thus we have to imitate water.

Furthermore, sainthood is love. Love means to celebrate the intensity of a heightened flow of energy. The peak of celebration culminates in the ocean of oneness, meaning celebrating *tawhid*. Furthermore, sainthood is adoration. The religion of Islam is the religion of adoration. The sweet scent of the Hereafter is reserved for the adorers. The saint dwells in a state of continuous wonderment, awe, and perplexity. The supremest adorer was the Prophet Muhammad, upon him be peace and blessings. In his heart-melting prayer he supplicated;:

O Lord, let me marvel at you!

Furthermore, sainthood is divine light. The whole question of human existence is regulated by the light of the religion! We will see with the divine light, we will be guided with the divine light, and we will heal through the divine light. The light of faith turns everything from wrong into right, and it will enable us to distinguish falsehood from sincerity. The sacred book, the Qur'an, is God's eternal Light. It is God's light leading the Pen of Truth. It is God's light revealing the mysteries behind creation.

Everyone is in need of unity, because our souls belong to God! There is no rest, no satisfaction, and no resolution except in Him. The solution to all problems; the remedy for all burning hearts; the salvation for all needy creatures; and the fulfillment of the true lover, is emptying one's heart of the world and filling one's heart with God most High.

In an ecstatic state, the great saint, Abu Yazid Bistami, felt himself dwelling in unity with the Only One, and when he took a step back towards creation he fainted. He could not bear the separation. But he was inspired:

Go out to My creation in My form, so when they see you they see Me.

This is what is meant to be vicegerent, to represent God on earth, as a *Khalifa'tullah*, to fulfill His agency on earth in our daily lives. In the words of the Qur'an:

He who was dead, to whom We gave life, and a light whereby he can walk amongst men... (6:122)

And moreover, I wish to say that you are only in union with God when you are in union with people. This is the state of unity desired by God most High. You enter His heaven, the paradise of intimacy, by serving His beloved creatures. You are close to Him in the measure of your closeness to people. As it says in the holy Qur'anic verse:

Enter you, then, among My devotees! Yea, enter you My Heaven. (89:29)

Nothing can surpass God's Own Heaven, which is exclusively reserved for those who are living in union with their fellow beings.

Prophet Muhammad, peace and blessings upon him, lets us know, that only believers are allowed to enter paradise. But there is a condition for sincere belief. We have to love each other in order to become true believers. Yet true love for God's sake—true brotherhood—only becomes real when we are related to each other by what we know, taste and love. The Prophet Abraham, upon him be peace, said:

Only the brotherhood of milk is important, which unites those who drink, because they have acquired the same knowledge!

In this case, the believer becomes the mirror of the believer, because in the centre of his heart is reflected what is placed in the centre of his brother's heart. Only the truth unites! If we drink the same drink, we become one with each other—we become lovers of the same Beloved. As the famous Arab poet, Umar Ibn al-Farid, says:

We have drunk to the remembrance of the Beloved a wine, where with we were drunk before the wine was created.

May we earn a portion of divine friendship! The Prophet, peace and blessings be upon him, said:

A man is with whom he loves!

To close this chapter, the following has to be said: it is the reason for creation, the glory of the universe, our spiritual master, the most beloved of the Beloved, the most desired of the Desire, the Prophet Muhammad Mustafa, peace and blessings be unto him, who is given by our all-Merciful Lord of Majesty and Bounty to the believers all over the world, so that we might reach abundant surrender, heightened contentment, sweet harmony, pure servanthood, intense pleasure, sincere submission, and loving union.

THE GIVING HAND

When will people realize that there is no happiness in the taking hand? If one's lifestyle is built on consumerism, the result lies in frustration. The only act which brings people everlasting happiness is true servanthood, the giving hand, which means to offer love.

Everybody wishes to be rich. Why don't we wish for the richness of a noble character, for the richness of an illuminated mind, or for the richness of excellent behavior? Everybody complains about their sicknesses. We say, "O my head hurts"; "O I have pain in my stomach"; and "O my liver is poisoned." But each of us has sicknesses of the mind and heart as well. Why do we not complain about them? We never say, "O my distortion hurts"; "O my insufficiency gives me pain"; "O my helplessness disturbs me"; "O my mistakes hurt me"; or "O my sins depress me."

We are always busy with our failures, with our downfall and with our losses. So why aren't we busy celebrating God's beauty and perfection instead? We usually revolt against the tyranny of politicians and businessmen. So why do we not revolt against the tyranny of our own egos? We never forget to feed our body. So why do we forget to feed our souls? We mostly exaggerate in eating, sleeping, talking, and shopping. So why don't we exaggerate in worship and service? We always run for excitement of our senses. So why don't we excite ourselves with God Himself? Is there anything more satisfying, more joyful, more fulfilling and greater than occupying oneself with Him? The Qur'an says:

> Let us flee onto God. (Dhariyat 51:50)

Knowing God is the greatest celebration:

Why do people prefer to walk around dead,
When they could fly around in the heavens of divine bliss?
Why do people prefer their own pain,
When the keys of paradise of eternal happiness have been given to them?
Why do people prefer to sleep,
When they have been given the water of life?
Why do people refuse to eat from the banquet of heaven,
When it is spread right in front of them?
Why do people prefer to stay in boredom and baseness,
When they are offered the scent of heavenly ascension even while in this earthly life?
Why are people indifferent to the pearls of wisdom,
Which are given to them in abundance?
Why do people not contemplate death more frequently,
Although it is the most important event in everyone's life?
Why are people not affected by the jewels of beings,
Which are sitting right in front of them?
We take this life as being accidental,
Whereas existence is celebrating the oneness of being every moment.
We mainly walk, talk, eat, sleep,
Whereas the span of our lives from birth to death means heavy learning.
We are full of self-importance,
Whereas our biggest treasure is pure modesty and nothingness.
We pretend to be owners of knowledge, property, and capital,
Whereas divine wisdom and wealth is pure mercy,
A generous gift from our beloved Lord to His servant.

Our great saint, Jalal al-Din Rumi, comments:

You have an escape from God, but not from food. You have an escape from religion, but not from idols. O, you who cannot bear to be without this despicable world! How can you bear to be without Him Who spread it as a carpet? O you who cannot be without luxuries and comforts! How can you bear to be without the Generous God?

When someone hears that in a certain city that a generous man is bestowing tremendous gifts and bounties, naturally he will go there in the hope of receiving a share. Since God's Bounty is so famous and the whole world knows about His Kindness, why do you not beg from Him? Why do you not desire robes of honor and of gold?

Because the eyes of our head only look at the surface of things, our eyes, ears, mouth become increasingly selfish. It is the ego which is looking, hearing and talking. Additionally, the mind believes in what the eyes perceive and the ears hear. Our organs have become violated by our selfish concerns.

The greatest damage can be done by our tongues. The salvation of man depends on how he uses his tongue. If we combine the way we look, hear and talk with the knowledge of our Creator— that is to say, if we live according to the divine order—we save ourselves from the dangerous and low places of human existence. When we neglect what we cannot comprehend easily, what we cannot touch with our hands, what we cannot see with our two eyes, what we cannot control with our willpower, and what we cannot rationally grasp with our mind, we fail to realize the hierarchy of existence, we fail to sincerely believe, and we fail to see the hidden treasure. In other words, we lack humanity.

There is enormous misunderstanding: it is human existence. This is our tragedy. Man can not grasp the meaning and value of himself. He has lost the true purpose of his existence. Man is deceived by his own existence. Man is deceived by his ego. Man is deceived by his senses. Man is deceived by the circus of this world. Man is deceived by his own business and activities. In Jalal al-Din Rumi's words:

This 'I-and-we-ness' is a ladder that all men climb—in the end, they all must fall. Whoever goes higher is a greater fool, for his bones will break the worse.

The meaning of the mundane world is unawareness of the divine Presence; it is not money, women, dress. Understand this well!

There are as many degrees of 'heart-knowledge' as there are people. The elite, the lovers, acquire thirst, whereas the majority look for water. The elite go through forty changes a day, whereas the ordinary man does not know one change in forty years. The lovers repent for their distraction, forgetting God for one moment; whereas the majority repent from sin. The great Sheikh, Muhyiddin Ibn Arabi, says:

> *How many a one praying experiences nothing of his prayers save stress, exertion and a view of the* Mihrab, *while another is constantly blessed with intimate divine converse, even though he seems to be simply fulfilling his ordinary religious duties.*

Jalal al-Din Rumi says:

> *In the eyes of the elect, love is a tremendous eternal light, even though the vulgar see it as but form and sensuality.*
> *On guard against drowning, men of intellect flee from it; but lovers have no work or profession except drowning in the ocean.*

God Most High says:

> *Know that every day, 70,000 mysteries from My Majesty pass through the heart of the Knower, never to return...*

On the other hand, an ignorant person dwells in his soup of unconsciousness his whole life. Let us leave the lower places of existence! Let us reach to the ones above us and learn!

Man has to understand his potential gift. He has to know who he is before he can remedy any problem. Prophet Muhammad, upon him be peace and blessings, said:

> *Man is the enemy of what he does not know.*

It is the unawareness of the divine Presence, and the lack of divine thirst, which is the root of all our problems. There is not one human being who does not want harmony. The heart can only be satisfied with God. If the heart is sick, the whole body will be sick; but if the heart is healthy, our whole self will be healthy.

Probably the greatest ignorance of man is that he is not able to see, and does not wish to see, his own self. Jalal al-Din Rumi quotes:

> *If only you could see your own beauty! For you are greater than the sun. Why are you withered and shriveled in this prison of dust? Why*

not become fresh from the gentleness of the heart's spring? Why not laugh like a rose? Why not spread perfume?

Human ignorance is the greatest veil. To ignore the hidden treasure inside ourselves is equal to spiritual blindness. So short-sightedness, unawareness, forgetfulness, narrowness, unconsciousness, and heedlessness are, in fact, the essential problems that separate human beings from God most High. That is to say, being deprived of seeing one's own beauty is equal to man's forgetfulness and ignorance. Jalal al-Din Rumi gives us fabulous descriptions of man's ignorance:

A basket full of bread sits on your head, but you beg for crusts from door-to-door. Attend to your own head; leave aside all dizziness. Go, knock upon the heart's door! Why keep on knocking from door-to-door?

Up to your knees in the stream's water, you are heedless of yourself and seek a drink from this person and that.

Would that you could know yourself for a time! Would that you could see a sign of your own beautiful face! Then you would not sleep in water and clay like an animal. You would go to the house of joy and all lovely spirits.

In the Holy Qur'an God reminds us repeatedly:

Will you not be mindful? (2:44, etc.)
"God gave us authority."

And our blessed Prophet tells us:

One hour of contemplation is equal to sixty years of worship.

But it has to be mentioned that man is not completely unaware of his state. God gives every single individual a conscience.

Indeed, human will be an eye-witness against himself, even though he puts forth his excuses. (75:14-15)

So nobody can take refuge in himself, or hide behind his argumentation, his reasoning, his pretension, his cleverness, or his self-fabricated rationality.

The great Sheikh, Muhyiddin Ibn Arabi, tells us in two statements how things are determined by the strength of our personal
will:

> *It is the tree of our own soul that gathers the fruit of its culture.*
> *Nobody receives something from God which does not come from himself.*

And a wise man named Kubra once said:

> *God wishes for nothing without the servant wishing for it, and the*
> *servant wishes for nothing without God wishing for it.*

God most Gracious says:

> *God changes not what people have, until they change it for them-*
> *selves. (8:53)*
> *I conform Myself to the opinion My servant has of Me.*

Our beloved Prophet, peace and blessings upon him, said:

> *Struggling makes one witness the Sacred Essence.*

In turn, Jalal al-Din Rumi comments:

> *Indeed, in a hundred thousand years, you will not arrive at the first*
> *station. However, when you travel this road until your legs are*
> *exhausted and you fall down flat, until you have no more strength*
> *to move forward, then God's grace will take you in its arms.*

For the believer, it means that God exists as far as he is capa-
ble of being in His Presence. In Jalal al-Din Rumi's words again:

> *God will give you what you seek. Where your aspiration lies is what*
> *you will become. For the bird flies with two wings, but the believer*
> *flies with his aspiration.*

In other words, man determines his own worth.

It is need, aspiration, search, longing, which differs the lovers
from the common folk. The average man is full of himself and does
not feel a thing outside of himself. He is drunk from his own selfishness. Meanwhile, there are the people who never cease weeping

before God's Court. They become beggars in front of God's door-step. Begging is their daily bread. Their pleasure derives from being hungry. They never can be satisfied. Their hunger is insatiable. They are in need of God and God's attributes and names are infinite!

Here, the immense significance of 'dua,' the personal supplication, has to be mentioned. To plead with God is the shortest way to God. The business of man in his earthly life is to take refuge in Him. There is nothing more valuable, than for man to entrust everything to Him. For the believer, there is nothing more valuable than to arrive at the door of intimate conversations with Him.

Things are very simple: restlessness, confusion, heaviness, indifference, laziness, complaint, insecurity, fear, and rebellion belong to the ego—leading to bitterness, frustration, hate, dissatisfaction, depression, arrogance, envy, ugliness, heartaches, and cruelty. Conversely, humility, beauty, goodness, generosity, compassion, love, and surrender belong to the soul—leading into security, harmony, contentment, peace, felicity, sincerity, happiness, faith, and beauty. The attributes of goodness are light which generates divine guidance, while the attributes of evil are darkness which leads astray.

I like to conclude by saying that happiness and contentment are not achieved where we think they are. And suffering is not given for the reason we think it is. That is why the majority of people flee from it. But nobody who has tried to avoid calamities did not receive a bigger portion than what he fled from in the first place. The select people of God know that the suffering is a means to bring them closer to their Beloved.

Humankind has to acquire this most important peace of wisdom, which Jalal al-Din Rumi teaches us:

> *The spirit of all science is only this: to know who you will be at the day of Resurrection!*

BEAUTY

O ur great Saint, Jalal al-Din Rumi, says:

When the spirit was annihilated in contemplation it said,
"None but God has contemplated God's Beauty!"

We can only truly love God most High if we realize divine
beauty within ourselves. In our present time, it is a duty for the
truthful followers of the Prophet Muhammad's community to
rediscover the beauty of the religion of Islam. The modern world
is suffering a tremendous sickness. I like to call it externalization,
meaning that man has lost the dimension of inwardness. The
world has lost its mystery, grace, vision, charm, blessedness, love,
and beauty. We have lost meaning and value, and we lost the
sacredness of all life. That is to say, man has lost the sensitivity
which makes him a human being.

Especially today, our task is to revive the treasury of eternal
light within our hearts. It is the inner wealth of the religion. In
other words, we have to rediscover the beauty of the light of our
own soul. There we will reside in the paradise of intimacy—the
believer's total bliss—because the light of our own soul will meet
God's light. We will look at it with the light coming from it. A
heart without illumination is empty, disgraced and narrow. An
illuminated heart can receive its most beloved Lord as a guest,
because the house of this heart is infinitely expanded, elevated and
purified with His love.

The origin of love is beauty. And the origin of beauty is the
divine light. The divine light represents the source of existence.
Starting from the source, we see that divine light generates beauty,
and beauty generates love. And divine love brings us to the desired

realms of nearness of our Supreme Creator. Love always looks for beauty. It is essential for a true believer to be in love, because a lover is always in search for the beauty of his beloved.

What is beauty? Closeness to God. What is love? Intimacy with God. What is perfection? Admiration towards God. What is wisdom? Knowledge of God.

We are creatures of light. We are the fruit of God's all-embracing love for the jewel of servants, Muhammad Mustafa, peace and blessings upon him, we are created from the noble light of Muhammad. So the spiritual reality of man is light. The divine light is the essence of all creation. This light generates beauty through its nature. So beauty is never separate from God, and beauty is never separate from the human being.

In order to become who we are, how God meant us to be, in order to realize our true self, we have to be able to see our own beauty. Therefore, the spiritual growth of man goes backwards to the roots of his being, unfolding into a gradual process of illumination leading into purity. Witnessing one's own beauty is equal to knowing one's true self. Therefore, everyone in his life feels an irresistible power of attraction towards beauty. We are drawn to it like moths to light. In the words of Jalal al-Din Rumi:

> *When the flaming candle sends its invitation,*
> *The moth's spirit does not hold back from being consumed!*

Furthermore if we know ourselves, we will be able to know God. So if we see our own beauty, we will get familiar with God Himself. It is the paradise of intimacy which is nothing else than the infinite beauty of His light. This means that the soul is in search for the perfection of eternal beauty, which is its own divine light. It means that the soul is in search of joy. The soul is in search of the sweetest sounds. The soul is in search of intimate loving whispers. The soul is in search of the sweet taste of awareness. The soul is in search of the beauty of His Face.

All beauty pertains to God. Beauty is a divine attribute of God. It is reported that the prophet Muhammad, upon him be peace and blessings, said:

God is beautiful and He loves beauty.

Only an eye with higher perception can see Eternal Beauty. It is nothing else than the full awareness of seeing God most High. This eye looks at the mirror of sincerity with the illuminated power of belief. It sees the luminous brightness of the divine secrets of God shining at him.

Eternal beauty is everlasting. Such beauty is faultless; such beauty does not permit any ugliness. The beauty of God's light has such a power—it transforms matter into light. As Jalal al-Din Rumi says:

This person eats food and gives out filth. The other also eats, but his food is transformed entirely into the light of God.
    He who has not seen Your beauty, makes the intellect his qiblah.
A blind man carries a can instead of a lamp.

The eye with a weak and false perception sees only the worldly, external beauty which is borrowed, of a second-hand quality, declining, and short-lived. The beauty appearing in the physical realm is a veil covering the light of eternal beauty of our most merciful Lord. Jalal al-Din Rumi says:

The moon-faced beauties of the world have stolen beauty from Our beauty. They have stolen a mote of My beauty and goodness.
Since tresses and cheeks show a sign of that drop,
Kings keep licking the ground.
Delicate earth has received a drop of beauty,
So you kiss it night and day with a hundred hearts.
All this beauty and attractiveness in the face of the black earth has shone forth from the moon of the Unseen. It is a ray of Perfection's Light.
The moonlight returns to the moon,
Its reflection leaves the black wall.

The Sufi saint, Sidi Hamza al-Qadiri al-Butchichi, comments:

> *Defect and ugliness are not in things or beings, but in the impurity*
> *of our vision of them. The more the soul is peaceful, perfect and pure,*
> *the more it will become disposed to see in all beings a luminous*
> *Divine manifestation: All is beautiful. Only the non-polished heart*
> *of the disciple renders things ugly.*

Divine beauty is reached through closeness with the One and Only. When a soul is traveling towards God, the more it ascends to the realms of His intimacy, and the more it descends into the realms of meanings, the more it will see the beauty of His mysterious Presence. Melting in the divine Truth will reveal divine beauty.

So, to see beauty necessitates closeness to the Almighty God. Complete closeness to God necessitates self-annihilation, non-existence. It means to be consumed by the One and Only. Human perfection, the highest station of human evolution, lies paradoxically in self-extinction leading into non-existence. So the perfection of divine beauty is only fulfilled through the believers self-annihilation. That is to say, only through nothingness can divine beauty appear in its fullest splendor. Jalal al-Din Rumi comments:

> *What sort of Beloved is He? As long as a single hair of love for your-*
> *self remains, He will not show His Face. You will be unworthy of*
> *union with Him, and He will give you no access. You must be com-*
> *pletely repelled by yourself and the world and be your own self's*
> *enemy, or else the Friend will not show His Countenance. So when*
> *our religion resides in a person's heart, it stays right there until it*
> *takes his heart to God and separates it from everything unworthy.*

God Himself desires His creatures to such an extent, that He wishes their complete annihilation in His eternal beauty. We should be consumed in the beauty of His light like a moth in the flames, because His love and desire for human beings is infinite.

So all existence is His wisdom, because it reflects the perfection and beauty of God most High. Therefore, the manifestation of the Truth is beauty. God revealing Himself is an act of beauty. This means that the sheer fact of God creating creation, is an act of infinite love and beauty. It shows the unconditional divine generosity of the All-Merciful. The whole universe is flooded with infinite blessings, with His mercy and compassion.

Whenever we witness the truth of the divine revelations of the holy Qur'an, or we witness the mystery of His divine Presence within all of creation, we will be in admiration and awe of the radiance of overwhelming beauty.

God's desire to manifest Himself is an act of pure mercy and gentleness towards His creatures. It proves His love and desire for humankind. It is divine love which makes the universe manifest; that is to say, the act of manifestation is love manifesting itself.

In manifesting Himself, God makes us know ourselves. Man's consciousness of himself is the consciousness of God towards him. Furthermore, God manifesting Himself is an act of generosity and an act of mercy towards Himself. To know one's self and to know God represents the greatest happiness and fulfillment for a believer. In turn, to know Him and to return to Him the love He has for us is the greatest celebration.

Sainthood is the wellspring of spiritual beauty. A perfect man lives in God's eternal richness. Perfection is reached through closeness to God, and closeness to God generates beauty. That is to say, perfection generates beauty through its nature. In other words, through annihilation in God, man will become a perfect mirror of divine beauty. Therefore, the ultimate goal of a lover is seeking God's Beauty.

Being honored to enter the school of love, I discovered that spiritual maturity is attained through beauty. We taste the everlasting values through divine beauty, whereas in one's childhood, one learns generally through orders, instruction, commands and dictation. I believe that, as human beings, in order to grow towards purity, we need the beauty and goodness of a true lover which will help us to understand God most High. In other words, I think that we learn through the beauty and richness of a perfect man, through our intoxication with the perfection and beauty of pure servanthood. The richness we feel is the light shining from his pure soul. The beauty of this divine light nourishes the depths of our hearts. Therefore, I feel that we have to enter the school of saints because the spiritual progress happens to the degree we attach ourselves to saints! Jalal al-Din Rumi comments:

> *All goals are Your Beauty.*
> *The lover's teacher is the Beloved's Beauty.*
> *Their book and lessons are His Face.*
> *Where do angels find food? From the Beauty of God Presence. The*
> *moon and planets seek nourishment from the world's sun.*

True sainthood is never absent from love! And love is never absent from divine beauty; divine beauty from healing; healing from divine guidance; and divine guidance from servanthood. The inner richness of a perfect man, the light of his purified soul, will ceaselessly nurture, serve, heal, beautify and guide the ones who are in utter need of such an enlightened presence.

To reach divine beauty, we have to overcome our body in order to reach the light of our own soul. An enlightened soul will celebrate the bliss of its gained freedom, being delivered from the cage of its body. The richness of such a soul radiates divine beauty. The richness originates from the light of goodness; the goodness of human character features; the generosity of being; the treasury of pure modesty; and the perfection of servitude. This is the sublime secret of the human heart, radiating unceasingly with unconditional love. This is the most excellent beauty, the beauty of being! In other words, the expression of the inner treasury of a man's heart, the wealth of human goodness, is beauty.

The light of human goodness is nothing else other than the beautiful attributes and names of the Lord of all the Worlds. The Qur'anic expression, "the most beautiful names," refers to the divine qualities, the divine attributes of God most High. At the time of creation, God taught man all of His names. The Qur'an states:

> *He taught Adam the names, all of them. (2:31)*

The reality of man is rooted in the beautiful attributes of God most High. That is to say, internally, in his innermost being, his essence, man contains a deeply rooted eternal beauty. It is the form that mirrors God's beautiful names. The spiritual attainment of man lies, therefore, in the realization of the beautiful names. The Prophet Muhammad, peace and blessings upon him, said:

Assume the virtues of God!

Jalal al-Din Rumi says about the perfect man:

Know that from head to foot the sheikh is nothing but God's attributes, even if you see him in human form.

This means that high ethics, such as patience, thankfulness, sincerity, truthfulness, humility, kindness, compassion, love, and respect—which are nothing else than the deep-seated reflections of some of God's names—will illuminate our relationship with the One and Only. In other words, the more man descends into the realms of meaning of the divine attributes, the more divine beauty will reveal itself.

The attributes of goodness, then, are a hidden substance within the make-up of a human being. They are veiled by ambition, envy, greed, arrogance, and sensuality. If man does not travel on the road towards spiritual perfection, which will help him to remove the selfishness covering his own soul, his personality will be infiltrated with animalistic behaviors. When such a believer is not illuminated with the light of goodness, he will lose his grace and attraction to the divine. Jalal al-Din Rumi comments:

Beauty returns to its Source;
But a body remains putrid, disgraced and ugly.

Man's heart is the best of God's creation because it is a divine mirror. It is destined to reflect the beauty of God's light. Caliph Umar, upon him be peace, the owner of such a pure heart said:

I saw my Lord with the light of my Lord.

And a wise man once said:

Beware of the Arif,*
He sees with the light of God!
* [wise one]

God most High created man as a vicegerent in order to represent Him on earth. Man becomes a mirror of the all-merciful Creator, and man can see his Creator through his own existence. Jalal al-Din Rumi comments:

> The Prophet said: 'He who knows himself knows his Lord.' Just as this copper astrolabe mirrors the heavens, man's existence is God's astrolabe. When God causes a man to have knowledge of Him and be familiar with Him, moment-by-moment, he observes the theophanies of God and His ineffable Beauty from the astrolabe of his own existence. That Beauty will never be absent from his mirror.

Manifestations of the Divine Names appear in the pure mirror of man's heart and man can have knowledge of himself in the divine mirror; that is to say, when man looks at the mirror, he sees himself. A believer who is able to look through his own mirror becomes the possessor of a purified look. When he looks at creation, he sees the glory and grace of God's light reflected. And when he looks at beings, he sees the appearance of their mirrors, either shining in beautiful luminous brightness at his own mirror, or in darkness and filth through their own ego substance. As stated in a famous divine tradition, our blessed master said:

> The faithful believer is the mirror of the faithful believer.

And Jalal al-Din Rumi comments:

> He is neither this nor that, He is plain.
> He has set your own reflection before you.
> The saint's own bodily form has been annihilated and he has become
> a mirror. Within are reflected the faces of others.
> You see an ugly face, that is you.
> You see Jesus and Mary, that is you.

If you spit, you spit in your own face.
If you strike the mirror, you strike yourself.
Whoever looks upon spiritual men with the eyes of his own weakness,
you must laugh at his own crooked eyes!

When divine mystery is perceived, beauty appears; when the unseen is seen, divine beauty appears. When the place of "no-place" is seen, when the unheard is heard, when the unspoken is spoken, and when the incomprehensible is perceived—divine beauty appears. When the beauty of God's Majesty shines in luminous brightness, the water of mercy will flow; the sweet fragrance of the news will reach the lover; the merciful breath will be breathed; the sweet scent of the hereafter will be tasted; the perfumes of intimate friendship will please hearts; the tears of utter joy will be shed; the child of the heart will be born; the sweet scent of remembrance will be inhaled; the perfume of existence will be tasted; the freshness of the eyes will be given; the silence of the heart's speech will be heard; the divine bliss of self-annihilation within the prostration will be experienced; and the pouring of inexhaustible treasures will be witnessed.

Beauty is a divine gift. We cannot choose to see eternal beauty. We cannot choose to fall in love. We cannot choose to see vision. We cannot choose to perceive the divine mysteries. It is God's infinite grace, and it will be given to His beloved servants as a divine favor.

We gain love from Love. We gain vision from Vision. We gain beauty from Beauty. We gain light from Light. Divine inspiration, ecstatic experiences, burning love, and pure vision are a gift from the Giver, the Lord of Majesty and Bounty.

On the one side, human beings receive unconditional mercy, blessings, grace, and generosity, infinitely spreading throughout the whole of creation. God most High imposes on Himself a law to be merciful towards His creatures according to His words:

He has inscribed for Himself (the rule of) Mercy. (6:12, 6:54)

My Mercy embraces everything. (7:156)

On the other side, there is conditional mercy, which involves a divine condition; all spiritual gifts, favors, and the bounties we have been honored to receive from our Lord are in relation to our efforts and hard labor, and the good intentions we show towards Him, respectively, in reward for our good works. The holy Qur'an states:

A man shall have to his account only as he has labored. (16:111)

If we show thankfulness in our actions, loving surrender, unconditional love, firm intention, and infinite generosity, God will clothe us with the robe of sainthood, which are His beautiful attributes. We give Him our lives, and He gives us divine vision, beauty and love; that is to say, He gives us being. There is no greater bliss for a living soul than the vision of the Beloved—to experience His Presence. Our great saint Jalal al-Din Rumi, the lover par excellence, gives us the perfect expressions to capture this experience:

> *Seeing other than Your Face has become torture!*
> *Everything other than God is vain.*
> *Where the paradise of Your Face to reveal itself in theophany,*
> *Neither hell nor its wretched inhabitants would remain.*

> *I swear, by Your Spirit!*
> *Be it sovereignty over the world—*
> *Anything other than seeing Your Face*
> *Is but fairy tales and deception.*

> *The light of the sun's face cannot do what Your Face does;*
> *The tumult of the Resurrection cannot do what Your Love does.*

If we would see and hear to whom we are praying, all hindrances and veils would dissolve between the worshipper and the Worshipped. It is truly seeing our Creator, where unity will flourish and all the divine secrets will gush forth to the pure hearts. Seeing Him means dissolving in Him. Seeing Him means knowing oneself. Seeing Him means knowing that only God exists.

God created man in His form which means we have an intimate relationship with God; that is to say, the human being is created to love. So all is in love with God, and God is in love with all.

Man's goal is to know God as a Lover and to participate in His love. So the goal is to love the God of Love! Moreover, the love of a human being derives from the love that God has for Himself and His creatures. So man participates in God's love for His creatures. Most of all, man participates in the love God has for His most beloved, the Prophet Muhammad, peace and blessings be unto him. The world is born out of the love God has for His beloved. Jalal al-Din Rumi comments:

> God said to love: *"If not for your beauty, how should I pay attention to the mirror of existence?"*

We only can realize God if we combine His Beauty with His Majesty and Might. As darkness is needed for the appearance of true beauty, negation is needed for the affirmation expressed in the fundamental declaration of faith in Islam, the *shahadah*: There is no god but God, and Muhammad is His Messenger. There is the power of opposition within the whole of creation. The manifestation of these opposite attributes is necessary for the subsistence of the world. In Jalal al-Din Rumi's words:

> *When gentleness would remain without severity,*
> *How would that display the King's Perfection?*

So temporality is needed for the appearance of eternity; rebellion is needed for the appearance of obedience; arrogance for humility; falsehood for truth; separation for union, heedlessness for awareness; cruelty for faithfulness; and severity for beauty. The opposites mirror each other; that is to say, severity mirrors beauty, and beauty mirrors severity. The believer in his life is constantly shifting between these polarities. His main concern culminates in the opposition between his selfishness and his selflessness; devil and angel; fire and light. In the prophetic tradition, it is reported:

When the believer places his foot upon the bridge over hell, the Fire
says, "Pass over, O believer, for your light has extinguished my fire."

If the believer is able to overcome the attraction of the attribute of fire, the devil, then he will gain the light of faith. This means that for a believer, the experience of suffering, loss, and cruelty is, in reality, his remedy, salvation, gain and good fortune.

Furthermore, God most High hides His mercy in the guise of His wrath, His beauty within severity, and union within separation. He constantly heaps calamities on His servants so they might plead, lament, grieve, weep, and ask for help from Him. This is His divine policy. God delays His gifts, blessings, favors, and generosity, that we might shed tears for His sake. These tears will bring us to the realm of His perfection and beauty. Our exalted saint, Jalal al-Din Rumi, provides a description of his own lamentations:

Whatever You do, Your lips tell tales of sugar!
Whatever movement You make, Gentleness is buried within!

Be cruel! Your cruelty is all Gentleness!
Do wrong! Your wrongdoing is all right-action!
The stone thrown by You is a pearl!
Your injustice better than a hundred faithfulnesses!

I make collyrium for my eyes from the dust of heartaches,
So that these two seas may be filled with pearls!
The tears people shed for His sake are pearls,
Though they think they are tears.

Tears shed for the sake of God are the divine treasury of the human heart. When a believer arrives at the root of his being, he will be endowed with the vision of eternal beauty and he will shed tears of pure joy in the face of the beauty of the divine light. Infinite love will strike him in his innermost being and his heart will turn into an ocean of tears. As beauty and light are inseparable, beauty and love are inseparable, and beauty and tears are also inseparable. Tears are the pearls of the heart. Tears are love's expression; tears are love's language. Tears of admiration in the face of His all-Encompassing Majesty and Perfection— these are the tears that will bring us to the perfection of love. Shedding tears is a direct expression of witnessing divine beauty. In the face of the eternal light, our hearts will become soft, we will tremble, and we will humble ourselves. This is the state most desired by God most High.

Within all of creation, there is nothing more opposed to God's divine light then the devil, the accursed. That is to say, within the whole of humanity, the devil is a great power besides God most High. In front of God's light, he argued and proclaimed false righteousness, trickery, deception, cruelty, and envy. With his false behavior, he represents the peak of shamelessness, arrogance, deception and ugliness. The devil is the most ugly of all creatures and completely opposed to the angels and saints, the personification of divine beauty. That is to say, selfishness generates ugliness, and selflessness generates beauty. We can, therefore, observe that the evil-doers are the most envious, arrogant, power-hungry and ugly.

To reach true beauty, the enlightenment of our being, we need darkness, we need ugliness, we need denial, we need evil, and we need cruelty. That is to say, we need the devil, whose duty is to lead humanity astray. So man in his earthly life has to fail, makes slips of error, sin and disobey. That is to say, he has to be deprived of goodness, beauty, love, grace and blessings, in order to undergo hunger, thirst, suffering, and poverty. So he will go on searching for his lost treasures. If he experiences losses, hardships and trials, he will be able to regain the bounties, gifts and favors of God the Almighty. Additionally, man will have to regret his wrongdoings, his insufficiency, his weaknesses, and his incapacities and begin wholeheartedly to ask for forgiveness. True repentance will create the need for goodness and love and, eventually, he will be able to regain the treasury of his human qualities which will bring him to exalted heights of human existence.

The majority of people pretend to flee from God's *jalal*, His might and majesty, and wish eagerly for His *jamal*, His beauty. They pretend to fear His grandeur, power and majesty; and they pretend to need His tenderness, love, compassion and beauty. But, in reality, on the worldly stage, things look very different. People seem to flee from His *jamal*, hiding from the beauty of His light; and they seem to prefer His *jalal*. This is the tragedy and paradox of being human. Due to man's duality, being created of light— which represents his divine origin and clay, his physical existence— he moves in the opposite direction from his true self. He flees from the divine realms of everlastingness and prefers to dwell in his animal instincts, sensuality, and disgrace—the dark side of the devil's domain. He flees from God's invitation, the beauty of His light and plays his games in the worldly circus, gaining nothing else than God's wrath. He does not want to see, he does not want to know, and he does not want to hear.

The majority of people hide from the truth. To face the truth is very uncomfortable for them, because light is shed on their own ego-substance. Their weaknesses, trickery, lowness, and ugliness become apparent. Therefore, they hide in their own ignorance and refuse to see clearly; they refuse to possess a purified look. They prefer to stay in a never-ending devil's circle for the rest of their lives. Short-lived, artificial happiness, and the constant repetition of suffering and torment, will be their long-life companion.

Sehl Ibn-i Abdullah et-Tusteri gives us the following description of people living in their own misery:

> When God loves a person, He makes this person's sin appear great and opens to him the door of repentance. This door opens to the gardens of intimacy with God. And when He becomes angry with a person, He makes his sins appear very small in that person's eyes and He punishes him with a variety of calamities; but because the person is unfortunate enough to see his sins as small, he does not take advice and the result is frustration and disappointment.

We should know that eternal beauty can strike us with a far greater power than God's Might and Majesty. The more man approaches its divine source, the roots of his existence, the more the power of the eternal light of God the Majestic will be revealed. In other words, God most High has hidden His might and majesty in His beauty, and His beauty in His Might. Only His lovers are able to see and discern the inner workings and countless levels of God's attributes of *Jamal* and *Jalal*, because they see with His light.

There is no greater effect on the human soul than the perfection of God's Beauty! It is the jewel of servants, the most noble of men, the reason for creation, the prince of the universe, the Prophet Muhammad, peace and blessings be unto him, which represents the perfection of realized love and the perfection of absolute beauty. The great saint, AbuYazid al-Bistami said:

> If a single atom of the prophet were manifested to the creation, nobody beneath the Throne could endure it.

And the great saint, Said Nursi, gives us a commentary regarding the incomprehensible reality of the Prophet Muhammad, upon him be peace and blessings:

> And since the Prophet Muhammad [upon him be peace and blessings] and the Qur'anic revelations are like the spirit and intelligence of life, it may be said that their truth is as certain as the existence of life... If the light of the Prophet Muhammad [upon him be peace and blessings] was to depart from the universe, the universe would die. If the Qur'an was to depart, the universe would go mad, and the earth would lose its head and its reason; it would even strike its now unconscious head on a planet, and Doomsday would occur.

The lover's eye wishes to see the beauty of his beloved object. The beloved's object reflects itself in the human face in the most complete manner. The perfection of divine beauty radiated from the face of Prophet Joseph, upon him be peace, in greatest splendor. God did reveal his beauty to creation. Whereas the beauty of al-Bistami was veiled because of the immensity of its impact it could have on his fellow beings. Once lifting his veil to a student who repeatedly insisted to see his face, the student fell instantly dead. From the famous story in the holy Qur'an, we know that Joseph, upon him be peace, inadvertently showed his beauty to some female guests who had been invited to dine with the wife of Aziz, a prominent Egyptian. When Joseph walked by in front of them to serve their meal, they all cut their hands in complete bewilderment and awe, so distracted were they by his beauty.

The beauty of his countenance had such an impact, that they could not feel the pain of their cuts. The Prophet's beloved wife, Aisha, upon her be peace, completed this exemplary story and said that if Prophet Muhammad would have walked by in front of those ladies seeing his beauty, they all would have died immediately.

So when we visit Medina, the illuminated city, the Prophet Muhammad's resting place, upon him be peace and blessings, we can be overpowered by the might of his beauty. Whereas when we visit Mecca, the city of the holy Ka'ba, the pilgrim can be overpowered by the beauty of God's might. God the Merciful is our Host and invites His beloved servants to the realm of His Nearness. Does the Lord of all the worlds greet His most welcomed pilgrim guests with His Majesty and Power?

We do not even have to be in front of His holy house, the Ka'ba, in order to feel His constant mercy and blessings raining over us. By the sheer fact that He is our Creator and that His love for His creatures made Him create the universe and all it contains, we become aware that we exist because of the love He has for us. At the time of the creation of man, God most High showed loving tender care by making the human being into the most honored of His creation. At the time of creation of the universe, He showed that His Mercy by far outstrips His Wrath by balancing His Throne with His Mercy.

Sometimes God shows His Wrath to humanity because of the divine rules of His Justice. But again, what looks like punishment on the external level is, in reality, His gift to humanity. Whatever God has arranged is in His loving concern.

So let us look for the beauty that comes from God! Let us look for the sweetness that comes from God! Let us look for the intimacy that comes from God! If we are not in love with God's beauty, then we can not accomplish our destiny, and we cannot rise to the levels of purity, illumination and love. If we are not in awe, wonder and admiration with God's amazing infinity, we will have difficulty understanding truth. We will fall into the danger of living like a machine, working for a bargain with God. Jalal al-Din Rumi comments:

> *The dervish that wants bread is fish on land.*
> *He has the form of a fish, but he is fleeing from the sea.*
> *He loves God for the sake of gain.*
> *His soul is not in love with God's Excellence and Beauty.*

WHEN KNOWLEDGE BECOMES LOVE....

As our blessed master has advised us:

Part of the excellence of a man, is paying no attention to that which does not concern him.

Correct behavior means that the faults of other people should be of no concern to us and that our imperfections should be the only concern for us. Religion is not only a question of fleeing from evil towards good, or of choosing between right and wrong, obeying or disobeying. Reducing religion into a purely moral matter would diminish the value and meaning of the human being. The essential work takes place on the ontological level. To reach the level of a devoted life in sincerity, we are obliged not to betray our true self, and not be ignorant of our divine origin. That is to say, the work within our earthly lives requires the peeling off of falsehood in order to encounter the reality of our being. We need to wake up and remember what we have forgotten and discover our true origin. It is the unawareness of our true human nature which veils us from the truth and veils us from our Creator. Each human being has the duty to investigate how God meant him to be. The whole business of human life on earth is to become able to perceive one's true self and, therefore, we have to leave the purely moral understanding of man and broaden our awareness of true meaning in order to discover our very substance.

The spiritual journey to one's origin represents the path of consciousness. If we travel towards our divine roots, we will gain consciousness. The more we approach, the more we become aware. So to increase divine awareness is equal to becoming closer to the Truth. If we learn to see with heightened awareness in the precious desert of existence of this world, true love will begin to arise within the divine center of our hearts. So the precondition for love is consciousness of our innermost self and, at the source, we will discover that the underlying cause of existence is love—that the motivating force for all activity within the universe is love. Then the light of consciousness will unite with the lightning of love. The secret treasures of faith will illuminate our innermost self. So, to be conscious of our true self means to love God; loving God means carrying the burden of the divine Trust; and carrying the responsibility of the divine Trust means to represent God on earth as a devoted servant.

As we see, in order to be able to progress on the spiritual path, we have to take things back to their source, correlating them with their origin—we have to approach nearest to the Divine. In other words, religion is the science of approaching towards God most High. The art of approaching represents, therefore, the greatest of all the arts. It is called, *"jihad,"* the divine internal struggle. The Prophet Muhammad, upon him be peace and blessings, having returned from a war with his enemies, tells us in a well-known tradition:

We have returned from the lesser jihad to the greater jihad.

What he meant by the idea of the greater struggle is the war with the enemy within our own self, which outweighs by far the war with our physical enemies on a battlefield. We can call it a spiritual combat, undergoing afflictions, trials, and suffering entirely for God's sake. It is called "the greater holy war," the war with one's ego, low desires, and wishes—with one's sensuality and bad habits. Every human being has to undergo the greater *jihad* provided that it has set out for the path towards human perfection. Having fought this battle successfully, one will have attained the purification of one's inner state of the heart and reached human perfection.

In order to execute this greater holy war, our Prophet Muhammad, upon him be peace and blessings, gave us the most effective advice, without which no spiritual progress is possible:

If you know yourselves, you know your Lord.
Begin with your own self.

This wisdom from our beloved master is the essential message for mankind. For the traveler on the spiritual path, before anything else, is aiming to know himself. If we do not know who we are, we cannot love and, therefore, we cannot comprehend God most High. Only knowledge brings us to love, and love brings us to God. To become aware of God is the biggest celebration because knowledge and love unite.

Furthermore, loving God necessitates following God's beloved Prophet Muhammad, upon him be peace and blessings, and thus following his practices. Our blessed master said:

If you do love God, follow me and God will love you.

This means that the Lord of Majesty will not accept us at His door of intimacy if we do not submit towards the model, character, behavior, teachings of our beloved Prophet Muhammad, upon him be peace and blessings. This holy tradition teaches man that through practicing knowledge within our lives, we might reach true wisdom and arrive at the purity of being; that is to say, in order to earn the luminous fruits of awareness, we have to live what we know. Only then will our knowledge will become true love. In other words, only wholehearted submission to what we know creates love and affection.

Nobody was more truthful to what he knew than our beloved of hearts. His purity, his truthfulness, and his sincerity are the treasury of his being. There is a holy tradition of the Prophet Muhammad, upon him be peace and blessings, about sincerity, the highest and most noble ethic of a believer:

All men will perish, except the scholars; and all scholars will perish, except those who act in accordance with their knowledge; and all of them will perish except the sincere; and even the sincere are in great danger.

And Said Nursi gives us a precise description regarding this most worthy feature:

You should know that, in this world, sincerity is the most important principle in works pertaining to the hereafter. It is the greatest strength and the most acceptable intercessor; and the firmest point of support and the most wondrous means of achieving one's goal; and the highest quality and the purest worship—since, in sincerity, lies much strength and many lights....

Again, in order to know ourselves, we need to apply another piece of advice given by our beloved master:

Die before you die.

Without this practice, we will not be able to attain true self-awareness. Death in this sense means rebirth from the false life of this world and the false life of the ego, which is defined as the above-mentioned greater holy war. Without application of this most important piece of wisdom, we will fail to accomplish a true vision of ourselves, because discovering our true self necessitates sacrificing ourselves.

At the core of our being, there is no place for selfishness. Spiritual perfection culminates in nothingness, self-annihilation, without which no true union with our beloved Lord can be achieved. At the end of the spiritual journey, there is only Him. Therefore, all spiritual work is a question of being and non-being; existence and non-existence; self and self-extinction; selfhood and nothingness; willfulness and annihilation; personality and poverty; self and self-sacrifice; and ego and selflessness. Jalal al-Din Rumi enlightens us about man's secret of non-existence:

As long as you have not died and become living through Him, you are a rebel seeking a realm for your co-partnership with God.

Kill your cow of your ego as soon as you can, so that your hidden spirit may come to life and awareness!

What is the mi'raj of the heavens? Non-existence. The religion and creed of the lovers is non-existence.

I have been so naught in Your Love's existence that my nonexistence is a thousand times sweeter than my existence.

We will only accomplish the highest ascension, the supreme illumination, the sweet fruit of awareness, the full embrace with our Beloved, if we die a spiritual death. When we give away from our substance, when we abandon our sensuality, when we sacrifice our goods, and when we cut ourselves from worldly attachments, we will earn eternal riches and receive blessings back a thousand-fold, because we will receive new life. In the spiritual world, there is no sacrifice without receiving eternal life; no death without rebirth; no poverty without richness; no annihilation without resurrection; and no self-extinction without eternity.

When nothingness, the poverty of being, adorns a man, we can observe inexhaustible treasures arising from his source—it is the beauty of the divine light. Unfortunately, people do not realize that giving up the pleasures of this world means winning eternal life. In the words of Jalal al-Din Rumi:

> To experience the day of Resurrection, you have to die first, for "resurrection" means making the dead come back to life. The whole world has taken a wrong way, for they fear non-existence, while it is their refuge.
>
> How should we try to win real awareness? By renouncing all knowing. How should we look for salvation? By giving up our personal salvation. How should we search for real existence? By giving up our existence. How should we search for the fruit of the spirit? By abandoning our hands.
>
> Self-existence brings terrible drunkenness; it removes the intellect from the head and modesty from the heart.

For all these reasons, religion is not just a set of divine rules on which the believer has to orient himself. It is not just a belief system which one tries to acknowledge and memorize. Living religion is a state of being. It involves the whole personality on all its levels—mentally, psychologically, physically and spiritually.

Therefore, the eternal conflict of man does not consist entirely in choosing between good and bad; doing righteousness or abstaining from sinning; what is permissible and what is forbidden; or obedience and disobedience. The work of a true believer lies in the capacity to discriminate the false from the true being.

This is the crucial point: we have to sharpen the faculty of divine perception which will enable us to discriminate the world from the hereafter; infinity from determination; duality from oneness; sacredness from profanity; the spiritual from the material; the body from the soul; multiplicity from unity. And, finally, there is the ultimate discrimination, which is the ability to define the Creator from the creatures. More precisely, it is the ability to define the Greatness of our supreme Creator from the nothingness and impotence of His creatures. We have to investigate with the highest precision the mystery of the relationship of God to man. The more we realize and see with the inner eye of the heart God's supreme Perfection and infinite Beauty, the more we will be able to see our own insufficiency, weaknesses and helplessness.

The secret for the human being is to lose his heart and become senseless, that is to say, to become broken-hearted before the Supreme Divinity. Only a heart filled with divine love will become receptive to the vision of the Creator's Might and Greatness. Such a heart will be in constant awe, bewilderness, and admiration before the Might and all-Compelling Greatness of His Lord. In one of his poetic exclamations, Jalal al-Din Rumi laments:

> *Where is the heart that is not shattered in a hundred pieces by God's love?*

It has to be mentioned that the exalted joy which a believer's heart experiences when it is equipped with divine perception is indescribable! It is the sweet taste of awareness which overpowers all other spiritual satisfactions. Nothing can match the taste of pure illumination!

To finalize, divine awareness generates eternal beauty, and such beauty generates the bliss of a divine taste never known before. The masters of the supreme perception, the owners of heightened consciousness, are the ones which have arrived at their divine root. They have discovered their true self, and at the same time, they have encountered Him, the One and Only. They are possessors of the greatest intelligence because they have found God the Almighty! This is the teaching of the religion of Islam, the religion of truth and unity. It serves humankind to know itself and to know the Lord of all the worlds.

To finalize this essay, spiritual evolution does not mean mere perfection in obedience—it means perfection in love!

PART FOUR

Humanity between Salvation and Destruction

With this essay, I am desperately trying to find a language for the end of times. I put all my efforts in looking for the lost togetherness with our beloved Lord. Someone described the end of times as a war of all against all.

Our great Sheikh Muhyiddin, Ibn Arabi, said concerning the end of times:

> *The entire universe fell asleep when the messenger died. We are passing presently through the last third of the night of the universe.*

Humanity is faced with great tragedies, such as natural catastrophes like floods, earthquakes, the burning of forests, and hurricanes—meaning that organic nature is beginning to lose its balance; we face the war on terror and the centralization of political power—meaning the global directorate of economical and military suppressors; the bombardment of the mass media; the collapse of financial markets; the danger of nuclear war; a rise in mental illness; chaotic disorders of the mind and the world; the rape of nature; destructive technology; unemployment; the mechanization of human life; overpopulation; hunger; an increase of refugees; environmental problems such as the pollution of the air, water, earth, food, and vegetation; epidemic sicknesses; global warming; and so on. We have even gone as far as depleting the ozone layer.

The gap between rich and poor, status and underprivileged, educated and uneducated, military supremacy and minorities, weak and strong, and upper classes and lower classes is dangerously growing. The world sees a disturbed balance between man and nature, spreading into disharmonious relationships between man and woman; father and child; child and mother; sister and brother; relative and relative; neighbor and neighbor; owner and employee;

friend and friend; politician and population; teacher and student; doctor and patient; and so on. The real cause of the disequilibrium is always the disharmony between man and God. Who is not at peace with himself and his fellow beings, cannot be at peace with the One and Only. That is to say, living with ecological crises, family conflicts, psychological sicknesses, political unrest, scientific disputes, business corruption, religious clashes, and so on, will always be a reflection of our inner state.

For example, we threaten nature, and now nature threatens us. With the advanced technology, man manipulates the Earth at his will. He exploits nature and its resources. The so-called progress of the highly industrialized societies heads backwards to our own ruin. Modern technology has created the potential for total destruction. The result is climate change. The damage brought to nature and the cosmos is definitely a mirror of the present inner state of man losing his own substance, the quality of life in himself and in his environment. We can say that the root of all problems always lies deep, because outward problems are always a reflection of the inner disequilibrium of man.

In addition, in our present time, people are witnessing an intense degeneration of moral human values. Modern life has lost its roots! Our roots are the moral human values of goodness, which are the attributes of God Most High. The majority of the world's population is running for the love of things. The god of the modern world is wealth. Material heaviness stops the flow of life. Heavy consumerism hinders any reflection or sublime sensitivity. The only destructive force is materialism. Under the rootless materialism of man, religion suffers tremendous degeneration. In other words, the elimination of religion in our lives is the root of all problems. It is the problem of modern man, who is caught up in his daily business affairs, forgetting about God. He is intoxicated with the world. Materialism is like a virus, a worldwide epidemic spreading throughout the world's arteries. That is to say, materialism is the obstacle between God and ourselves. Material progress necessarily results in a cost of religion.

Unfortunately, the moral strength of the majority of people has decreased to a tragic degree. When true faith has left people's hearts, the foundation of the regulation of life gets shaken. In other words, human existence itself is threatened. Man finds himself in a spiritual crisis. Bediüzzaman Said Nursi once described the growing greed for wealth in modern Turkey with his fabulous critical statement:

> *O miserable pseudo-patriot who fervently encourages Muslims to embrace this world and forcibly drives them to European industry and progress. Beware, do not let the bonds with which certain members of this nation are tied to religion be broken! If, thus foolishly blindly imitating and crushed under foot, their bonds with religion are broken, those irreligious people will become as harmful for the life of society as fatal poison.*

We should direct our attention to eternal love, unconditional love! The unconditional love is what God desires from every human being: loving without any boundaries; loving without any reason; loving without ulterior motives; loving without expecting something in return; and loving without any self-serving benefit.

As we see, modern society is purely oriented by profit thinking, which leads into aggressive actions against nature and mankind. It is called exploitation. On the one side, power-hungry politicians take advantage of underprivileged populations. On the other hand, man exploits the resources of nature and the cosmos. Man effectively rapes nature. Like Seyyid Hossein Nasr comments:

> *Nature has become desacralized for man. Moreover, nature has come to be regarded as something to be used and enjoyed to the fullest extent possible. Rather than being like a married woman from whom a man benefits but also towards whom he is responsible, modern man's nature has become like a prostitute, to be benefited from without any sense of obligation and responsibility towards her.*

Through the misuse of nature, the universe and our human bodies in our present world, humanity experiences staggering consequences. The harmony of creation is disturbed. For many centuries, man conquered nature, ruled over it, and used it with his rootless greed. But Alas! Today, the conquered becomes the conqueror, and the destroyed becomes the destroyer. Today, nature hits back. Today, nature starts ruling people's life. Today, nature makes history, performing the final acts, and having the final saying. The wisdom to be drawn from this inevitable catastrophe is that man has to become aware that all the acts done by him will eventually turn back to him, either in his earthly life or in the hereafter. He will reap the fruits which he planted.

There is an intimate connection between nature and God. Planet Earth, the universe, and our bodies are all divine property. They are entrusted to humankind by the One and Only. They are all governed by the same laws of nature. If we treat our bodies with carelessness, we will have an immediate response. The way we treat our body is the way our body will treat us. Physical and mental illness will befall man if he neglects the divine rules of creation—if he rebels against nature, the cosmos and himself. The result will be moral and physical damage, and environmental destruction.

Today we live in the age of natural catastrophes because we have exploited nature and its resources. Earthquakes, floods, hurricanes are becoming the language of nature threatening humanity. If we wish to find salvation, and if we wish to regain our lost balance, we will first have to give nature the grace of living spirituality; we will have to apply higher awareness, the divine perception, which will reveal the sacredness of all life; and we will have to increase our sensitivity for the divine Presence in all that exists. This means that we will have to contemplate each thing in its universal aspect, in its divine purpose. Only such all-embracing vision can explain existence.

And, furthermore, we should apply this wisdom in our daily lives with respectful and loving behavior towards nature, our fellow beings, and ourselves.

Additionally, modern scientists deal with nature on a purely materialistic, rational, measurable quantitative level. They deal with sheer facts, cut off from any meaning. They refuse to acknowledge the endless hierarchy of existence and refuse to penetrate into the infinite layers of meaning. The main principle is to recognize that knowledge of the universe does not lie exclusively within science, but within metaphysics. Man has to rediscover the spiritual significance of his environment, the cosmos and himself. Modern science has to be seen in a universal perspective. Without any doubt, modern science draws its achieved quantitative knowledge from a far higher, infinitely complex, and richer reality.

We have to flee from the quantitative aspects of life and we have to "take refuge in God" it says in the Qur'an:

None will you find as a refuge other than Him. (18:27)

That is to say, man has to realize, in all matters of his life, to take refuge from the devil the accursed in God the Almighty. The more materialism enters people's hearts, the more life gets desacralized. The result is avoid, the emptiness of the Divine.

For this reason, the worst consequences of the disequilibrium between man and nature is the loss of the relationship between creatures and their Creator. Once people have lost the link with God the Almighty, our supreme Divinity, and once human beings become unaware of the secret of His Presence, we have lost all and everything. It means that man is cut off from its own roots.

This is the tragedy of modern man. The sacredness of human nature can never be neglected. Man can never live separate from God! The human being is divine property. He belongs entirely to His all-Majestic Lord of all the worlds. For this reason, he has to connect himself to the metaphysical reality of creation; he has to give meaning and value to the universe, the world and himself. By the sheer fact that all things are created by God most High, existence becomes, in itself ,the biggest miracle. So all creation necessarily displays its Creator. Nature and man are carrying symbolism, revealing layers over layers of meaning. All existence speaks to man, conveying higher degrees of realities. The cosmos is a living organism stored with the most astonishing hierarchy of knowledge. There is a divine order in all that exists. Amazing wonderworks of nature, which produce, every moment, millions of living entities, phenomena over phenomena, supply all the needs of man. The human being has to confirm to this divine order, and he has to live his life accordingly. Then he will gain harmony with himself and his environment. As it says in the holy Qur'an:

> *The seven heavens and the earth and all that they contain extol His limitless Glory; and there is not a single thing but extols His limitless Glory and Praise. (17:44)*

Moreover, we can observe that the resolution of conflicts on the political, economical, religious, social, humanitarian, ecological, cultural, and scientific fields all turn into business deals. Human life is corrupted. Man becomes an article of trade, simple merchandise. Especially, the competitive world of multinational businesses, a product of the world's globalization, exercises complete control and abuses its power with its false, savage ideologies and increases, therefore, the corruption of human life. Instead of interacting with a creative dialogue to resolve the immensity of problems on all levels, religion makes politics; politics uses economics,; economics uses science; science makes business; business uses religion; and so on. There is nothing more dangerous than using God's sacred knowledge, His resources, His bounties, His gifts, and His favors, in order to gain military or economical supremacy over the whole world.

For example, for entrepreneurs to sell their products, human life becomes a target. Through the spiteful, faulty psychology of their seductive commercials, suggesting fake paradises, man gets brain-washed and experiences a total corruption of his senses. Human life gets bought and sold. One of the sicknesses of our time is that people are not primarily selling their crafts and their merchandise anymore; they sell themselves, their ideologies, their intelligence, and their attractive looks. They play seductive games as clowns in the supermarket circus in order to win large audiences. In religion, business, and politics these kinds of people are very common, selling themselves with their perverted propaganda speeches in order to attract new customers, voters, or community members. Modern societies are hosting these creatures like sand hosts the sea. They are called hypocrites.

Additionally, the world is under the bombardment of the mass-media. Unfortunately, people without the slightest resistance either willingly love to become subjugated by the cheapest, lowest entertainment industry, or to believe blindly the seductive and false advertisement industry. It is like they love to get hurt by cheap palaver, loud noises, and heavy attacks on their senses. In olden times, people hunted animals. Today, it is economical animals which hunt people.

In modern science, atomic physicians are able to manipulate the laws of nature and gain so-called "creative power"; but, in reality, they gain only destructive potential. God forbid, they use chemical weapons on this holy planet earth. The same is true for biology, biotechnology, medicine, and genetic manipulations. These fields go as far as reproducing life, calling it cloning. They artificially produce nutrition and animals. Not much is left until they may think that they are able to recreate human beings. There is nothing more dangerous than playing Creator, acting like the Great Will.

The problem is this: modern science , especially, has reached into the furthest and deepest regions of all existent things, but it is unaware of the reality of its own self. Our great saint, Jalal-al-Din Rumi, comments:

> *The great scholars of the age split hairs in all the sciences. They have gained total knowledge and complete mastery of things that have nothing to do with them. But that which is important and closer to him than anything else, namely his own self, this your great scholar does not know.*
>
> *He knows the properties of every substance, but in explaining his own substance he is like an ass.*

You know the value of every merchandise, but you do not know your own value; this is stupidity.

The virus of modernization has captured the whole world's population, and it was created by the technical and industrial progress of the Western societies. People's lives have become completely mechanized, losing grace and blessings. It means that peoples lives are robbed of their substance, losing meaning and symbolic intelligence. In modern societies, machines are beginning to dominate people's life. They decide what man does and who he is. Man becomes a slave of his own inventions.

Moreover, the old treasures of abundant love have vanished from people's hearts. The split between life and religion is dangerously growing. Modern man has lost the dimensions of inwardness. He suffers from a gradual desacralization of the cosmos, nature and himself. He has lost authenticity, originality, and integrity; in other words, he has lost his own verticality. Once of the greatest losses is the human quality of shame. In media, people expose their privacy to attract wide audiences and to enjoy successful businesses. They sell their most precious intimacy, which is certainly one of the worst sicknesses of modern society. They even engage in prostitution with children. Not much is left until man becomes either a living machine or a horizontal creature, an animal.

Unfortunately, the more material sophistication dominates modern societies, the more barbarian and aggressive man becomes, which is obviously a paradox. Whereas the increase of the material quality of life should necessarily lead to a cultural refinement of society, the human being becomes more "brainless," arrogant, and ignorant.

In the scientific age we live in, we can speak, therefore, of a spiritual crisis. The problem seems to be that the more man loses its own verticality, the more he feels the need to conquer "upwards" into the vast cosmos of our solar system. Through his animalistic greed, the earth is not sufficient anymore. Modern man in the scientific age has lost inwardly what he gained externally; namely, he has lost the inward spiritual ascension of his soul towards the realms of God's nearness, and he gained the external excursion into space with his technically highly sophisticated space shuttles. So, all actions in his life are aimed at catching up by what he is missing. He becomes a compensator.

With his purely materialistic world view, he identifies entirely with the physical reality and compensates for his internal losses with his greed and power-hunger. The more man gets stagnated into the material heaviness of his own life, the more he feels an urge to travel. Especially in our present time, we can observe this restless urge to fly around the world. We have lost the spiritual journey of our soul and the wonderment and admiration towards the infinity of God's divine knowledge. We have lost the hidden treasuries of our hearts and dream, therefore, for the material, fake paradises of this world.

We can observe that one of the worst problems of our modern societies is the distortion of the human mind! Through the vicious mind games of political leaders, the world has become a very dangerous place. The degeneration, deception, conspiracy, falseness, and hypocrisy of the modern mind has reached its peak. Humanity is under the threat of violation, abuse, corruption, exploitation, terror—which are all sicknesses of the mind caused by the sickness of the heart. Unfortunately, the possessors of such minds are the rulers of this world. This is true not just on the political, but on the economical, social, scientific level as well. We can define these kinds of people as "man-eaters," or "economical animals." Today, mentally disturbed, sick people have become leaders in politics, business, economics, and religion. It seems the more neurotic and pathological they are, the more they are likely to win—the more corrupted they act, the better are their chances of winning.

It is the collapse of human values that has brought the rise of mental illness which, especially today, leads to the use of deadly drugs. And such entirely morally bankrupt people symbolize nothing else than the deepest degeneration of our present societies.

On the political level, the distortion of the mind has reached such levels that, in the name of God most High, people kill innocent others with terror acts; or, in the name of God most High, they invade and destroy whole countries, asking our Creator to bless their terrifying actions, portraying, therefore, an image of righteousness and justice. Their filthy mind-games are manipulating the "Divine."

Self-fabricated ideology destroys the sacredness of all life, as man lives disconnected from God, and as he creates his own false 'absolute.' Especially in the Western world, new spiritual orders, occult sciences, and psychic circles are ruthlessly flourishing. We can call it pseudo-spiritualism. These externalized, disproportionate, selfish fabrications of the Divine bring humanity much more harm then materialism. The ego of man dictates a new world order which serves its own purposes. Man goes as far as playing God and brain-washing people to believe in him. As we are able to see, our time gathers plenty of such filthy mind-game leaders.

In the face of all dark events that we witness today, a feeling of helplessness is spreading world-wide. An earthquake of material and spiritual nature has shaken humanity to extremes. We are smitten with heavy destructive forces all over the planet. We live in a spiritual desert. We live in a time where corruption, abuse, falseness, distortion, injustice, perversion, exploitation, and aggression reached their peak. The world is bleeding. God has taken away the values of security, health, trust, order, comfort, and peace within ourselves. There is something like a threat of total war. Someone described the end of times as a war of all against all.

Today the whole world experiences a mourning. The mourning is of a universal nature. There is a crying need which is growing to global dimensions. The crisis has hit all the countries of the world with the same force. A globalization of problems has arrived. The time has arrived where the eastern reality meets the western reality. East and west have become inseparable. The world has turned into a global village, meaning that the distance between nations has vanished.

Moreover, the world's population is growing forcefully closer together due to modern transportation, such as airplanes, which has created mobility for everyone to be everywhere. A global communication such as digital electronic technology, computers, the Internet, and mass-media, such as satellite television, has created access to information for everyone at anytime. Therefore, the world's population is experiencing a rapidly growing consciousness due to the global communication system.

The planet has effectively turned into a library in which knowledge, information, science, education is available for anyone at any time. The worldly stage has turned into a movie-theater in which we are able to follow and watch all events anytime as they happen. At the same time, we can encounter all the diversity of beliefs, cultures and rites; we can participate in their spirituality and gain any sacred knowledge. For these reasons, the human being is able to enjoy the achievements of modernity from the West, as well as the achievements of ancient treasures of the East. It means, for the individual, that globalization opens up infinite opportunities to unify with the rest of the world's population at any time, in any region, in any way. Man should see himself as an inhabitant of the world, living in a global conscience, enjoying a multi-cultural education.

This is exactly Islamic consciousness is—seeing humanity as one community, one body, one brotherhood. This is the universal perception of a true believer in God most High. With this mentality, globalization becomes purely positive. It brings food to the poor, offers health care to the sick, and sends help to the politically suppressed. That is to say, a true believing servant participates in the suffering of his fellow brothers and sisters because he is part of this one body. He runs in every corner of this world in order to help!

But unfortunately, the fact that the world's population is able to face and witness each other, makes us aware of the enormous gap which divide people from people, nations from nations, and races from races—namely black from white, underprivileged from privileged, rich from poor, educated from uneducated, healthy from sick, war from peace, and so on. Geographical closeness makes us aware of the huge distance, the seemingly insurmountable gap, which divides us from each other. In other words, we can observe a crying injustice all over the world.

Additionally today's globalization reveals an unfortunate paradox. The world is suffering from a globalization doctrine, which is purely materially profit-oriented, because globalization is a super-product of Western civilization through advanced technical and industrial progress. The world has turned into a marketplace instead of a place where we can reach spiritual fulfillment by representing our compassionate Creator who embraces all things.

As we see, eastern reality and western reality are meeting each other today, unfortunately through terror, natural catastrophes and the greatest corruption of human life. It is not just the awareness of the higher knowledge that unifies the whole of humanity and makes east and west face each other; it is the latest negative events of human history that makes the world into a global village.

The mind-games of the political and economical rulers have reached the peak of distortion. The mastermind of total deception creates ideologies to maintain a globalization which secures worldwide control and economic domination of financial markets. Distortion becomes an ideological weapon for globalization.

This is the irony of our time: the United States presents itself as a model of justice in its fight against terrorism. But, in reality, it terrorizes the whole world and threatens to attack any other nation who does not support their corrupt ideology and their false fight against terrorism. Their policy is this: if you are not with us, then you are against us.

Said Nursi documents this very accurately:

Tyranny has donned the hat of justice; treachery has clothed itself in the garment of patriotism; jihad has been given the name of rebellion; captivity has been called freedom. Opposites have changed forms!

Especially today, we can observe that power hunger is called "liberal democracy," and terrorism is called "fundamental justice"; or global fundamentalism is called "free-trade multi-national business," and so on. There is a famous and very reliable hadith which reports:

At the end of time, justice will be in the place of injustice, and injustice will be in the place of justice.

Due to these corrupt policies, all decisions are made behind closed doors to secure the unrestricted use of worldwide corrupted business trade practices. With such secret policies, very little remains of any humanitarian or social services. And even under the name of charitable organizations, there is exploitation of populations.

Now, America has apparently found its desired identity and is trying to become a universal Empire through the globalization process. It can finally exercise supreme and unrestricted authority on a worldwide level in military, technical, economical and political terms—a global dictatorship of multi-national business trade. American global policies are served by uncivilized, brutal, dehumanizing, and barbarous strategies. It is the insanity of our age. I like to call it global fundamentalism. They are the strong against the weak, the rich against the poor, the owners against the suppressed. The eternal problem of this world has became the number one problem! The criminal actions against humanity are the exploitation of the powerful against the helpless!

Within our global age of political, economical and military corruption, the religion of Islam has become a target! In the subconsciousness of the powerhungry global invaders, the infinity of the eternal light of Islam has become their most hated object. The ultimate power of the universal religion has become unbreakable resistance. Opponents resent the unsurmountability and superiority of

Islam and, therefore, act as invaders to gain supreme victory. For though they seem to be driven by their addiction to petroleum, their soul is envious of the glory and grace of the perfected religion.

Did not the devil talk in the front of God's light, portraying an image of false righteousness and justice, because he felt he was the greater than anything his Lord had created? It was envy that distorted his heart, and he disobeyed; and it is the envy of the global invaders that distorts their minds and hearts, so they threaten the religion of Islam. On the surface, they seem to be the supreme authorities who have gained victory over the whole planet; but in reality, they are crushed by the divine light of truth. It is for this reason that we have to apply the light of unity of God's religion against the torments of our global age.

Since September 11th, humanity has found itself between destruction and salvation. The manifestation of the absolute evil has reached its highest level. There is nothing left but darkness and light! The darkness of complete ignorance meets the purity of belief. The peak of evil meets the highest illumination. The destructive potential meets the illuminated power of belief. The devil is face-to-face with God. Through events in human history, God has brought the far distant opposites together. God has shaped us up for holy experiences, in order to become ready for higher awareness. For this reason, man finds himself between truth and falsehood. He has to decide to which side he belongs.

Since the 11th of September, 2001, Our Creator has been waking up every single human being on this planet so that we might learn to see. God makes us live the effects of distorted jihad because we do not live His given, desired, divine internal struggle. God gives universal suffering because we do not live His all embracing universal religion. God confronts us with death, the highest number of losses of human life and material bankruptcy, taking away all property, belongings, and health, because we do not apply and undergo the experience—'die before you die'—our beloved Prophet Muhammad's advice to humankind. Human history repeatedly shows us that humanity does not change, until it is forced to do so.

God's language has such an intense, shattering impact on humankind that there is a divine Presence arising within our lives. It means that God is teaching His closeness to us! I can tell you like never before—I can smell the sweet scent of lovehood within our present time. This very century we live in is talking to us. It shows that we are not living how God meant us to be. Every pain, every suffering, is caused by the separation from God. Jalal al-Din Rumi comments:

> *The cruelty of time and of every suffering that exists is easier than distance from God and heedlessness. For that cruelty will pass, but distance from Him will not. No one possesses good fortune but he who takes to Him an aware spirit.*

Especially today, humanity has a great need for answers of an eternal nature, such as what is the purpose of human life on this earth? Why has man to undergo such suffering? Where does man come from before birth, and where does man go to after death? Before we can solve any problem, we have to think about who we are. We have to know our significance on this planet. Why are we here? Man's forgetfulness has caused the greatest problems, which is nothing else than his ignorance and refusal to see how things really are.

Humanity is in urgent need for the truth because we are dangerously far away from it. Now it is time for an interactive dialogue. Humanity is in need of global solutions and eternal values. We urgently have to create a fruitful dialogue between East and West. We are in need of eternal values and, therefore, the solution has to be universal. It means that it is time for the universal religion, the universality of the truth, to know God's pure religion. There is only one religion, the religion of absolute truth. We have to realize that God is the solution for all and everything.

Let us leave this black and white thinking. Let us leave the circle of permissible and forbidden, *halal-haram*. Let us finish this running after good deeds. Let us leave this first-class school thinking. Let us leave superficial worship. Let us leave these bargain supplications. Let us shatter our willful religious thinking; our spiritual pretence; our manipulated divine aspirations; our vicious mind games; our blurred, contaminated worship; our divine illusions; and our false religious appetites. Our beloved Prophet Muhammad, upon him be peace and blessings, used to pray:

I cannot count Your blessings.

Let us stop counting; let us stop wasting our lives away; let us stop rejecting our own selves; let us stop our fantasies; let us stop our shamelessness; let us stop our disgracefulness; let us stop living like ignorant thieves; and let us stop the dominance of our lower senses.

The problem is this; if we do not live as true believers, we do live like thieves. With every breath, we take away the things given by God most High. When we violate the rights of other people, using them like slaves, we become like thieves. When we lose time, the most valuable gift God gave us, we become like thieves. When we exploit nature without any sense of responsibility or respect, we become like thieves. Additionally, if our worship, our actions, are not oriented towards the eternal direction, the absolute *"sirat-al-mustaqim,"* the straight path—that is, the perfection and beauty of our glorious Creator. And if our worship contains the smallest deviation from the path, we fall into the danger of idol-worshipping. That is to say, ulterior motives within all our doings as believing servants creates hypocrisy, and hypocrisy creates idol-worshipping.

Let us not become body-worshippers! Let us not inherit the vision from the devil, or see things in his perspective! We are so happy with contaminated water, whereas we are given to drink from the purest source, the speech of saints! Like our great saint, Jalal al-Din Rumi, says, people call the veils of the heart, the heart. The majority of people are deeply caught up in their own narrowness of mind and heart. They live in the prison of their own existence. Let us clean ourselves from false perceptions. Let us direct ourselves to eternity, to the glorifying unity, to the supreme beauty and perfection of our beloved Lord of all the worlds. Mevlana Jalal al-Din Rumi nourishes us with supreme pearls of wisdom:

> *Know that the World of Unity lies in the other direction from the senses. If you want Oneness, go in that direction.*
>
> *The spirit of all the sciences is only this: to know who you will be on the day of Resurrection.*
>
> *The wisdom of the world increases opinion and doubt; the wisdom of religion soars beyond the heavens.*
>
> *When knowledge is revealed to the heart, it becomes an aid; but knowledge by the body is a heavy load.*

And in a well-known hadith Prophet Muhammad, upon him be peace and blessings, said:

> *Whoever is humble, God raises him up; whoever is arrogant, God will bring him down low.*

The human being cannot live without guidance, without spiritual nourishment, without healing, without education. Only the religion can give the human being what it needs. Without religion, the human being is lost in the jungle in this world. We have to realize that God is the solution for all and everything.

Today, most of all, man is lacking the awareness of the divine reality within himself. Modern man is ignorant of his true self; he is uninformed of the treasures within his breast; he is deaf and blind of his divine origin. This means he is unaware of his total dependence towards his Supreme Creator, the Lord of all the Worlds. It is the unawareness of the divine Presence and the lack of divine thirst that is the root of all problems. Man is a stranger to himself. A wise man said:

> *You are the cloud veiling your own sun.*

And Prophet Muhammad, upon him be peace and blessings, said:

Man is the enemy of what he does not know.

Man is an immortal being. Human life is purely an inner matter. We are created for eternity, because our soul belongs to God. That is to say, we are created dependent; we are a creature of total need; so, therefore, we are in need of intimacy. Acting independent in this world means human irresponsibility.

Modern man has to wake up from his unconsciousness and encounter the divine reality of his being. Man represents the hidden treasure in its totality. The whole wisdom of the religion of Islam is based on *"Ikra!"*—"Read!" (96:1)—the first revealed word of God most High to His beloved Prophet Muhammad, upon him be peace and blessings. There was no book, Our beloved master was unlettered. Yet our Creator wished to teach His creatures to read for themselves, to read human existence, to learn to know themselves, and to learn about their value and meaning. It is an undisputable fact that it is for no other reason that we are brought into this world but to gain knowledge—knowledge of ourselves, the universe and God the Almighty.

The greatest knowledge is the knowledge of your own selves, because the heart of man is the macrocosm. Self-knowledge means to penetrate through the layers of our being until we reach the light of our own soul. And then all the doors to our divine Majesty will open and we will look at His light with the light coming from it. Knowing ourselves will enable us to know and see His Face, our Lord of Majesty and Bounty.

What do the current events on the worldly stage tell us? Why are all this great disasters happening on the ecological, political and sociological level? Humanity is experiencing such heavy lessons, such threats, and such suffering. So much blood is running, and so many tears are being shed.

Primarily, we have abused our trusteeship with God. We have abused nature. We have abused human relationships. We have abused the divine order of the cosmos. We live in a humanitarian crisis. A global malaise has spread through the worlds arteries. Secondly, it is through experiencing the hardships and trials in this world that we will become needy for the truth and wake up from our sleep of ignorance.

The constantly occurring disasters in our present age of the world's history demonstrate that human beings are being stripped of all worldly traits. They become poor before God the Almighty; they become naked in front of His eyes. When we have lost everything—when God takes away all of our property, possessions, status, fame, and even our health, friends and family, then we will experience true poverty. This state is the most elevated state of our Prophet Muhammad, upon him be peace and blessings, who said:

> *My state is utter need and my poverty is my pride.*

If man offers himself completely towards our All-Merciful Lord in sincere need and poverty, He answers with His endless grace. God most High will reward His beloved servant with the beneficence of His beautiful attributes.

The truth is that man has nothing to cover his nakedness other than the beautiful attributes—the divine names of God. That is to say, man's only clothing is the robe of sainthood. This is God's divine policy; that is to say, He rewards loss with gain; poverty with richness; helplessness with help; brokenness with wholeness; impotence with strength; and nothingness with true faith. This is the wisdom of our time. God most Merciful is teaching His Closeness to us!

To become poor before God means to die before dying. The present disasters are not His punishment; they are His gift to humanity. To lose in the eyes of God means being honored to wear the robe of sainthood. This is why we have to realize that our loss is our gain. In other words, humanity is able to wake up to a higher consciousness, true wisdom, and gain the luminous fruit of awareness. Our great saint, Mevlana Rumi, comments:

> *No origin resembles its effect, so you do not know the root of pain and torment.*

> *But this retribution is not without an origin. How should God inflict pain on an innocent person?*
>
> *Though a thing's origin and producer do not resemble it, they still give rise to it.*

The events on the worldly stage show us that our present state in history is not about accumulating knowledge; perfecting ourselves in all the modern sciences; the highest sophistication of the human mind; the brilliance of academic speeches; demonstrating perfect professionalism; pretending to have magical super powers; polishing high profile media images; or proclaiming supreme and absolute knowledge in every field, over every man. Mevlana Rumi comments about the danger of learned men:

> *Enough—for knowledge is a veil upon knowledge.*
> *If you knew that you were the king,*
> *Why would you remain the interpreter?*

In our time, man has to decrease the piled up internal libraries, detach his inner self from stored academic knowledge and start to empty out quantitative knowledge to replace it with qualitative eternal knowledge. All knowledge comes from God the Almighty. Modern man acting as the owner of all achieved knowledge represents one of the worst sicknesses of the heart. Man has to step down from his authoritarian position and process whatever he has learned in his past life. He has to wake up from his sleep of ignorance and regret that he spends his life in sleep. Today, the teaching from the pulpit is coming gradually to an end.

We can observe that the present century is experiencing a material bankruptcy. The forgetfulness of modern man has caused the greatest problems. The whole of the world's population is facing aggressive threats from the environment they live in. So many people are losing all and everything they possess and, additionally, they are experiencing the greatest losses of human lives. The more the modern world grows into wealth and luxury, the more we can see a counter-movement of material bankruptcy.

Wealth creates superficiality. Humanity has lost the dimension of inwardness—that is to say, we have lost the meaning and value of human life, which means nothing else than creatures losing the connection with their Creator. But as we see, history has started the process of purification. We live in the end of times. Now, we are being taught by the events on the worldly stage. Humanity is experiencing a spiritual earthquake. Great lessons are to be drawn from the ongoing affairs of this present world. It is as if the time speaks to mankind. Man has little to say in the face of the tragedies he witnesses. They speak for themselves. Our great Sheikh, Muhyiddin Ibn Arabi, said, concerning the end of times:

> *The entire universe fell asleep when the messenger died. We are passing presently through the last third of the night of the universe.*

Additionally, we can observe that God most High has taken away the majority of His illuminated saints. He has emptied out the world of the light of unity of His lovers and friends. It is as if human beings are left on their own, facing each other. Moreover, through the process of globalization, people have started to face each other on a worldwide scale as well. East meets West, and vice-versa. In the 21th century, we are brought close through the events of human history and what we discover is the most tragic fact: we are dangerously distant to each other. Separation among human beings is like a virus, a disease, spreading from man to his family, neighbours, working colleagues, friends and communities, to his city and his country. We can never put enough value or take enough care for inner peace, especially in the world today, where human life on all levels is very fragmented. The separation of hearts is the real catastrophe of our present time! Therefore, we can see that the globalization of our planet earth has became a major lesson for all of mankind.

That is why today, the events on the worldly stage, on the political, social, economical, scientific, business, military, and ecological levels, are gaining spiritual significance. The seemingly political and ecological crises are, in reality, the spiritual crises of humanity. Human life has become a divine affair, which it has been, in fact, from all eternity—but, in the present century, we are being reminded of our divine origin more frequently and with increased intensity.

This is the orchestration of God's affairs. This is His teaching, and His examination. The present world is experiencing an increase of suffering, turmoil, disaster, and devastation, with which our Creator wants to train His creatures for mercy, compassion and love. It is God's message to humankind.

The greatest teacher of our time is pain. Only pain can transform and wound our nature. On the one hand, God is teaching lessons to humanity which are mixed with the salt of pain; and, on the other hand, we can observe an increase of His endless mercy and blessings spreading throughout the whole world. Human suffering is only given because we forget the One and Only! Jalal al-Din Rumi gives us excellent description about the necessity of human suffering:

> Look not at time's events,
> Which come from the spheres and make life so disagreeable!
> Look not at this dearth of daily bread and mean of livelihood!
> Look not at this famine and fear and trembling!
> Look at this—in spite of all the world's bitterness,
> you are passionately and shamelessly attached to it.
> Know that bitter tribulation is a Mercy!

In consequence, through the gradual process of human history, we will arrive at a time of higher awareness and heightened sensitivities. And we will live in a time of transformation on a global scale, burning and washing away our impurities with our losses, tears and blood.

Things are relatively easy. Man has to turn away from the false appetites for this world, the false occupations which do not concern him, and the bad habits which pull him down towards to animalistic sensuality. He has to direct himself towards the divine realms of everlastingness. This means that man has to knock on the heart's door and achieve, as God wills, spiritual enlightening. In this way, he will be able to acquire divine wisdom, '*marifa*,' the illuminated power of belief.

The highest form of life is belief! Today, it is time for the celebration of believer-hood, because the believer knows with certainty. The sweet taste of awareness is given to the ones who are able to see that they cannot see. These are the ones who have been woken up from the sleep of unconsciousness and have been equipped with God's greatest gift to humanity—namely faith, true belief. And the organ with which one increases the sight of the hereafter is the eye of the heart. This eye has been opened through the divine efforts of a believer continuously knocking on the door of hunger—meaning true need. There is nothing more valuable for a human being than to wake up towards higher consciousness, to the eternal realms of His Nearness, as Jalal al-Din Rumi teaches in the following supreme wisdom:

> *The inhabitants of hell are happier in hell than they were in this world, since they are aware of God, but in the world they were not. And nothing is sweeter than the awareness of God. So the reason they wish to return to the world is to perform works in order to become aware of the locus of manifestation for God's Gentleness. It is not that the world is a happier place than hell.*

True religion is to see God most High! The highest vision is to see God, and this most exalted consciousness demands closeness to God. Closeness to God is only reached when we increase our human tears, our sweat, and our trembling, which will soften our hearts. That is to say, in order to arrive at the station of purity and illumination, we have to process all of our knowledge until it becomes a reality in our being. Religion is not only a belief system. It is a state of being. The believer travels from state to state, backwards to his roots, his original home, the home of absolute contentment and peace. That is where the truth of Muhammad, upon him be peace and blessings, is gathered.

This is the teaching for our modern societies. On the one hand, we will wake up and learn to see; on the other hand, we will gain our lost treasury of intimacy— the intimacy with each other and the intimacy with the highest of priceless jewels, Muhammad Mustafa, upon him be peace and blessings, and finally, the intimacy with our most beloved Lord of all the worlds.

To conclude, the learned man, the scholar, is called an *Alim*. The enlightened man, the saint, is called an *Arif*. The enlightened man sees with the light of God, because he has washed away all his impurities. The cleaned, spotless mirror of his heart reflects the secrets of the divine light. *Inshallah,* as God wills, we will gain the visionary strength of the heart and regain a purified look where God Himself becomes the eyes with which we see.

We should learn from the lessons God is teaching us and try to break the circle of human suffering. This possibility is inherent in man. We can deliver ourselves from the suffering of existence, meaning the cage of our bodies. With the perfection of the religion, our beloved master, the Prophet Muhammad, upon him be peace and blessings, gave us a secret prescription for eternal happiness in this world and the next:

Die before you die.

Before we accumulate further increases of human suffering and increases of material bankruptcy by God most High, we should take the splendid advice of our beloved of hearts and put it into practice. Like never before in history, it is more urgent to realize that we are all children of Almighty God; we all are descendants of Adam, upon him be peace; and we are brother and sisters of the hereafter.

Islam teaches that the whole of humanity, the world's population, has to be like one body. We have to see ourselves as one community inhabiting the whole world. This is universal consciousness. A true believer feels one with all creatures. He has to cultivate brotherhood, being available for needy people at anytime. He lives in universal dimensions; he has to take on a global role. He feels at home anytime, anywhere, because he knows God most High is everywhere, being infinitely aware of His Presence. He looks up in order to learn from people who know more, and he looks down in order to help people who possess less.

Islam teaches that if you help one human being to realize the truth, you help the whole of humanity. And if you murder one human being, it is as if you murdered the whole of humanity. If we do not feel the injustice done to people living in another part of the world, we do not belong to the one body of humankind. A true believer cannot go to sleep easily when he knows his neighbor is hungry. Islam teaches the highest sensitivity for everyone. It teaches the art of giving. It teaches the art of living for others. It teaches the highest ethics, total self-sacrifice, the treasury of pure modesty. The law of the religion forbids the deliberate crushing of an ant or causing it pain or pulling out flowers, plants, trees, giving the highest value and respect towards all of creation, because they are God's bounties and favors to humanity.

In a divine tradition, Abu Darda reported the Prophet, upon him be peace and blessings, as saying:

> *Seek me among your weak ones, for you are given provision, or are given help, only by reason of the presence of your weak ones.*

And Abu Huraira reported God's Messenger, upon him be peace and blessings, as saying:

> *When one of you looks at someone who is superior to him in property and appearance, he should look at someone who is inferior to him.*

The highest ethics, namely the treasury of pure modesty, is the inner wealth of the religion. It is through the beauty and goodness of our characters that we become real representives of God most High on this earth, culminating in the highest station, servanthood, 'ubudiyya.'

Islam has produced such countless luminous fruits, such a treasury of beings, with infinite and heroic generosity. Islam makes sultans into slaves; wealthy people into servants; ignorant, vulgar people into saints; and murderers into believers. Beggars gain dignity, slaves gain honor, and poor people gain respect.

The miracle of creation culminates in in the noble character of the Prophet Muhammad, upon him be peace and blessings. The sincere followers of our beloved master were the most extraordinary people. Nowhere in history have such magnifying and beautiful personalities appeared on the worldly stage. There was power and generosity in a single person; leadership and modesty; high intelligence and submission; ownership and mercy; wealth and humility. These miraculous character features are nothing else than the true inheritance of the noble character of Muhammad.

This is what our modern world is missing—the luminous brightness of the light of unity which shines on the world from the deepest regions of a man's heart! May God most High allow us, within our earthly existence, to drink just a few drops of the light of Muhammad, upon him be peace and blessings! It will change everything. We will never ever return to what we were before, after tasting the sweetest of all drinks. The heights of the religion of Islam reflects itself in the most valuable statement of the Emperor of the world in his time, Yavuz Sultan Selim Khan:

> *Becoming the king of this world is but a useless struggle.*
> *Being the slave of a saint is superior to all else.*

A ruler who is the slave of a saint becomes automatically the slave of his people. In other words, the true master of a people is their servant.

Religion is a matter for the heart. It teaches heart knowledge. The whole work is a practice of love. The religion of Islam is the religion of moderation, balance, submission, harmony, equality, and justice. Especially, the Prophet Muhammad, upon him be peace and blessings, always taught the middle way, aiming for inner harmony. Islam rejects excessive asceticism, fundamentalism, and conjectural speculations, in order to secure a perfect balance between the material and the spiritual, between this world and the next.

Through the current events on the worldly stage, religion has lately become a great issue. Especially, the religion of Islam is in the spotlight. When religious authorities meet religious authorities from the same or different religions, we can observe that opinion meets opinion; or philosophy meets philosophy; or ideology meets ideology; or argument meets argument; or theory meets theory. In the worst case, distortion meets distortion. When theologians and academic professionals meet, it can become confrontational; it can lead into a war of words.

Yet arguments and disputes are signs of selfishness, arrogance, envy and ambition. Instead of mutual sharing, people separate people from each other. I believe strongly that in our present time, we have to rip off status, professional clothes, official representatives, and academic status, in order to arrive in a place of mutual, respectful dialogue, to have an effective and beneficial conversation. The believer has to talk to the believer. The human being has to talk to the human being. Man has to address his most primary needs, which are the common good for all. Man has to find a universal language which will create a true love-talk. In other words, need has to meet need. To finalise these elaborations, we can mention this excusite piece of wisdom from our great saint, Mevlana Jalal al-Din Rumi:

Your noise is my silence.

There is a basic principle especially in the religion of Islam: there is only remembrance. All knowledge comes from God. Therefore, God's eternal knowledge of the holy Qur'an is timeless. Its embodied values are absolute. The roots of the divine revelations are from eternity. The source of knowledge does not need words. The eternal wisdom of our supreme Divinity does not need proof.

The holy Qur'an teaches mankind:

*Do not fall into dispute lest you lose heart and your power depart.
(4:174)*

So strive as in a race in all virtues. (5:48)

Help one another in righteousness and piety. (5:2)

Said Nursi gives us great insight about the idea of moderation in Islamic thought:

> *Too much or too little of anything is not good. Moderation is the middle way. O Sunnis, who are people of truth, and Alawis, whose way is love of the Prophet's family! Quickly put an end to this meaningless, disloyal, unjust and harmful dispute between you.... Since you are believers in divine unity, it is essential to leave aside unimportant matters which necessitate division while there are a hundred fundamental sacred bonds between you which command brotherhood and unity.*

How extremely valuable is his statement in our time! And he further comments:

> *Since the noble Prophet Muhammad [upon him be peace and blessings] was created with a most moderate character and in the most perfect form, his actions all proceeded from moderation and equanimity. In all his practices, daily conduct and the injunctions of his Sharia, he chose the way of moderation and avoided excess and negligence.*

In order to live our earthly life in harmony, our beloved master never ceased to advise his community not to allow discrimination between poor and rich; the judge and the servant; the academic and the peasant; husband and wife; man and woman; Arab and European; and so on. All human beings are equal because they are from one God, which makes them brothers and sisters of the hereafter. We have to see ourselves as one living organism. All our worship and voluntary good acts, done for God's sake, bring human beings together, like little streams of water which eventually flow into the great ocean of infinite Oneness!

Mutual sharing of true wisdom for God's sake will culminate in the reality of the statement:

> *The faithful believer is the mirror of the faithful believer.*

Man will experience total bliss in seeing the light of divine secrets shining at him from the pure surface of the mirror of the heart. There is nothing more comforting than to listen to people who speak from their hearts, because they make you feel the underlying unity of all human beings. They speak out your own heart's wishes. The source of their words is the place of pure love. There is nothing more beautiful than sharing love between human beings!

God created and brought us into this world so that we might love each other, serve each other, and help each other. We know from a tradition of our blessed master that there is a condition involved if we wish to be accepted in paradise. Only believers will have the permission to enter. Additionally, there is a highly important condition we have to satisfy in order to become believer. We have to love one another for God's sake, in order to reach the state of a believer; that is to say, we fulfill the conditions of true belief only if we love humankind. And as we are in need of breathing, we are in need of God.

THE CELEBRATION OF THE TRUTH
IN THE TWENTY-FIRST CENTURY

And they left a very powerful seed!
I was always attracted to the religion of Islam through its beauty and its universality and its all-embracing love!

When love and knowledge unite, the religion becomes a celebration. To know God is the greatest celebration! That is why religion is pure joy!

Jalal al-Din Rumi says:

> The intellect does not know and is bewildered by the religion of love,
> even if it should be aware of all religions.

The biggest miracle is the miracle of creation. Due to the present standard of modern science, we are able to perceive the whole of creation as a scientific miracle. Today, scientific researchers explain nature mathematically and, therefore, humankind is witnessing the enfolding of inexhaustible teachings of the truth.

In the present moment in history, we can observe unusual encounters. Primarily, the modern knowledge of scientific research meets with the divine, ancient knowledge of the religion: the Western heritage of analyses bridges the Eastern heritage of illumination. Secondarily, globalization encounters universality: the global age of our century meets with the universal religion of Islam. That is to say, there is an encounter between East and West, religion and science, universality and globalization.

As far as modern science is concerned, we can observe that the modern mind has reached the borders of human perception. Modern science is encountering a certain substance matter, which is unweighable, immeasurable, uncountable, unperceivable, and seemingly timeless and spaceless. In other words, scientific research has entered into stages where experiments become improvable and, therefore, unknowable. Researchers are faced with the incomprehensible. It is the reality of infinity. There is no end to the furthest reaches of outer space, the mysteries of the universe; and there is no end to the furthest reaches of inner space, quantum and atom physics. Scientific experiments show that nature reveals a highly dynamic interplay of subatomic particles.

Especially, quantum physics has advanced into the deepest realms of matter and begun to realize the interconnectedness of all existence on the one side, and the highly dynamic character of the universe on the other side. In other words, this field has begun to realize the oneness of the universe. The field of atomic physics provided the first glimpses of the essential nature of things; that is to say, it started to discover the spiritual reality of the universe. Now modern science is moving towards the origin of existence. This is the daily bread of the lovers and wise men. Eternal life reveals itself from the source. The mystics contemplate the hidden treasures of divine beauty hidden in the depths of their beings. When they arrive at the roots of their being, they find illumination—what was veiled from their eyes becomes manifest, and what was hidden becomes apparent.

From whatever perspective modern scientists are looking, perfectly working organizations of the inner and outer reality of the universe, the micro-cosmos and the macro-cosmos, are increasingly becoming manifest. They observe laws of the greatest regularity; the harmonious interplay of millions of perfectly organized living entities; and the most complicated and astonishing processes of cause and effect related to living particles. The perfection is of such immense incomprehensibility that it transcends ordinary awareness. It is as if the ground of modern science has started moving. For the more science advances, the more subjects become unknown!

And this is where the modern mind meets with the consciousness of the pure states of the mystics. The higher awareness of the religion meets in a harmonious manner with the new discoveries of modern scientist. They complement each other in the perception of the true nature of things. Mystical and scientific worldviews are discovering similar results. The scientific mind has arrived at the source of existence and complies with religion in contemplating the eternal rules, the laws of perfect order that shape the universe.

Today we see an encounter of the West and the East, as modern science encounters religion, and religion, in turn, reveals scientific knowledge. Through breakthroughs in science, evidence for belief is given; the process of human history unifies rational science with divine wisdom. We can even say that modernity meets eternity!

So the truth of God's Revelations gets confirmed by the modern mind. The unseen gets confirmed by rational proof. Logic looks at transcendence. The material meets the spiritual; the external meets the internal; and the body meets the soul. The two opposites come together. History brings union, and history closes the circle—because we can observe that the universe, on the one hand, can be tested mathematically; and, on the other hand, religion can be scientifically explained.

The eternal argument between East and West—namely reason and faith, the profane and sacred, the seen and unseen, the physical and metaphysical, the quantitative and qualitative, ratio and belief, world and eternity, and the transitory and infinity—has diminished. Summing up, the conflict between science and religion is able to come to an end. This is the beauty of our century.

The idea of the West and East facing each other means that we need to recognize that West and East complement each other; that is to say, the East and West have arrived at the point where they need and, depend on, each other. So West and East can get to know each other and profit from each other and be, therefore, useful to each other.

Especially, in our present time, it is obvious that the West is lacking eastern qualities, and the East is lacking western qualities—on the material as well as on the spiritual level. For example, the West desperately needs to give sense to its scientific achievements. And even more so, it needs desperately give sense to its own life.

The staggering void of spirituality for many centuries has left people in the greatest desperation. They are suffocating in grave materialism. Western societies have the greatest rates of suicide and consumption of narcotics. The void left by de-throning God can never remain empty!

Conversely, the East especially needs, on an official level, to increase reflection, analyses, and psychology, in order to structure and organize the people's social lives and working lives. The sectors of education, health and social services, politics, science, economics need reorganization and reconstruction. Moreover, on an internal level, the capacity of the mind has to be used more extensively as well, in order to fully live the capacities of one's heart. The complexity of the soul is such that it needs the highest intelligence. The majority of Eastern people unfortunately take their spiritual treasuries for granted.

Western civilization is able to offer the highest specialization and sophistication in every field and, therefore, to possess the highest standard of industrial and technical achievements. The modern mind studies the human being through philosophy, psychology, biology, astronomy, medicine, anthropology, psychoanalyses, and sociology. In other words, the present standard of science can help to enlarge insights about the reality of man.

In turn, Eastern civilization can offer mystical contemplation, the power of unification, the light of belief, and the beauty of surrender and, therefore, bringsout the most magnified jewels of beings—uncountable saints of the highest grade. The truth of the religion offers the deepest way of thinking, the highest illumination of the mind and soul. Religion recognizes the fact that all knowledge comes from God. Religion offers the true vision of how things really are. Religion is the science of the root of existence. Religion is heart knowledge. Religion gives the strength to face the problems of the modern world. Religion explains the purpose and meaning of the human being on all levels. Religion gives the ability to see behind form and descend into the realms of meaning. Religion offers all-embracing love with the principles of unity. Religion is to see the unseen, to hear the unheard, and to know the unknown.

Due to these reflections, we should recognize that mystical intuition, belief, contemplation, and submission should mach with scientific analysis, systematic precision, experimentation, and research—and vice-versa. It is not just the scientist who should become a believer in front of the amazing complexity of his discoveries; it is of utmost necessity for the religious person to become a researcher of the complexity of his soul. A scientist might or might not become religious in the face of his amazing discoveries, but a believer's duty is to become a seeker of God's infinite realms of knowledge and perfection and beauty. He has to study the infinite realities of the universe and the world and he has to research the complexity of his own soul. As the modern scientist researches the immense fastness of the macro-cosmos, the universe, and the immense smallness of the micro-cosmos, the sub-atomic particles, so the believer has to contemplate the micro-cosmos of his heart, and he has to contemplate the macro-cosmos of the universe. If the believer approaches the divine center of his indestructible secret, he will see that, in reality, his heart is the macro-cosmos and the universe is the micro-cosmos, because the human being is created in the concept of the perfect man.

Today, modern experts of time management in the West have recognized and acknowledged the practices of the Prophet Muhammad, upon him be peace and blessings, just to mention one of thousands of examples of the statements of the present scientific experts. This acknowledgment of seemingly ancient eastern practices of the Prophet from highly sophisticated western professionals demonstrates that there is true fusion of Western and Eastern mentalities.

Said Nursi wrote countless essays about the best of what Europe has to offer from an Islamic worldview. He encouraged an open, interactive dialogue between western and eastern civilizations. With his penetrating vision resonating from the early nineteenth century, he gave the following comments:

There are numerous virtues in modern civilization, but they are neither the property of Christianity, nor the creation of Europe, nor the work of this century. Rather, they are the property of all. They rise from the combined thought of mankind.

The Ottoman state is pregnant with Europe, and it will give birth to a European state one day. And Europe is pregnant with Islam; one day, it will give birth to an Islamic state.

All knowledge derives from God. In reality, at the foundation, scientific knowledge and divine knowledge are one; they are two aspects of the same reality. Both fields, religion and science, investigate internal subjects. Through experimentation in laboratories, science researches the inherent laws, functions, structures, mechanics, organization, and orders of substance and matter—the physical realities—whereas religion gains insight in the world of meaning, and studies the metaphysical realities of man, the world and the cosmos. Science is researching the visible physical existence of the universe, whereas religion contemplates the invisible spiritual realities of the hereafter. Both fields are concerned with sacred matters or physical matters and have to penetrate the inward structures and realms of their desired subjects.

Moreover, to study science means to try to study the laws of God most High, and how God makes creation work. The universe becomes a mirror for discovering the eternal beauty, perfection and wisdom of its Maker. One becomes aware of God Himself, and starts to see His Greatness, Might and Majesty. Again, divine knowledge and scientific knowledge are one. The more scientific knowledge and religious knowledge is revealed to a believer's heart, the more respect he will give to all of creation, to his fellow creatures, and to his most beloved Creator.

This is the great opportunity of our time. The West can give to the East what it needs, and vice versa. Summing up, West can bring analysis, and East can bring illumination.

On the other hand, in today's modern societies, where religion and science are separate, we can observe that materialistic world views, philosophical speculation, quantitative values, hostilities, gross egotism, power-hunger, and self-fabricated spirituality start to dominate peoples' lives, which, in turn, creates regional wars, wide-world terror, oppression of the weak, political and economical corruption, the downfall of moral values, and so on.

In other words, human beings are losing the dimensions of inwardness, the meaning and value of their lives on earth. When we study human history, we can see that the separation of religion and science always results in a disaster. When religion is gravely undermined in the population and, moreover, when religion does not exist for economical, scientific and political authorities—wherein are rulers charged with high responsibilities—the disastrous consequences are almost granted. In politics and business, on the worldly stage, we watch daily 'godless' animals in human form, with their pathological greed for power. In total contrast to our time, we cannot mention enough the honorable utterance of the great Sultan of his time, Yavuz Selim:

> *Being the king of this world is a useless struggle.*
> *Being the slave of a saint is superior to anything else.*

When modern scientists refuse to interpret their information and knowledge in the light of metaphysics—effectively splitting with religion—they end up giving a distorted view of reality, neglecting the internal richness of all existent things. With their purely quantitative, materialistic interpretation of reality, they are merely exploit nature and its resources.

Especially in the West, the dreams of capitalism, fame, status, wealth, and the standard of highest technical sophistication, determine people's lives. The desire for material luxury creates selfishness, and selfishness creates the separation of hearts. The modern mind is growing into monstrous proportions. The greed for power knows no limits, leading into the cultivation of a personality cult. The western man feels that he is the owner of his material achievements. He acts as though he were self-sufficient. Like Jalal al-Din Rumi comments:

> *For in self-sufficiency, man becomes rebellious; he becomes disobedient like a dreaming elephant.*

Man believes that he is the center of the universe. Therefore, he becomes unbearably distressed to see that someone could be above him—meaning that someone possesses more, or possesses a higher social status. He feels an ongoing urge to control and dominate other people's lives, and he acts either as a conqueror or as a rebel. And, especially, in terms of religion, modern man ignores the eternal wisdom of the messengers. Accepting God's revelations, he would have to acknowledge the divine rules which shape the universe and shape his own life. Additionally, he would have to recognize divine authority above himself, from which he would have to learn and take advice. Therefore, he shows either total ignorance towards religious influences, or he creates his own occult sciences, his own fake spirituality. We can say that modern man suffers from the illness called 'self-centeredness.'

Additionally, as religion is removed from the modern society and the rise of secularism starts to dominate people's lives, time has become like dynamite. We see heightened tensions between East and West, between continents, and between nations, and we can even see internal political frictions between tribes.

This is the tragedy: in the western world, life has little to do with religion and religion has little to do with life. Whereas, in reality, looking with the eyes of the heart, we can perceive that all life is divine. The cosmos is a divine creation, the world is a sacred place, man is a holy being. There is no separation between the world and the hereafter, the profane and the sacred, the material and the spiritual. All creation is immersed in continuous worship, and all existence is bursting with divine knowledge.

The religion of Islam has preserved a wholesome view of the universe through its absolute refusal to accept anything as being separate from God—namely that all knowledge and all creation derive from God the Almighty. Islam does not separate man from nature, the body from the soul—or, especially, science from religion. Knowledge of God most High can be found in any leaf that falls, in any spark of fire, in any drop of water, in any grain of sand. Man and nature are perfect mirrors of the divine Reality, the

Lord of Majesty and Bounty. And, most important, Islam means the absolute refusal to acknowledge any created realities, and any knowledge devoid of meaning—thereby teaching the inseparable link between science and religion, man and the cosmos. It sees all of creation as a symbolic intelligibility, continually referring the outward manifestation towards the inner reality, the physical form towards the inner meaning. All existent things are a reflection of the perfection, grace and beauty of the Creator.

Islam possesses in its heart the essence of all other religious traditions. Therefore, like no other religion, it stresses the principle of unity which circulates throughout the entirety of God's creation, culminating in the fruit of the universe, the saint, *Insan,* the perfect man. The light of unity becomes the ultimate guidance and the driving force for all of humankind. Seyyed Hossein Nasr goes as far as saying:

> *Man is the channel of grace for nature; through his active participation in the spiritual world, he casts light into the world of nature. He is the mouth through which nature breathes and lives. Because of his intimate connection between man and nature, the inner state of man is reflected in the external order. Were there to be no more contemplatives and saints, nature would become deprived of the light that illuminates it and the air which keeps it alive. It explains why, when man's inner being is in darkness and chaos, nature is also turned from harmony and beauty to disequilibrium and disorder.*
>
> *Men who live only on the surface of their being can study nature as something to be manipulated and dominate. But only he who has turned toward the inward dimension of his being can see nature as a symbol, as a transparent reality, and come to know and understand it in the real sense.*
>
> *Revelation (the Qur'an) to man is inseparable from the cosmic Revelation which is also a Book of God. Islam, by refusing to separate man from nature, and the study of nature from gnosis, or its metaphysical dimension, has preserved an integral view of the universe, and sees in the arteries of the cosmic and natural order the flow of divine grace.*

These reflections of our great scholar and author are revealing precisely the interconnectedness of all existence; the proof of the sacredness of all life; and the danger of modern man living in darkness and ignorance. Islam, therefore—due to its unifying and universal view of reality, and its refusal of the quantitative culture produced by the materialistic mind—enforces the awakening of the divine nature of man, planet Earth and the universe, a view without which the world and its inhabitants will turn into a state of secularism, which will spread, unfortunately, like a virus.

A true believer, who can unify science and religion, becomes a perfect man. He has unified his own mind and heart, his own reality of east and west, his earthly life with the hereafter. If humankind remains unaware of the sacredness of all life, we will stay at the narrow and low level of human existence. Reflection on people's lack of acknowledgement of an integral and universal perspective of human life, a wise man once remarked:

> *The eastern people pray but do not read books.*
> *And the western people do not pray but read books.*

The greatest problem of man is his own ignorance and heedlessness! Only when man wakes up from the sleep of his unconsciousness will he be able to grasp divine Existence. The truth of Islam is always material and spiritual progress, a true union of heaven and earth. Without earthly perfection, there is no spiritual perfection. Man has to live the perfection of an earthly plentitude, and combine the fruit of life and his practices with the fruits of his contemplations; that is to say, he has to combine the intellectual wisdom with the wisdom of his heart.

The human being can only fly with two wings. Man has to combine the inner and outer realities; he has to combine the profane with the sacred; he has to combine knowledge with love; he has to combine his worship with servanthood; he has to combine his contemplation with charitable works. What is contemplation without remembrance? What is the ecstasy of a lover without the higher awareness of the Only One? What is contemplation or profound reflection without sincere actions and true experience? What are our human lives worth without knowing the Only One, our supreme Creator? What is love without knowledge? What is knowledge without love?

If man does not live wisdom in his life, he cannot ascend vertically to the realm of God's nearness. He will stay forever on the dark side, disconnected from the sacred reality, retaining his old identity.

Having described the ideal man in contrast to the insufficiency and incompetence of the so-called modern man, who is living blindly on the surface, it is also important to mention some rather alarming facts in terms of the Eastern civilizations in our present time. Throughout Eastern countries, we can observe that the virus of modernization has entered people's hearts as well, due to the modern Muslim trying to "catch up" with the West. The old treasures of illumination and abundant love have diminished to a great degree, and we can observe plenty of moral decay. People are also weakened by long-lasting poverty, technical and industrial backwardness, political tyranny and oppression, internal political unrest, and so on. In one of his books about Prophet Muhammad, upon him be peace and blessings, the modern Islamic scholar, Fethullah Gülen, devotes a chapter about the Prophet's predictions for the distant furure:

> *The Prophet Muhammad, upon him be peace and blessings, predicted and explained the principle reasons for the Ottoman State's destruction and the condition of the Muslim world after the First World War: "Nations will call each other, as people make invitations to a meal, to make a concerted attack on you." Someone asked: "Will this happen because there are only a few of us?" God's messenger answered: "No, your numbers will be vast, but you will be as powerless as wood-chips or straw carried in a flood. God will remove your enemies' fear of you, and implant within you a fear of death and a love of the world.*

And Fethullah Gülen remarks:

> *The prediction, which became a reality during the First World War, also describes our current situation. We are divided into many factions, while our enemies seek closer unity based on mutual interests.*

Today, in certain circles of the Eastern populations, there is something like an identity crises leading into an inferiority complex among the Muslim. What a paradox! In the Qur'an, God most High says:

I have perfected My religion. (5:3)

But God will not allow but that His light should be perfected. (9:32)

And We taught them knowledge from Our Presence. (18:65)

Islam opened up all the doors for the spiritual fulfillment of human life. The perfected religion was, for 11 centuries, the greatest civilization on earth, and only since the 18th hundred century has a decline started to happen. Instead of being concerned with its own losses, the Muslim world should remember what made the Ottoman Empire into the great civilization that it was. For example, everyone knows that so many sciences originate in Islamic civilization.

Unfortunately, as we witness today, the material and spiritual decay never ceases to head into the deepest regions of Eastern societies, and we are facing, at this moment, the greatest tragedies, such as political and economical corruption, the war on terror, internal civil wars, staggering poverty, economical inflation, epidemic sicknesses, and so on. Of course, these negative events are darkening the whole planet earth. Worldwide chaotic and destructive events are shattering modern societies to pieces. Many people are collapsing under negative influences such as threats of atomic bombs, environmental pollution, the war on terror, unbearable injustice, natural catastrophes, political corruption, and the total collapse of moral values.

Due to this global situation, the belief of each individual is questioned. His self-esteem, and his own worth is weakened. The feeling of insecurity and distrust puts him in a vulnerable position. Man's deepest moral foundation is shaken. He sees himself drowned in his own failures and losses and in the misconduct and failures of ruling officials such as government, administration, business, religion, science, and so on.

Unfortunately, the majority of people wish to neglect any severe problems in their own lives and they withdraw their interest and participation in any distressing news from the rest of the world. But they only can turn their back on worldwide disasters as long as such calamities do not threaten their own lives, leaving them no choice but to endure it out of necessity. But nevertheless, more and more, every individual on earth is required to cope with environmental pollution and the results of the climate change.

It has to be said that if we wish to resolve and answer any problems occurring in our present societies, it is exactly the right time to take this great opportunity of reconciliation of one's deepest needs, wishes, longings and goals in life. Everyone in today's general insecurity has to reaffirm his own faith, reorient himself, and reevaluate his place in his own life—that is to say, to give new sense to his life. What are my values? Why am I here on this planet? What is my goal? What do I wish to accomplish? To which belief do I belong? Due to the lack of such answers and the immense lack of unification, brotherhood, embrace, and love, man, especially today, feels urged to look for its opposite. It is precisely our time which urges us to fill the gap. Time gives man some troubles only to get rid of them. In Jalal al-Din Rumi's words:

> *If I speak bitter words to you, it is only to wash you clean of all bitterness.*

In other words, it is God Himself making His creatures reevaluate their own lives. We should respond to His call without resistance. We should adapt a heart-wakefulness, equipped with infinite alertness, to be ready at any time, in any place, to feel His Gaze, to hear His Call, and to receive His merciful Guidance. This state of heightened divine awareness should turn into our lifestyle.

Moreover, another time-related fact has to be mentioned. Modern man possesses a great deal of knowledge about an increasing number of things, but unfortunately, only within a small minority of men we can witness some realization. This is our tragedy—

the lack of putting our knowledge into practice. Only man with a wholesome awareness will not fail to place his knowledge into his heart and realize its wisdom in his daily life.

To conclude, today we can observe, like never before in human history, a great need for the universality of the truth! In old times, East and West had a separate existence. Now, we are forced through the current global events to get together and find answers, solutions, and salvation on a worldwide scale. Things are very easy: we have to look at Adam, upon him be peace, the first human being, the prototype of humanity, and we have to look at our blessed master, Prophet Muhammad, upon him be peace and blessings, the fullness of realized love!

Due to these above-mentioned elaborations, I would like to conclude that the achievements of the East and the West should not belong exclusively to either one nor the other. We have to combine the knowledge of all mankind. Everything belongs to everyone. But the ultimate wisdom is this: nothing belongs to the human being, not even his own self!

As we see in our present time, the horizons of knowledge have opened up to the fullest dimensions. The reality of infinity, the eternal truth, is occuring on the spiritual level as well as on the scientific level. That is to say, we live in the perfection of knowledge of the religion, and we live in the perfection of the knowledge of science. We are able to celebrate the achievements of the West, modernity—and, at the same time, we are able to celebrate the achievements of the East, eternity.

When science and religion unite, when the divine heritage of the East combines with the intellectual heritage of the West, humankind can experience an absolute spiritual fulfillment and become aware of an outstanding concentration of divine Presence, and we will witness the perfection and oneness of all existence. For this reason, not only is the modern mind faced with a revolutionary breakthrough due to their newly discovered inventions reaching beyond direct sensory experience as far as to necessitate reformulating their world view, but the awareness of the universal religion, Islam, is experiencing a revival due to the present fusion of eastern and western knowledge.

As we mentioned, the level of today's top researchers meets with the contemplative states of the mystics. In the present time, every day, new and revolutionary discoveries are released, and these astonishing scientific results are able to confirm the divine knowledge of the religion. Let's just mention the famous scientist, Jean Jacques Cousteau, who discovered the barrier where the two seas, the salty and the sweet water, do not meet, which was revealed in one of the Qur'anic verses:

> *It is He Who has let free the two bodies of flowing water: one palatable and sweet, and the other salt and bitter. Yet has He made a barrier between them, a partition that is forbidden to be passed. (25:53)*

And another highly astonishing discovery, quantum physicists, together with paranormal investigators, have recently discovered an underlying energetic field throughout the whole universe. It is termed the 'Zero Point Energy Field.' They found that at Absolute Zero, minus - 273 Centigrade, where previously it was thought that all activity ceased, there is still vital life. Due to this underlying energetic field, modern scientists and metaphysicists have embraced a new understanding. Quantum physicists talk of subatomic particles being forever linked, known as 'entanglement.' If the energy of this field could be trapped into a cupful, it would boil an ocean! It can be called a timeless sea of energy. One researcher at a recent conference summarized her view of the energy field as:

> *There is nothing that is not God!*

With their new breakthrough, some 'zero-point energy enthusiasts' pretend to have generated the invention that would, without any doubt, save the world. In an exposé, they make the following statement:

> *Based on the quantum physics discoveries, the time has come for a technological rebirth in the new energy field! At the global level, it*

represents the possibility to develop, at last, a super-ecological society in all the corners of the earth, with the help of a discreet, powerful, clean technology. A brand new society will appear, characterized by omnipresent and all-encompassing electric energy sources.

As we see, the highly sophisticated sciences of astronomy, chemistry, biology, medicine, and physics can give evidence to belief. In simple words, the results of their newly discovered studies were written 1400 years ago in the holy Qur'an.

Like no other prophetic book, the Qur'an reveals to humankind the miracle of creation. As the final divine scripture sent to humanity, it represents the completion of God's revelations; and the Prophet Muhammad, upon him be peace and blessings, as the last Prophet to be sent, represents the seal of prophethood. With the final messages and the final messenger, the cycle of time is closing. The passage of time returns to its starting point—the end leads towards its beginning. We can, therefore, witness that the divine verses repeatedly stress the source of creation.

The eternal light of God penetrates through all levels of creation in order to reveal their mysteries. It is the hidden Treasure, which is nothing else other than God Himself. The divine messages, therefore, represent a restoration of the origin, making transparent the purity and oneness of all existence. They enlighten the beginning of existence, which reveals the miracle of creation. That is to say, the holy Qur'an teaches the reality of the universe, the world and man in its most pure and basic sense. And it is precisely modern science which gives evidence to the revealed mystery and wonders of God's divine revelations, and gives evidence of the miracle of creation of the universe and all it contains. For this reason, we can observe today that man is experiencing a revival of the infinite treasuries of the holy book, the Qur'an—an affirmation of its all-encompassing, all-embracing Truth. The community of believers is experiencing something like a second birth: it is the birth of renewed awareness, of realizing and recognizing the beauty and strength of the religion of Islam.

Moreover, the historical processed of humankind have lead us into a global age. The world's population has become like one state, one community. This is exactly the treasury of Islam. The believer lives in a universal consciousness, because our blessed Prophet Muhammad, upon him be peace and blessings, was not send to a particular nation—he was sent to the whole of humanity, as a mercy upon the whole universe As the last messenger to come, he brought the completion of all the revelations; he, therefore, represents the seal of prophecy.

A bridge between East and West was established. This bridge symbolizes the unification of the whole world. Because of the messenger's finality, Islam is, in its true sense, the all-embracing universal religion. The essence of all other religions is contained in it. In other words, the finality of God's messages and the finality of God's messenger encompass the whole universe. So the universality of the truth is established with the final and perfected religion of Islam.

Again, we can see through the globalization of the whole world in our present century that the religion of Islam is experiencing a revival due to its universal nature. The pure treasury of Islam encounters the treasury of our time. Universality meets globalization. Globalization compresses and diminishes the world into one state, and unifies the world's population into one community. On the one side, there is the inward movement of reduction to oneness; on the other side, there is the external movement of expanding, the rapidly growing of the human consciousness towards the infinity of God's knowledge.

Universality is nothing else than God's all-embracing light of unity. The religion of Islam bears His light of universal unity to all humanity. This is His Greatness. The power of His creation is an act of His love, grace and oneness. That is why He is the All-Merciful and his most beloved prophet, Muhammad, upon him be peace and blessings, is a mercy for the whole world. Bringing the light of unity to the world means His love is running through the world's arteries, and infinite grace, mercy, and blessings are bestowed for all of His beloved servants.

Our Lord of all the worlds invites us to His religion of all-embracing love. Again, like a handful of wine grapes becomes a single mass of liquid when squeezed, it also means that God unifies every single one of His living creatures into one body of loving brotherhood. It means that all human beings are united in the universality of the Islamic faith and become brothers and sisters of the hereafter.

Through the occurrence of the global age in our century, man finally becomes ready to grasp and realize the truth of the global religion. Islam becomes the ultimate guidance for every truthful believer for his life on earth.

Due to the celebration of the truth, it has to be said that our time demands a revolution of human consciousness, an increase of awareness towards the infinity of God's knowledge—in other words, the application of a universal consciousness.

Unfortunately, the word global is used to describe worldwide disasters, terror and catastrophes. Additionally, globalization is treated exclusively as a process of worldly affairs with no connection to religion whatsoever. This fact reflects obviously a great tragedy, a complete lack of human awareness. As it is so, it is even more urgent to answer the problems of globalization with global answers, with global salvation, and with global healing. The cause can be treated with its root. The negative effects of globalization can be resolved with the truth of the global religion of Islam.

For this reason, Islam is absolutely successful in our age, because it gives to our time what it needs. Now we are able to grasp the truth. We are able to understand Islamic consciousness. Islam is a universal religion embracing all nations all over the world. Its knowledge is universal, its message is universal, and its guidance is universal. Islam sees every individual as an inhabitant of this world.

On the external level, it seems disastrous with the war on terror, severe poverty, identity crises, epidemic sicknesses, political and economical corruption, economical instability, and so on. That is to say, we can observe insurmountable problems throughout the eastern Islamic countries. In reality, however, Islam smoothes out any conflict between people, nations, cultures, races and color. It unifies the mind, heart, body, soul, conscious, and belief. Islam matches the human heart in its comprehensive nature and capacity. It nurtures the macro-cosmos of the heart. For all believers, there is not a single thing left unanswered or unfulfilled. It treats man as a being of glorifying unity. It teaches moderation, equality, justice, balance, and peace. With God's true religion we are woken up to perfect consciousness.

It is time to wake up to higher awareness. Only higher awareness can build a bridge between East and West. Only through higher awareness can the truth have a voice in the world. Only higher awareness can generate the soul's ascension to the realms of Gods nearness. If we manage to gain a universal consciousness, we will be able to survive in the jungle of our modern societies. A true believer is living in a global consciousness. The bridge between East and West was built long time ago. The absolute truth was given a long time ago.

Like no other religion, Islam represents the religion of unity, oneness, wholeness, harmony, inwardness, brotherhood, togetherness, and embrace. This is what the modern world misses; today, we are deprived of charm, beauty, vision, tenderness, kindness, and love. As a result, the modern man feels worthless, useless and low. In order to save ourselves from drowning in the sea of disorder and distortion of modern societies, and of our own minds and hearts, we have to apply the science of unity. It is the science of unity which teaches mankind the art of life. Unity gives wholeness to human life. It is teaching the ascension of the soul; it gives the sweet taste of awareness; it nourishes all basic needs; it gives eternal happiness; it opens the eyes of the heart; and it answers all questions. The solution to all problems is inwardness—to leave the form, the surface, and descend into the realms of meaning. Living true inwardness generates the harmony of being, which is the science of unity.

The eternal message and wisdom is this: we have to understand that Islam is not limited to the Middle East! It is not the exclusive property of Muslims, and it never was. With its all-embracing truth, it nourishes the whole of humankind with what they need. Because Islam recognizes the fact that all needs of human beings are universal, it thus nurtures all living creatures on a global scale. Islam, with its deep-rooted tradition, manifests eternal laws and propagates eternal values. It transcends history, status, cultural, geographical, and educational differences. The religion of Islam is absolute victorious in the sense that it does not make any distinction between nationality, race, or country.

Our blessed master was sent to the whole of humanity. He was the living truth of religious universality. We can say that the truth is Islamic consciousness, because the truth is, in its nature, universal. There is no partial truth. Therefore, the absolute truth of God is Islam.

Only sainthood can heal! Only selflessness can illuminate the universe! Only selflessness can change the world. It is time to listen to saints. They teach inwardness and divine love, which is the hidden treasure within us. With their light of unity, they heal our spiritual wounds. Sainthood is the answer for the problems of the 21st century. We have to listen to universal saints, because they represent the universal religion of Islam; therefore, they speak in a universal language. They speak to all people, all times, all cultures, all beliefs, and all nations. Universality is directly connected with the beauty of God's light of unity. And all the universal saints operate with this light; they see with the light of God! So when the saints speak, it is as if one hears fresh news given from the Prophet Muhammad's mouth.

In order to nourish our profoundest humanitarian needs, we have to realize that we have to take refuge in the spiritual blessings of our beloved Prophet Muhammad, upon him be peace and blessings. We have to nurture ourselves with his light of eternal beauty. In our present time we have an urgent need to understand Prophet Muhammad, upon him be peace and blessings. We become ready to know the worth and meaning of the honor of the universe. It is time to be slaves to his compassion, beauty, generosity, and goodness. There are no virtues other than the virtues of the Prophet Muhammad, upon him be peace and blessings. All virtues are comprised in his noble character.

Prophet Muhammad, upon him be peace and blessings, ruled the world through his selflessness. His most noble character reflects the purest, the most supreme sainthood. His humility reached such a degree, that he became the slave of his community. As the jewel of servants, he guided the whole of mankind with his light of goodness, his treasury of pure modesty, and the eternal richness of his soul. This means that all human beings who have ever lived in this world are able to nourish themselves with his endless mercy, with his spiritual blessings, and with the light of his goodness.

Here is one of the essential messages of the religion of Islam: the true miracle is not in bringing a dead body to life—it is that God accepts your prayers because of your goodness and closeness to Him. That is to say, real goodness is not attributing goodness to oneself.

We have to know that it is not through speeches, proclamations, and orders that our blessed master taught the world the truth. Whatever pearls of wisdom he gave to humanity has, first of all, a healing effect. Our beloved of hearts is the mercy for all the worlds. He cures all our spiritual wounds. He brings salvation for every problem. He offers a remedy for all broken hearts. His inexhaustible blessings are pouring upon every living soul. He gives abundant comfort to distressed hearts. He nourishes all crying needs. And he sends infinite grace to the suppressed.

In our modern societies, human beings have these needs to the highest degree, because this world and man are deprived of the divine beauty and blessings; they are robbed of its own substance. Prophet Muhammad, upon him be peace and blessings, brought a religion which teaches perfection in love. He brought a religion where knowledge becomes love. That is to say, we learn from eternal beauty. We reach the spiritual heights of human existence by nourishing our soul with the light of goodness, which is loving servanthood. Our blessed master demonstrated like no other human being, that we only reach spiritual perfection through living a life of earthly plentitude.

He demonstrated that religion means realizing the Greatness, Majesty, Mercy, Love and Beauty of our Creator—and due to this divine vision, being drawn without resistance to loving surrender. In other words, submission to God's Will has to be done with love and admiration. The sacred duties have to be executed with pleasure and joy to serve Him.

They left a very strong seed. The seed was planted with the first human being, the Prophet Adam, upon him be peace. It is the seed for the religion Islam. With his descent to the earth, Adam, upon him be peace, became a humble student, and God most High became his majestic Teacher. This means that the religion of Islam exists since the beginning of human life on this earth.

God most High says in the holy Qur'an:

> *Today I have perfected the religion, I completed My favours unto you. (5:3)*

> *You have indeed, in the Messenger of God, a beautiful pattern (of conduct) for any one whose hope is in God and the Final Day, and who engages much in the Praise of God. (33:21)*

Prophet Muhammad, upon him be peace and blessings, brought the perfection of the religion, the union of the internal and external revelations, the union of worldly and spiritual matters, and the union of meaning and form. Heaven and earth got married. It says in the holy Qur'an:

> *Soon will we show them our Signs in the (furthest) regions (of the earth), and in their own souls, until it becomes manifest to them that this is the Truth. (41:53)*

This means that the religion of Islam reached its perfection when our beloved master honored the world with his holy appearance. The perfection on earth can be reached with servanthood, and the perfection of heaven can be reached with the ascension. This means that our Lord of all the worlds nurtures the minds as well as the hearts of His believing servants, the honored members of His beloved's community. A perfect balance of inner and outer knowledge was given, which leads to the unity of being.

On the one side, humanity received the gift of infinite divine knowledge, supreme consciousness, endless illumination, the inheritance of the "truth of Muhammad," and on the other side, humanity received the highest standard of morality, the wisdom of the Prophet's noble character. This means that with the coming of Prophet Muhammad, upon him be peace and blessings, into this world, the ascension of the soul beyond the unsurpassable limit was given—respectively the knowledge and possibility of endless levels of spiritual evolution got revealed to man, so he is able to travel beyond the beyond, exploring the infinity of God's divine attributes and names.

Our blessed master brought a religion of infinite elevation, ascension, purification, illumination. All the doors for the ultimate fulfillment of spiritual life opened. Sheikh Muhyiddin Ibn Arabi said:

> The words revealed to Mohammed [upon him be peace and blessings] set order everywhere, from the East to the West. Moreover, the prophet was not sent as the prophet of a particular nation, but as a mercy upon the whole universe. So the soul is meant to regulate not just a part of our human nature, but the whole of it.

With this wonderful comment of our Sheikh, Ibn Arabi, we are told to carry the responsibility as believers to discover the whole complexity of our soul and reach human perfection. When we accomplish the ultimate goal, the complete annihilation in God the Almighty, we will experience the bliss of the absolute fulfillment, which lies in the holy tradition where God Most High says:

> When I love a servant, I become the eyes with which he sees, I become the ears with which he hears, I become the tongue, with which he talks, I become the feet, with which he walks, I become the strength in every part of his being.

The holy Qur'an says:

> And God will perfect His Light. (61:8)

We are part of the religion—Light upon light. God's divine Light meets the purified light of the believer's soul. God gives us His Light to see His truth. God shed His Light throughout the whole creation, which enables us to see through all the veils which are covering our soul. Belonging to the religion of truth means being guided by the Light of God. Endless subtle secrets became revealed. We have given access to the hidden divine treasury. The brilliant radiance of the mirror of sincerity reveals divine secrets to infinity. He spoils us with brilliance of His light. He gives us direct knowledge, the power of perception:

And We taught them knowledge from Our Presence.(18:65)

We are able to wonder in His Kingdom, dwell in the highest awareness of Him, with Him, towards Him, and in Him. The marvelous sun of discovery is rising to the utmost limits and dispersing all darkness of unconsciousness. And God has brought the good news of togetherness, the loving union with Him. He has given the good news of the power of the affirmation of divine unity. And God has given the good news of:

God was well pleased with them, and they are well pleased with Him.(5:119)

On their faces the cheerful radiance of bliss.(3:107)

God most High says in the holy Qur'an:

We are part of the religion of the heart, the religion of love, the religion of infinite mercy. At the time of creation of man, we learn:

And He blew onto him His spirit.(32:9)

This is God's breath of mercy. The whole of creation is infused with His merciful breath, meaning that His mercy is omnipresent through out the whole universe. God most High says:

My Mercy embraces all things.(7:156)

The motivating force for creation is love and mercy. God's most essential attributes towards humankind are mercy and compassion. His infinite mercy is pouring ceaselessly through His most beloved Prophet into the world. The most distinctive quality of a believer is mercy and compassion. The essence of morality is compassion. The only medicine which can heal the wounds of our present time is active compassion. With our most beloved Prophet Muhammad, upon him be peace and blessings, God's endless blessings and grace are pouring in abundance all over the world.

All existence is nurturing itself with the glorious utterance: *"Bismillahirahmanirrahim,"* in the name of God the Compassionate and the Merciful. All praises, all divine discourses, and all actions begin and end with this divine utterance. For every human being, *"Bismillahirahmanirrahim"* represents the eternal link with our beloved Lord, the true home of our soul, the key to eternal happiness opening the doors to paradise:

"Bismillahirahmanirrahim" is the sacred word for the secrets of His infinite treasures.

"Bismillahirahmanirrahim" opens the doors to His bounties and favours. *"Bismillahirahmanirrahim"* gives the guaranty of His all-Encompassing protection.

Mentioning *"Bismillahirahmanirrahim,"* as His creatures, we offer ourselves in sincere humility towards our all powerful Creator. And mentioning *"Bismillahirahmanirrahim"* within our lives, in all our doings, shows our voluntary submission, our thankfulness, our striving, our yearning, our love, and our praise for the One and Only.

Only human beings can realize God, realize the truth, and realize their unity with the Creator. Only human beings can mention His name outright, and can comprehend His reality, which is His mercy and compassion. Thus, we need His ruler-ship, and we need His Lordship. We have to bind ourselves to His infinite power, His infinite protection, and His all-embracing compassion. Our soul needs eternity, the treasury of His beautiful names. We need to drink from His infinite ocean of mercy. We need the Bestower of bounties, to act in His name, to pray in His name, and to reflect in His name. The ones who realize the need for His infinite power, will submit without resistance towards His all-graceful Presence and live willingly and lovingly in His name.

Within our present time, there is an urgency, a crying need. Humanity is in utter need for the truth and experiences a desperate thirst for divine compassion, because we are dangerously far away from it. I wish to say that, especially today, we need to cling to the beauty of the noble character of Muhammad, upon him be peace and blessings, because he is the mercy for the whole world. God says:

He singles out for His mercy whomever He will.(2:105)

And we need to cling to the truth of Muhammad, upon him be peace and blessings, because he is the source of light. God says:

God guides all who seek His good pleasure to ways of peace and safety, and leads them out of darkness, by His will, unto the light. (5:16)

Today I believe we can comprehend the reality of Mohammad, upon him be peace and blessings, more profoundly than in the past. We are able to perceive his supreme value and beauty more fully because we are in greater need of him.

The prophet Moses, peace be upon him, used to pray to his beloved Lord:

By his mystery in Your Presence, by his journeying to You.

We have to realize that it is by Muhammad's reality that we exist. It is by his light that we illuminate our human nature. It is by his mercy that we nurture our hearts. It is by his truth that we reach the divine wisdom of our glorious Creator. Through the secret of his mystery in the divine Presence, we are able to reach our supreme Lord.

I wish to say that it is most urgent to win divine guidance. Now it is time to discover the light of our own soul. It is time to sincerely listen to the supreme saints, the purest of the pure. It is the moment to appreciate Ali, may God be pleased with him. Although he was the door of knowledge, he told us:

When you teach me one letter, I will become your slave.

And Abu Bakr, may God be pleased with him, who was made to see hell and its tortures was so extremely terrified, that he begged God to make his body big enough to cover hell, so that no one would be able to enter. Now it is time to relate to Prophet Adam's limitless purity, upon him be peace, to see the wonder and treasury of human love within his breast. Now is the time to celebrate human relationships again. Now is the time to realize complete dependence towards the One and Only, and to realize that we entirely belong to Him. Now is the time to understand the reality of intimacy with the One and Only. Now is the time to realize the hidden meaning of unity. Now is the time for the religion of admiration. Now we are ready to see the miracle of creation. Now is the time for rebirth, the sweet taste of awareness. Now is the time to realize the good news of eternal life. Now is the time for the good news that we are not bound to time and place. Now we have to give our souls the visa for immigration, to set ourselves free on a magnificent journey to our homeland. Now is the time to realize that our loss is our gain. Now is the time to realize that the faithful believer is the mirror of the faithful believer.